The Natural Foods Epicure

The Natural Foods Epicure

*The No Salt, No Sugar, No Artificial Ingredients,
All Natural Foods Cookbook*

by
Nancy Albright

(Author of *The Rodale Cookbook*)

Editor:	Charles Gerras
Design by:	Terri Lepley
Illustrations by:	Chris Magadini
	&
	Joe Charnoski
Special Contributions by:	Rita Reemer
	&
	Jerome Goldstein
	Anita Hirsch
	Faye Martin

 Rodale Press Emmaus PA

The Natural Foods Epicure was originally published in hardcover as *Rodale's Naturally Great Foods Cookbook.*

Copyright © 1977 Rodale Press, Inc.

Printed in the United States of America on recycled paper

Library of Congress Cataloging in Publication Data

Albright, Nancy.
    The natural foods epicure.

    Previously published as: Rodale's naturally
great foods cookbook. c1977.
    Includes index.
    1. Food, Natural. 2. Cookery (Natural foods)
I. Gerras, Charles. II. Title.
TX369.A42   1983   641.5'637   82-18959
ISBN 0-87857-468-9   paperback

2   4   6   8   10   9   7   5   3   1   paperback

The Author

The hundreds of thousands who bought and loved Nancy Albright's *The Rodale Cookbook* will be pleased to see that her imagination and adventurousness in handling food have been expanding deliciously since that book appeared. Credit the need for constant experimentation and curiosity required of her as Food Editor for *Organic Gardening and Farming* magazine and overall Food Consultant for Rodale publications. But credit also Nancy's basic concern about food and her conviction that most of us could be eating better than we do, and for less money if only we used more natural foods.

Rodale's Fitness House kitchen and dining room, which Nancy created to serve as the proving ground for new cooking procedures and recipes, are busier and more popular than ever. It's easy to see why. The meals are marvelous! Nancy Albright cooks every day—and for a "family" that is used to quality fare. She really knows her way around a kitchen and it shows in the clear way she discusses cooking methods and in the hundreds of intriguing recipes she has created for this book.

Special thanks to Irene Somishka and Ann Snyder for their concern and efforts in preparing *The Natural Foods Epicure*.

Contents

You Can Eat as Though You Had a Million

If money were no object, if you could afford to buy any kind—and as much—of any food you wanted for every meal of the day, what kind of food would you choose?

Imagine yourself ordering breakfast in the most glamorous hotel you can think of. Are you ordering Pop Tarts, Egg Beaters, Tang—or do you see the waiter serving fresh fruit, two beautifully fresh eggs, poached or sunny-side up with high, round yolks flanked by two perfectly toasted pieces of bread?

You're in the dining room for lunch. Are you thinking of a hot dog and cola drink or are you thinking of a cup of clear broth and a chef's salad with strips of lean ham or roast beef, slivers of cheese and chicken in a bowl of lettuce, tomato, hard-cooked eggs and topped with a fresh salad dressing?

You go out for dinner in an elegant restaurant. As you sit amid snowy napkins, flashing silverware and fine crystal, do you order canned fruit cocktail or fresh melon? Do you ask for breaded ground veal patties, instant mashed potatoes and canned peas—or will it be a piece of fresh fish, broiled and bathed in a butter and lemon sauce, served with freshly steamed asparagus next to a hill of fluffy rice with flashes of pimiento and green pepper mixed throughout? From the dessert cart will you have instant chocolate pudding topped with synthetic whipped topping or fresh made deep-dish apple pie with a dollop of real whipped cream?

Is there any real question about the choices?

No matter what the TV commercials and magazine ads would have you believe, to most informed people, good food means food that is as close to its natural state as possible. People who can have the best demand fresh foods, carefully prepared—whether for flavor or the additional nutrition they contain—and refuse to tolerate any synthetic or chemicalized substitute.

Dozens of celebrities in the worlds of sports, entertainment and big business are convinced that they feel better, look better and work better when they stick to natural foods. The so-called "fat farms" that charge a thousand dollars or more per week to whip their pampered guests into shape, indulge them with fresh fruits, beautifully prepared vegetables right out of the garden and broiled meats, fish and poultry. Serving canned soup or a frozen dinner to these clients is inconceivable.

1

Natural Foods Restaurants Are "In"

In New York City, the latest rage in restaurants is the "gourmet salad restaurant." Such places are not intended for strange types or for people who eat this way for spiritual reasons or to save money. These restaurants are featured in chic department stores and in fancy neighborhoods on the elegant East Side.

In October 1976 this is the way the *New York Times* Food Editor, Mimi Sheraton, described Healthworks!: "Here in a handsome white tile and natural wood setting, livened by hanging plants and fresh daisies on the tables with floating candles at night, customers choose from three or four daily salads that range in price from $3.25 to $3.75. The diner can choose whole grain bread, freshly made soup of the day and beverages that include wine, Perrier water, coffee, fruit juice or a VHP (very healthy person) shake ($1.25), made of skim milk, ice yogurt and fresh fruit whipped to a frosty froth."

Not exactly cheap, eating at a place like that. But that's the point. People who choose to eat there can afford just about any kind of food they want. And what they want is flavor, freshness, nutritional value and substantial food that will get them through the rest of the day without feeling overstuffed.

Along with the salad bars, New York is blossoming with "Yogurt-terias." These are a new version of the fast-food idea, where yogurt, not the hamburger, is king. The food that once stamped any American who ate it as a health nut has gone respectable. You can turn up at the checkout counter of a supermarket with half a dozen containers of yogurt and the checker won't bat an eye; you can whip out your cup of yogurt at your desk for lunch and find that half of the people eating at the office will be doing the same thing; you can even order yogurt at restaurants as a dessert.

Real Food Fits Any Life-Style

For too many Americans the fact that natural food is naturally great is a well-kept secret. They hear that fresh fruits and vegetables are too perishable, too expensive and too much trouble. They hear that processed foods are better because they've been "enriched" with extra vitamins and minerals (no mention of the many lost in manufacture and not replaced) for improved nutrition and better health. They hear that only food faddists and health nuts bother with yogurt, brown rice, wheat germ and the like, and, anyway, none of these foods fits into the ordinary American menu.

Several years ago the editors at Rodale Press set out to disprove those myths when they published *The Rodale Cookbook*, one of the first full-length cookbooks devoted exclusively to recipes using only natural ingredients. The enormous success that book has had (over 250,000 copies in print) clearly shows that the public is dissatisfied with no-flavor fill-up foods and determined to have tasty and nutritional meals instead.

These are the people who keep small gardens because they long for the inimitable taste of vine-ripened tomatoes or the snap and sweetness of just-picked green beans. They search out farmers who raise free-ranging chickens and grass-fed cattle and patronize the nearest farmers' market for produce raised in the area. Their kitchens are stocked with varieties of fresh whole grains and beans; they make their own yogurt and bake their own bread. And when they eat out, they eat well on fresh, carefully prepared food; reheated, precooked offerings just won't do. They don't merely fill up on food; they experiment with its infinite varieties. To them cooking and eating are rich, creative experiences!

Anyone who has missed out on the joys of natural foods makes an enviable discovery when he or she bites into a slice of home-baked, whole grain bread, for the first time, or tastes a chunk of fresh pineapple or spoons into a bowl of homemade soup thick with garden-fresh vegetables! Don't wait another minute to join the New Food Generation. You owe it to yourself to share in the pleasures of Naturally Great Foods!

Yes, You Can Afford to Eat This Way!

Those who worry about the cost of this kind of eating learn by experience that the amount of money spent for food is an unreliable measure of its quality. Often as not, the less the cost, the more the quality in terms of nutrition and flavor. Fortunately for all of us, the opportunities for stocking up on home-grown, high quality food at attractive prices are increasing with every passing day.

For example, it used to be that if you wanted to buy direct from a farmer, you had to drive into the country for miles, hunting around for a roadside stand.

No more. If you live in or near an urban area, there's bound to be a farmers' market near you that's open at least one day a week. Invariably, buying direct from the farmer means fresher, more flavorful food often at lower—certainly comparable to supermarket—prices.

Of course, the advertising by the major food companies in the United States is mostly for supermarket junk foods—foods that are highly processed and stuffed with artificial flavors and artificial colors and which make the most profit for the manufacturer and generally offer the least real food value. For example, recently the annual advertising allowance for General Foods ran to $189 million, and we all know that money did not go to encourage us to eat more fresh fruits and vegetables, whole grains, or inexpensive meats. It went for four-color ads and TV commercials to entice us to drink laboratory-made orange drinks and fill out our meals with synthetic meat extenders and heat 'n' serve rolls. The simple and reliable rule is: The greater the profit margin for a food, the more advertising it gets.

But we consumers are not so easy to sell as we once were. Quality and flavor are making a comeback as requirements in food. We've had it fast; now we want it good!

Business analysts and opinion polls confirm an increase in purchases which reflects an appreciation of good cooking and natural foods. When consumers turn away from high-priced supermarket specialties, they turn to fresh vegetables and fruits—and consumers are making a firm commitment to natural food cooking by buying appliances such as blenders and grinders which are useful in preparing such foods.

Who Are the Food Faddists?

Most authorities agree that our good health depends upon our total environment—the air we breathe, the clothing we wear, the jobs we have, how much we walk (even where we walk), the water we drink and, especially, the food we eat.

Many people simply make it a policy to avoid foods that contain additives. They reason that a lot of these chemical substances are already recognized as potentially carcinogenic and the jury is still out on a large number of the others being used. To them, eating processed foods is a risk they choose not to take. It's certainly not an unreasonable position, yet many Americans are conditioned to think of such eating habits as food faddism.

A few years ago *Nutrition Action* (March 1975, p. 1), a publication of the Center for Science in the Public Interest, ran an editorial, "Stamp Out Food Faddism," which dealt with that misconception. The following is an excerpt:

"Food faddism is indeed a serious problem. But we have to recognize that the guru of food faddism is not Adelle Davis, but Betty Crocker. The true food faddists are not those who eat raw broccoli, wheat germ, and yogurt, but those who start the day on Breakfast Squares, gulp down bottle after bottle of soda pop, and snack on candy and Twinkies . . . . If any diet should be considered faddist, it is the standard one. Our far-out diet—almost 20 percent refined sugar and 45 percent fat—is new to human experience and foreign to all other animal life . . . . It is incredible that people who eat a junk food diet constitute the norm, while individuals whose diets resemble those of our great-grandparents are labeled deviants."

The Co-op Experience

A couple of years ago, some of the employees at Rodale Press started a natural foods co-op. The co-op is open Wednesdays from 5:00 P.M. to 7:30 P.M. It's unpretentious, but the shelves, refrigerator and freezer have ample supplies of fresh vegetables, fruit, grains, nuts, oils, dried fruits, cheeses, juices, frozen meat, and yogurt.

One family that spends about $25 to $30 weekly there is constantly pointing out how the simple act of shopping in a "store" like the co-op has dramatically changed the family menu—all for the better: "Frozen vegetables, for example, are a thing of the past for us. Green beans take no time at all to prepare in a *wok*. The short-grain brown rice, grown by an organic farmer in Arkansas, puts fast-cooking rice to shame—and actually costs less than the abandoned big name brand.

"Since colas and candies and the flashy snack foods are not stocked on co-op shelves, the children content themselves with munching on cashews, almonds or dried apricots.

"Meats are not the main dish nearly as often as they used to be. And no one in the family minds it. The hamburger we buy at the co-op—when we do serve it—has much less fat. The poultry (purchased at a local farmers' market) is featured—along with fish—in a variety of ways."

The point is this: There's nothing odd or sacrificial about the way this family eats. They enjoy good food, they like to save money whenever they can, and they don't resent the extra effort required now and then to prepare certain dishes.

What they are doing, anyone can do. Of course, having good meals at home does raise the standards for evaluating food eaten out. But good old American enterprise is taking care of that.

Help for the Harried Shopper

Clever businessmen are aware that there is a growing demand for well-prepared natural foods in snack bars and restaurants. And the sharpest of them are cashing in on this trend.

Several years ago the management of New York's famous Bloomingdale's officially recognized the natural foods revolution by becoming the first department store where the tired, thirsty and famished shopper could forego the usual hot dog and soda syndrome to enjoy the likes of fresh carrot juice and a curried egg salad sandwich served with lettuce and bean sprouts on whole grain bread.

The most popular luncheon dish served at this restaurant, Forty Carrots, is the deliciously satisfying homemade soup served with a tossed salad, warm whole grain carrot muffin and butter. The soup of the day depends upon what the market provides. It could be mushroom, cream of spinach, cream of tomato, vegetable or split pea.

If you want just a healthful "pick me upper," you could choose the Protein Booster, a drink made with ricotta cheese, apple cider, lecithin and brewer's yeast; a Pink Cloud made with raspberries, milk and yogurt; a Banana Whisk made with banana, milk and yogurt; or a Sunshine Drink made with cantaloupe or pineapple, milk, yogurt and honey. Of course, you can try these out on your own blender.

Another new concept, the "gourmet salad restaurant" opened with a splash in October 1976, on New York's 57th Street. Called Healthworks!, its owner Bruce Zenkel said he could give Ronald McDonald a run for his money. And the current trend seems to bear him out.

No need to wait for a Healthworks! or a Forty Carrots to open in your town. You're probably enjoying the taste and texture of real food right now! And if you've been curious about some of the less familiar natural foods such as sprouts, carob and millet, but hesitant about using them, this book will put you at ease. Dozens of natural foods are discussed with fascinating details on how they are used in this country and throughout the world, plus money-saving hints on shopping for them and ideas for including the foods in everyday menus.

The cooks of the Rodale Press experimental kitchen at Fitness House, under the direction of Nancy Albright, have created and tested hundreds of new recipes that take advantage of the appeal and versatility of these natural foods. Some dishes, such as Curried Potatoes with Yogurt, are unique to this book; others, like Beef Stew with Plums, are variations on old favorites with new interest added by some unexpected flavor or a change in texture.

We confidently welcome you to these fresh experiences in cooking and eating. They are sure to outshine the dreary dining experiences that spring from supermarkets and fast-food outlets, bringing even greater anticipation and pleasure to the meals served at your house from now on.

Natural foods cooking has evolved from a hobby for a few to a way of life for an important segment of our population. Rodale Press has always been in the vanguard of this movement toward better eating and we believe that our Fitness House kitchens reflect the most imaginative yet practical use of natural foods. In *The Natural Foods Epicure* the cooks and editors present the state of the art at its best. We believe this book will challenge those experienced with natural foods cooking to new heights of excellence and will encourage those who are new to the idea to explore the happy surprises awaiting them in natural foods creatively prepared.

C. G.

Recipes by Category

Rice Flour Muffins
Sally Lunn
Sauerkraut Onion Rolls
Scottish Scones or Bannocks
Simple Rye Bread
Skillet Cornbread
Sourdough Pumpernickel Bread
Sourdough Rye Bread
Sourdough Starter
Sprouted Wheat Bread (unleavened)
Sunflower Seed Muffins
Tibetan "Prayer Wheel" Barley Bread
Triticale Buns
Triticale Egg Bread
Unyeasted Rice Bread
Wheat Germ Muffins
Whole Wheat Popovers

CEREALS

Buckwheat Porridge
Cooked Bran Granola
Hot Bran Cereal
Hot Cereal Mixes
Hot Cream of Rice
Hot Rye and Peanut Cereal
Millet Mush
Never-Fail Cooked Rice
Uncooked Bran Granola

**CRACKERS,
BREADSTICKS,
CREAM PUFFS**

Bob Rodale's Corn Pones
Bran Sesame Crackers
Cheddar Chips
Chive Wafers

Garbanzo (Chick-Pea) Sprout Snack
Oatmeal Crackers
Old Country Soft Pretzel Sticks (rye)
Peanut Cornmeal Snaps
Soul Food Crackers
Sprouted Wheat Sticks
Tiny Cream Puffs
Whole Millet Crackers

DIPS AND
SPREADS

Avocado Spread
Basic Yogurt
Cottage Cheese
Cottage Cheese, Date and Nut Filling
Eggplant Dip or Dressing
Fitness House Spread
Hummus
Kidney Bean Dip
Lima Bean and Sesame Dip
Messmor (whey spread)
Sunflower Seed Spread or Dip
Walnut Cheese Spread
Walnut-Onion Dip or Spread
Wheat Germ Spread
Yogurt Cheese

FISH

Baked Stuffed Whole Fish
Carp Patties
Catfish Baked in Dill Sauce
Fish Filets Sauteed in Egg
Fish Kebabs

Florida Baked Catfish
Fried Carp
Gefilte Fish (fish balls)
Kedgeree
Stuffed Rolled Flounder
Sushi (rice and fish wrapped in seaweed)

**MEATLESS
MAIN DISHES**

Asparagus and Eggs with Sesame Seeds
Baked Onions and Bulgur with Raisins
Baked Tomatoes and Eggs
Black Bean and Rice Bake
Broccoli Cheese Pie
Broccoli Timbales
Buckwheat Groat Patties
Buckwheat-Groat Souffle
Buckwheat-Stuffed Cabbage Rolls
Bulgur and Lentil Pilaf
Bulgur Soybean Loaf
Carrot Peanut Loaf
Carrot Soy Loaf
Cheese Fondue
Chick-Pea and Lentil Curry
Cornmeal Puff
Corn Souffle
Cottage Cheese Buckwheat Squares
Dried Lima Bean Casserole
Dutch Peanut Croquettes
Egg Foo Yung
Eggplant Souffle
Eggs on Curried Rice

Eggs Moppioli
Fresh Herb Omelet
Fresh Vegetable and Fruit Stew
    with Soybeans
Frijoles Refritos
Gnocchi
Grainburgers
Green and Red Pepper Casserole
Indian Lentil *Dal*
Kale and Kidney Bean Bake
Kidney Bean Curry
Lentil and Potato Pie
Lentil, Rice and Prune Pilaf
Mexican Garbanzo Beans
Millet Lentil Loaf
Peanut and Cabbage Curry
Pfannkuchen (a large German omelet)
Rolled Eggplant Italian
Rye and Lentil Pilaf
Scroggin (backpacker's food)
Soybean-Cabbage Casserole
Soy Cheeseburgers
Soy-Potato Dumplings
Spinach Lasagna
Split Peas with Barley
Sunflower Carrot Patties
Swiss Cheese, Egg and
    Green Bean Casserole
Tomato Quiche
Wheat Soybean Casserole
Zucchini Frittata

MEATS
Muscle Meats
Beef

Applesauce Meat Loaf
Beef and Sprout Patties
Beef Stew with Plums
Bran Vegetable Meat Loaf
Buckwheat Cholent
Millet-Stuffed Peppers
Mushroomburgers
Steak Tartare
Stir-Fried Beef and Watercress
Stir-Fried Turnips with Beef
Wheat Berry and Beef Casserole

Chicken

Baked Chicken, Quince and
    Butternut Squash
Chicken Breasts in Sour Cream Aspic
Chicken Paprika
Coq au Vin (Chicken in Wine)
Madras Chicken Curry
Pennsylvania Dutch Chicken Pot Pie

Lamb

Braised Lamb Shanks
Bulgur *Couscous*
Lamb Cassoulet
Lamb Chop Quince Saute
Lamb Korma
Ragout of Lamb

Pork

Dutch Kale with Potatoes and Sausage
Hopping John (black-eyed peas,
rice and pig's feet)
Lecso (Austrian Tomato, Sausage,
Pepper Ragout)
Orange Marinated Pork Roast
Oven-Baked Sausage
Pork Mango Saute
Pork Prune Roll-Ups

Turkey

Grapes Turkey Mornay (an
aristocratic sandwich)
Turkey a la King
Turkey Bulgur Casserole
Turkey Divan
Turkey Tetrazzini

Veal

Curried Apple and Veal
Mango-Topped Veal Chops
Veal a la Madelon (Veal and
Mushrooms in Sauce)

Organ Meats

Brains

Brain Fritters

Gizzards	Braised Chicken (or Turkey) Gizzards Gizzard Chili
Heart	Hearty Hash Stuffed Beef Heart Sweet-Sour Beef Heart
Kidneys	Kidneys en Brochette Steak and Kidney Pie Stir-Fried Kidneys Veal Kidneys Bordelaise
Liver	*Beef Liver* Beef Liver a la Suisse Chanfaina of Liver *Chicken Livers* Chinese Chicken Livers *Pork Liver* Liver Pate

Stomach

Pennsylvania Dutch Pig's Stomach

Sweetbreads

Breaded Sweetbreads
Sweetbread Mushroom Curry

Tongue

Boiled Fresh Tongue
Tongue Salad or Sandwich Spread

Tripe

Spanish Tripe
Tripe Lyonnaise

PANCAKES AND CREPES

Baked Banana Pancake
Barley Flour Pancakes
Buckwheat Crepes
Catfish Crepes
Cheese and Bean Crepes
Convenience Crepes
Cornmeal and Rye Pancakes
Crepes Suzette
Mushroom Crepes
Oat Crepes
Rice and Soy Crepes

Turnip and Potato Salad, Grated
Watermelon and Onion Salad
Zucchini, Pepper and Tomato Relish

Main Dish
Salads

Apple, Beet and Tuna Salad
Blackberry and Cantaloupe Salad
      with Cottage Cheese
Fish Salad or Sandwich Filling
Gado Gado (Indonesian)
Herbed Soybean Salad .
Jellied Avocado Tuna Loaf
Navy Bean Salad
Salmon Kidney Bean Salad
Whole Wheat Macaroni Salad
      with Cheese Dressing

Salad Dressings

Avocado Banana Dressing
Basic Oil and Vinegar Dressing
Beet Dressing
Cottage Cheese Dressing
Emerald Dressing
Lemon Dressing
Lemon-Sesame Dressing
Lime Honey Dressing
Savory Yogurt Salad Dressing
Soy Salad Dressing
Spicy Yogurt Dressing for Fruit Salad
Sunflower Mayonnaise

Sunflower Oil Dressing
Tomato Dressing
Watercress Dressing

SAVORY SAUCES
AND CONDIMENTS

Apple and Apricot Chutney
Basic Gravy
Basic White Sauce
Cheese Sauce
Fig Sauce for Meat Loaf or Pork Roast
Garam Masala (Indian spice mixture)
Green Tomato Pickle
Scottish Egg Sauce
Tomato Sauce
Wheat Germ Breading Mix
Wheat Germ Giblet Stuffing

SOUPS

Alfalfa Sprout Gazpacho
Black Bean Soup
Brain Soup
Cashew Carrot Soup
Cheese Soup
Chick-Pea and Cabbage Soup
Cold Beet and Cucumber Soup
Cold Whey Soup with Potatoes
    and Zucchini
Court Bouillon (fish stock)
Dashi (Japanese fish stock)

Fish Chowder
Garden Soup
Kohlrabi Soup
Mexican Dry Rice Soup
Oatmeal Soup
Okra Soup
Orange Borscht
Peanut Butter Soup
Russian Barley Soup
Sweet Potato Soup
Swiss Chard Soup
Winter Squash Soup

Fruit Soups

Apricot Soup
Avocado Grapefruit Soup
Avocado Soup, Creamy
Blackberry Soup
Caribbean Banana Soup
Cherry Soup
Hot Rhubarb Soup
Peach and Cantaloupe Soup
Strawberry Soup

SWEETS
Cakes

Banana Sweet Potato Cake
Carob Bran Cake
Carob Honey Cake
   (Carob Nut Frosting)
Cherry Custard Cake
Danish Apple Cake

Holiday Fruitcake
Honey Spice Cake
Jelly Roll
Peach Almond Torte
Walnut Torte

Confections

Carob Carrot Candy
Carob Potato Bonbons
Carob Raisin Clusters
Carrot Confection
Molasses Bran Candy
Molasses and Peanut Butter
    Log Confection
Oat Candy
Quince Paste (old-fashioned
    quince candy)
Super Fudge
Wheat Sprout Candy

Cookies

Banana Cookies
Basic Oatmeal Cookies
Bran Cookies
Carob Nut Brownies
Oatmeal Cookies
Raised Peanut Cookies
Sesame Cookies
Sunflower Seed Cookies
Triticale Nut Drops

Dessert Sauces

Apricot Sauce

Carob Syrup
Cranberry Yogurt Sauce
Foamy Sauce

Fruit Desserts

Apfelkuchen Souffle
Applesauce (unsweetened)
Apple Strudel Slices
Blueberry Yogurt
Cold Berry Souffle
Cranberry-Applesauce
Cranberry Galette
Lemon Orange Gelatin
Peach Fritters
Plum, Peach and Nectarine Compote
Raw Apple and Black Walnut Cream
Spiced Plums in Wine
Strawberry Cream Roll
Wheat Berry *Muesli*
Winter Pear Crunch

Ice Cream, Sherbet

Carrot Yogurt Sorbet
Cherry Ice Cream
Lemon Sherbet (milkless)
Strawberry Soft Yogurt Ice Cream
Yellow Plum Ice Cream

Pies

Apple Pie with Whole Wheat
    and Rice Pastry

Apricot Prune Apple Tart
Carob Cottage Cheese Pie
Coconut Yogurt Cheese Pie
Cranberry Apple Tart
Crumb Crust
Gooseberry Meringue Pie
Green Tomato and Apple Mince Pie
Key Lime Pie
Mock Pumpkin Pie
Oat and Rice Flaky Pastry
Oat and Wheat Pastry
Pear and Orange Custard Tart
Plum Custard Tart
Quince Tart
Rhubarb Custard Pie
Soybean Custard Pie
Strawberry Cheesecake Pie
Strawberry Custard Pie
Sweet Potato Pie
Whole Wheat Flaky Pastry
Whole Wheat and Walnut Pastry
Zucchini Lemon Pie

Puddings

Barley Apple Pudding
Bulgur Raisin Custard
Carob Peanut Butter Pudding
English Plum Pudding
Indian Pudding
Noodle Kugel
Pineapple Pudding

Pumpkin Pudding
Rhubarb Fool
Rye Bread Berry Pudding
Thick Custard
Thick Vanilla Yogurt

VEGETABLES

Amaranth, Sauteed
Asparagus with Yogurt Dill Sauce
Bean Sprouts, Stir-Fried
Broccoli and Carrots, Curried
Brussels Sprouts with Brazil Nut Sauce
Brussels Sprouts in Mushroom Sauce
"Bubble and Squeak" (English cabbage
    and potato hash)
Cabbage, Curried
Cabbage, Stir-Fried
Cauliflower with Garlic-Crumb Topping
Celery, Green Bean and Tomato Toss
Celery Hearts, Braised
Corn, Baked Pennsylvania Dutch Dried
Green Soybean and Corn Succotash
Jerusalem Artichokes, Fried
Jerusalem Artichokes au Gratin
Kohlrabi, Herbed
Mushrooms, Stuffed
Okra Curry
Okra, Fried
Parsley Pesto
Parsnip Patties
Parsnips and Carrots, Baked

Parsnips, Glazed
Potato Starch
Potatoes with Apples *(Himmel und Erde)*
Potatoes with Yogurt, Curried
Potato Pudding, Lithuanian *(Kugelis)*
Pumpkin Ring, Baked
Pumpkin, Sauteed
Swiss Chard, Braised
Swiss Chard Loaf
Turnips, Glazed
Turnips and Peas au Gratin
Zucchini, Corn and Tomato Saute
Zucchini Dollar Cakes
Zucchini in Yogurt Sauce

The Best Foods to Use

The most exciting thing about food is the extravagant variety of it! Think of bread and you don't have to have a loaf made with wheat in mind—you can be thinking of the tasty breads that are made with oat flour, cornmeal, triticale, millet, rye or barley. Mention cheese and while one person gets a mental picture of the well-known yellow slice by Kraft, another is savoring the idea of a cracker spread with Brie, or a chunk of feta, a slab of Stilton, a slice of provolone. To some people beans mean only a can of Campbell's Pork 'n' Beans; others conjure up dishes made with limas, kidneys, soybeans, black-eyed peas, and a dozen other delicious legumes.

Generally speaking, people stick to the foods they know best. But what a waste that can be! There's luscious flavor, delightful texture and true visual beauty—not to mention exceptional nutrition—in markets full of natural foods that are passed over only because they are unfamiliar. People say they don't know what to expect in cooking with yogurt for the first time; they are insecure about serving organ meats and they worry about the time it takes to cook with any flour but wheat flour. We believe these people are missing some of the great joys of the table for the flimsiest reasons. And more important, they're not being fair to themselves.

The following pages deal with dozens of interesting foods that have plenty to offer in taste and goodness, as well as savings. Nowadays it's surprisingly easy to shop for them, store and prepare them, and we supply some useful tips on how to introduce unfamiliar foods into your regular menu plans.

27

Cooking with Cereal Grains

Having a good selection of cereal grains on your kitchen shelf is your assurance that a meal is always on hand. The grains all store well, so you can maintain a well-stocked kitchen. Buy the freshest grain available and keep it in a tightly covered container in a cool, dry place. Held in this manner, whole grains will keep for about a year. Because insects thrive on healthy grain, the well-closed container will protect your supply against infestation as well.

When cereal grains are cooked, they absorb liquid and swell; millet and barley increase to four times their original amount, while all other grains swell two and a half to three times their size. Plan on serving half a cup of cooked grain per person for breakfast or as a side dish, and one cup cooked grain for main dish servings.

The same basic cooking method can be applied to all the cereal grains:

1. Rinse raw grain in cold water and drain well. This will help remove both surface grit and excess starch, as well as start the swelling process.
2. Bring correct amount of cooking liquid to a boil (see chart), in a pot large enough to accommodate the increase in volume after cooking. Meat or vegetable stock, juice, milk or water may be used. The more flavorful the cooking liquid, the more flavorful the cooked grain will be.
3. Add grain to the boiling liquid. Stir once.
4. Allow the liquid to return to boiling, then turn heat down to the lowest possible setting, cover and cook grains slowly until they are soft. This will take anywhere from 10 minutes to one hour (see chart).

To determine if the grain is cooked, use the bite test: well-cooked grain will be chewy, but not tough or hard. If not quite done, add a little more water, cover and continue cooking.

If you'd like a creamier product for porridge or pudding, do not heat the cooking liquid initially, but combine it first with the uncooked grain, then bring the mixture to a boil. Cover and continue as above.

The addition of salt slows the cooking, so it is best to wait until the grain is tender, then season.

Too much stirring makes the grain gummy, so stir only as suggested.

Cooked grain can be held in a covered pot off the heat until needed. It will hold its heat for quite awhile.

Grain for Every Course

There's a place for cereal grain dishes in every course of the meal from soup to dessert. Grain prepared according to the basic cooking instructions can be served as an accompaniment to meat or fish or used as a base for vegetables or stew. Cook the grain in a pot of soup for a rich chowder. Knead leftover grains into dough for a very special bread. The cooked grain can be seasoned with honey, dried fruit, herbs or cheese for a breakfast porridge or a dinner pilaf.

If you like hot cereal, experiment with different combinations. You will experience new taste sensations and vary or increase the nutritional values because the amino acid patterns of different grains complement each other.

If you prepare a mix, you might want to make enough for more than one use. A relatively quick-cooking (15 to 20 minutes) mixture for about 20 half-cup servings is made from:

> 3 *cups oatmeal*
> 1 *cup rye flakes*
> ¼ *cup cornmeal*
> ¼ *cup raw wheat germ*
> ¼ *cup bran*

A cooking time of about 35 to 45 minutes is needed for the following nutritional mixture (for approximately eight servings):

> 1½ *cups brown rice*
> ½ *cup millet*
> ½ *cup barley*
> ¼ *cup soy grits*

The pages that follow provide some interesting specifics on several individual grain foods and some good ideas on how to use them in new ways.

Grain Cooking Chart

Grain	Amount Uncooked	Amount of Water	Cooking Method and Time[1]	Amount of Cooked Grain
Barley	1 cup	4 cups	Boil—30–40 minutes	4 cups
Buckwheat	1 cup	2–5 cups[1]	Boil—20 minutes	3 cups
Bulgur	1 cup	2 cups	Boil—15 minutes	2½ cups
Cornmeal	1 cup	4–5 cups[2]	Boil or Double Boiler—30–40 minutes	4–5 cups
Millet	1 cup	4 cups	Boil or Double Boiler—25–30 minutes	4 cups
Oatmeal	1 cup	2 cups	Boil—10 minutes	4 cups
Rice (Brown)	1 cup	2–2½ cups[3]	Boil—35–40 minutes	2½ cups
Rye	1 cup	4 cups	Boil—1 hour	2⅔ cups
Triticale	1 cup	4 cups	Boil—1 hour	2½ cups
Wheat Berries	1 cup	3–4 cups[1]	Boil—1 hour	2½ cups
Wild Rice	1 cup	4 cups	Boil—40 minutes	3–3½ cups

Notes

1.   All whole grains may be cooked by the thermos method. Place 1 cup grain in a quart thermos (preferably wide-mouth) and add boiling water almost to the top, leaving 1-inch headspace between water and stopper of thermos. Using a long wooden spoon handle, stir grain to distribute water evenly. Close and leave for 8 to 12 hours. (For rice, add only 1½ cups boiling water and leave only 8 hours.)

Another method for cooking grains is the "pilaf" method. This involves sauteing the grain, usually with minced onion, in oil and then adding stock or water, approximately twice as much liquid as grain, and cooking it, covered, over medium-low heat until the liquid is absorbed and the grain is tender. The time is about the same as above. Brown rice, bulgur, barley, millet and wild rice are especially good cooked this way. Buckwheat is traditionally cooked in this way, but a raw egg is usually stirred into the dry grains before adding the stock or water. This replaces the need for sauteing the buckwheat in oil, and is done to keep the grain separate throughout the cooking. The required amount of water is 2 cups for the "egg" method of cooking buckwheat, and 5 cups when cooking it to be eaten as a cereal. See the Index for Buckwheat Groat Patties and Buckwheat-Stuffed Cabbage Rolls.

The hard grains such as wheat, rye and triticale may be brought to a boil in the required amount of water, boiled for 10 minutes, then left to soak for 8 to 12 hours in this same water. After the long soaking, they may be cooked for 15 to 20 minutes and will be tender enough to eat. This is one way to shorten the cooking time.

The pressure cooker method offers the advantage of cutting the cooking time in the above chart in half. In general, use twice as much water as grain when cooking in the pressure cooker, although more water—four times the amount of grain—is needed for the harder grains, such as rye, triticale and wheat.

2.   When adding cornmeal to boiling water, it is best to first combine it with 1 cup of cold water and then stir this into the remaining 3 or 4 cups of boiling water. The lesser amount of water is to be used when you wish to have a stiff cooked cornmeal, as for cornmeal mush.

3.   The lesser amount of water is required for short- or medium-grain rice, the larger amount for long-grain rice.

A further tip on cooking grains:
To enhance the flavor and shorten cooking time, toast grains in a dry, medium-hot, iron skillet, stirring constantly, until they have a pleasant fragrance and take on a darker color. This also enables the grain to be "cracked" or coarsely ground in an electric blender.

Barley

In our culture people are more likely to think of barley as an important ingredient in beer brewing than they are to think of it as a basic ingredient in stuffing or dessert. Actually, it can be used in these and many other ways on the daily menu. In some countries barley is a major dietary staple.

Barley is a cereal that needs plenty of moisture to grow and the grain retains much of this moisture. Therefore it should be stored in a dry place. This is a fact that should be considered if people buy in bulk for a co-op.

Don't throw away the water drained from barley that has been cooked. Either drink it as is, or flavor it with honey, fruit or herbs to taste. It has been said that the flawless complexion of British women is due to their drinking barley water in quantities and regularly.

Here's one way to make barley water from scratch:

Simmer ¼ cup pearl barley in 1¼ quarts of water for about an hour. Squeeze 1 lemon and 2 or 3 oranges, and set the juice aside. Pour off the water in which barley has been cooked, add the fruit rinds to it and let cool. Then remove the rinds, add the fruit juice and refrigerate for future use.

It's a refreshing, healthful drink. The barley itself can be used for another dish.

Special Barley Recipes

Barley that has been put through a roasting and steeping process (malted barley) can be used to make a very fine beverage which is brewed like coffee, but has neither caffeine nor any other harmful ingredients.

There's an instant grain beverage, called Pero. In addition to the barley, it contains some chicory, rye and molasses. You can make a cup of Pero in the same way you'd make instant coffee.

For people whose stomachs don't react too well to chicory or who don't like its rather strong taste, there is *Kathreiners Malzkaffee*. It was first used and recommended by Sebastian Kneipp, a German priest who lived in the nineteenth century and was very concerned about people's health. The beverage that Kneipp introduced is pure malted barley, roasted, nothing added. It's brewed like coffee and can be drunk with or without milk and sweetener. It is tasty and easy on the stomach. In Germany it is an accepted beverage for the whole family, especially for children. You can get it in any grocery store handling imported food and also in some health food stores.

Barley Apple Pudding

½ *cup barley*	1 *tablespoon oil*
2 *cups sliced apples*	3 *tablespoons honey*
1 *tablespoon lemon juice*	½ *teaspoon cinnamon*
⅓ *cup orange juice*	¼ *teaspoon nutmeg*

Cook barley according to preferred method. (See "Cooking with Cereal Grains.") Drain and reserve liquid for soup.

Preheat oven to 350°F. Arrange apple slices to cover the bottom of an oiled casserole. Drizzle lemon juice over the apples. Mix remaining ingredients with the cooked barley and spoon over apple slices. Bake in preheated oven for 30 minutes. Serve hot or cold as dessert.

Yield: 6 servings

Russian Barley Soup

½ cup barley
1 small onion, minced
1 tablespoon butter
2 cups chicken stock
¼ teaspoon dill
¼ teaspoon ground
    coriander
½ teaspoon dried mint
salt to taste
1 tablespoon rye or whole
    wheat flour
2 eggs, beaten
1 cup yogurt
2 tablespoons lemon juice
fresh parsley, chopped
fresh mint, chopped

Cook barley according to preferred method. (See "Cooking with Cereal Grains.")

Saute onion in butter. Heat chicken stock to boiling and stir onion and cooked barley with any remaining liquid into stock. Add herbs and salt. Blend flour into eggs, then carefully stir in yogurt. Add a little of the hot soup to the egg and yogurt mixture, gradually stirring it in to avoid "scrambling" the eggs, then pour this back into the hot soup. Stir in lemon juice. Keep hot but do not permit to boil. Add fresh parsley and mint just before serving.

Yield: 6 to 8 servings

Barley-Buttermilk Biscuits

1 tablespoon dry yeast
¼ cup lukewarm water
1 tablespoon honey
1¼ cups barley flour
¼ teaspoon salt
2 tablespoons butter
¼ cup buttermilk
1 egg

Soften dry yeast in lukewarm water, add honey and allow mixture to set for approximately 15 minutes, or until frothy.

Combine barley flour and salt and, with two knives or pastry blender, cut butter into the dry ingredients. Combine buttermilk and egg and beat slightly, then stir into the flour mixture. Add yeast mixture, mix thoroughly and let the whole mixture stand for 20 minutes. *Preheat oven to 400°F.*

Drop dough by tablespoon onto an oiled baking sheet. Pat into 2-inch rounds and bake in preheated oven for 15 to 18 minutes, or until nicely browned.

Yield: 12 2-inch biscuits

Barley Flour Pancakes

Soften yeast in lukewarm water. Stir in honey and set aside for 5 minutes.

Blend together eggs and yogurt and add to yeast mixture. Then add flour and oil. Leave batter in a warm place for 20 minutes.

Ladle batter onto a hot, oiled griddle or skillet and cook until browned and puffy. Turn pancake and cook until the second side is nicely browned.

Serve with honey or maple syrup.

Yield: approximately 10 pancakes

4 *teaspoons dry yeast*
½ *cup lukewarm water*
2 *tablespoons honey*
2 *eggs*
1 *cup yogurt*
1 *cup barley flour*
2 *tablespoons oil*

Tibetan "Prayer Wheel" Barley Bread

Sprinkle yeast over lukewarm water, adding honey to mixture and leave to "work" while preparing the dough.

Put oil in a heavy iron skillet, and over medium-high heat, brown barley flour and sesame seeds in the skillet, stirring constantly, until flour is an even tan color. Take care to prevent it from burning.

Remove mixture from skillet and put it into a large bowl. Stir in salt and 4 cups whole wheat flour.

Mix the hot water and oil and stir it into the flour mixture until the ingredients are completely combined. Allow mixture to cool until it tests lukewarm to the wrist.

When mixture is lukewarm, stir in the yeast mixture. Using ½ cup whole wheat flour, knead dough for 15 minutes on a floured board, until it is smooth to the touch.

Place dough in large oiled bowl and turn it over to oil the surface. Cover with a damp cloth and allow to rise in a warm draft-free place overnight.

In the morning carefully place on oiled cookie sheet,

1 *tablespoon dry yeast*
½ *cup lukewarm water*
1 *teaspoon honey*
2 *tablespoons sesame oil or other oil*
2 *cups barley flour*
½ *cup unhulled sesame seeds*
2 *tablespoons salt*
4 *cups whole wheat flour*
3 *cups hot water*
2 *tablespoons sesame oil or other oil*
½ *cup whole wheat flour*
1 *egg, beaten*
1 *teaspoon water*
¼ *cup unhulled sesame seeds*

keeping the shape of the risen dough. Do not re-knead, punch down or reshape in any way.

Combine the egg with water and brush top of dough with mixture. Sprinkle sesame seeds over surface.

With the tip of a sharp knife, score a large cross on the surface of the loaf. Allow the loaf to spread on cookie sheet for an hour in a warm, draft-free place. *Preheat oven to 450°F.*

After an hour, when the loaf will resemble a large wheel, bake in preheated oven for 1 hour. The high temperature produces a crusty exterior and tender interior. Cool loaf on rack before slicing.

Yield: 1 large loaf

Buckwheat

Buckwheat isn't a wheat—it isn't even a grain. This Russian native is a cultivated member of the rhubarb family whose dark brown, pyramid-shaped seeds are used just as cereal grains are used. Buckwheat is less expensive than any of the grains, yet it is high in fiber and contains more high-quality protein than all other grains except rice and oats. It is a good source of the B vitamins and rutin and is lower in calories than rice or corn.

Most Americans think of buckwheat pancakes when buckwheat is mentioned, but that's only because they're not familiar with the tasty pilaf made from the buckwheat groats (kasha) and the casseroles in which buckwheat plays a major role. Try kasha in a stuffing for fowl, in bread or in Buckwheat Groat Patties.

When you buy buckwheat groats, remember that two kinds are sold—raw (light) and roasted (dark). Both kinds can be ground into flour. Most people identify only the dark one as buckwheat flour. If its rather distinctive taste does not appeal to you, experiment with the light kind. When steamed, it tastes similar to barley.

Brown the meat in oil in a Dutch oven or heavy pot which has a tight-fitting lid. Add onion and saute until lightly browned. 🍲 (If using crockery pot, omit the following steps and continue with method below.) Keeping the meat in the center of the pot, add the other ingredients. Cover and cook in a very slow oven (200°F.) for 8 hours or overnight. Serve with tomato sauce or catsup.

Yield: 6 to 8 servings

🍲 Transfer meat to crockery pot, add other ingredients. Cover and cook on low for 6 to 8 hours. Serve with tomato sauce or catsup.

Buckwheat Cholent

(This recipe can be cooked in a crockery pot. See marker 🍲 *for method below.)*

1½ to 2 *lbs. brisket of beef, or chuck*
  2 *tablespoons oil*
  1 *large onion, finely chopped*
  1 *cup navy beans*
  1 *cup buckwheat groats*
 ½ *teaspoon salt*
   pinch of pepper
  4 *cups boiling water*

Cook buckwheat groats according to preferred method. (See "Cooking with Cereal Grains.") Drain if necessary.

Put cooked groats in a large mixing bowl. Add butter, molasses, salt and cinnamon. In a small bowl, soften yeast in lukewarm water, add honey and set aside until frothy.

Combine the two mixtures, then add the flours, wheat germ and water. Beat for 3 minutes. Cover with a towel and put in a warm place to rise for 1 hour.

Stir the dough down and put in an oiled large loaf pan. Let rise for 1 hour. *Preheat oven to 400°F.* and bake for 15 minutes. Lower the heat to 375°F. and bake 55 minutes longer, until done. Remove from pan and cool on rack.

Yield: 1 loaf

Buckwheat Kasha Bread

 ½ *cup buckwheat groats*
 ¼ *cup butter*
 ⅓ *cup molasses*
  2 *teaspoons salt*
 ½ *teaspoon cinnamon*
  2 *tablespoons dry yeast*
  3 *tablespoons lukewarm water*
  1 *tablespoon honey*
  1 *cup buckwheat flour*
1½ *cups whole wheat flour*
 ¼ *cup wheat germ*
 ⅔ *cup warm water*

Buckwheat Groat Patties

1 *cup buckwheat groats*
1 *egg*
2 *cups boiling water*
½ *teaspoon salt*
2 *small onions,*
      thinly sliced
½ *lb. mushrooms,*
      chopped
1 *teaspoon oil*
1 *tablespoon chopped*
      parsley
2 *eggs, slightly beaten*
1 *tablespoon chopped*
      sunflower seeds

In a heavy saucepan combine groats with egg and cook until egg is completely absorbed. Add boiling water and salt. Simmer for 15 to 20 minutes, or until water is absorbed.

While groats are cooking, saute onions and mushrooms in oil for approximately 5 minutes. Mix sauteed vegetables with cooked groats, add parsley, eggs, and sunflower seeds.

Form into patties or drop by tablespoon onto oiled heated skillet. Saute both sides until nicely browned.

Yield: 8 3-inch patties

Buckwheat-Stuffed Cabbage Rolls

1 *medium-size onion,*
      finely chopped
½ *green pepper, finely*
      chopped
3 *tablespoons oil*
2 *cups buckwheat groats*
4 *cups boiling water*
½ *teaspoon salt*
  pepper to taste
½ *cup chopped peanuts*
¼ *cup chopped sunflower*
      seeds
1 *head cabbage*
warm water

Saute the onion and green pepper in oil until tender (approximately 5 minutes). Add groats and stir until coated with oil. Add the water, cover and simmer 15 minutes or until groats are tender and the water has been absorbed. Season and add peanuts and sunflower seeds.

While groats are cooking, core the cabbage and steam until leaves are pliable. Separate the leaves and place 2 heaping tablespoons of the groat mixture on each leaf. Roll up, tucking in the sides. *Preheat oven to 350°F.*

Place cabbage rolls in an oiled baking dish. Pour warm water over rolls to reach three-quarters of the way up the sides of the dish. Cover and bake in preheated oven for 1½ hours or until cabbage is tender.

Yield: 16 cabbage rolls

Cook buckwheat according to preferred method. (See "Cooking with Cereal Grains.") Drain if necessary.

Preheat oven to 400°F. Puree cottage cheese briefly in electric blender until smooth. Add cooked groats and mix well. Beat egg yolks slightly and add to cheese-groat mixture. Add seasonings and mix thoroughly. Beat egg whites until stiff and fold into the mixture. Pour into a buttered rectangular pan and spread to about ½-inch thickness.

Bake in preheated oven for approximately 30 minutes, or until top is brown. Cut into squares and serve as a side dish with meat or an all-vegetable dinner.

Yield: 4 servings

Cottage Cheese Buckwheat Squares

1 *cup buckwheat groats*
1 *cup cottage cheese*
3 *egg yolks*
½ *teaspoon salt*
1 *tablespoon chopped parsley*
1 *teaspoon chopped chives*
1 *teaspoon basil*
½ *teaspoon thyme*
3 *egg whites*

Stir groats into boiling water, add salt and cook approximately 20 minutes, or until soft. Add raisins and cook 5 minutes longer. Sweeten with honey if desired. Serve with milk.

Yield: 3 cups

Buckwheat Porridge

½ *cup buckwheat groats*
2½ *cups boiling water*
½ *teaspoon salt*
⅓ *cup raisins*

Combine all ingredients in electric blender and process until batter is smooth. Let rest for 2 hours to allow particles of flour to expand in liquid, resulting in a tender crepe. Just before baking crepes, process batter again briefly to blend ingredients.

Follow standard method for cooking crepes. (See Index.)

Yield: 16 8-inch crepes

Buckwheat Crepes

5 *eggs*
1 *tablespoon honey (optional)*
2 *tablespoons oil or butter*
1 *cup buttermilk*
1 *cup water*
1¼ *cups buckwheat flour*
½ *cup whole wheat pastry flour*
1 *teaspoon grated orange rind*
½ *teaspoon salt*

Buckwheat Muffins

Preheat oven to 425°F.

½ cup raisins
1 cup water
1⅓ cups buckwheat flour
⅔ cup finely chopped
       walnuts
½ teaspoon salt
2 tablespoons wheat germ
1 tablespoon molasses
1 tablespoon oil
3 egg yolks
3 egg whites, stiffly beaten

Soak raisins in water for approximately 10 minutes. While they are soaking, combine flour, nuts, salt and wheat germ. Separately, combine molasses, oil and egg yolks. Add raisins and soaking water. Combine the two mixtures and then fold in egg whites. Bake in oiled muffin tins in preheated oven for 20 minutes.

Yield: 12 muffins

Corn

If you are looking for a simple and appetizing way to add more unrefined grains to your list of cooking ingredients, you needn't look any further than cornmeal, the ground kernels of corn. It's a tasty, nutritious and economical food that can be used in a variety of ways, particularly in baking.

Most supermarkets sell cornmeal, but most of these products are "degermed" or bolted. It's best to buy the whole corn as freshly ground as possible. Natural food stores are the best source for this.

Robert Rodale, editor and publisher of *Prevention* magazine, has his own favorite way of using cornmeal:

"I have found that the most convenient and tastiest way to eat corn regularly is in the form of homemade corn pones. In fact, I have been eating them for years because I like the taste much better than the taste of bread, and only recently have come to value them even more for their bowel-bulking action. Here is the recipe:

"Heat several cups of water to boiling. While it is heating, put three cups of *white* cornmeal and a half teaspoon of salt in the mixing bowl. If you can get raw peanut flour, add about one-half cup of that, and you can also add some sesame seeds and/or caraway seeds.

"Slowly pour the boiling water and one-third cup of corn oil into the meal at the same time. Stir thoroughly. Use only enough of the water to make a firm dough, not too wet.

"After the mixture cools, form into about 15 cakes with the hands. I let the imprints of my fingers remain to save time. Bake on a greased pan for 35 to 40 minutes in a 375°F. oven. They are done when the edges get well browned."

The versatility of corn is readily demonstrated in dishes such as Gnocchi, an Italian specialty, and in Indian Pudding, where this popular grain food turns up as the basic ingredient of a dessert—and a very popular one, at that.

Banana Cornbread

Sprinkle yeast over lukewarm water. Add honey. Set aside for 10 minutes to activate yeast. Combine cornmeal, oat flour, soy flour and salt.

Mash bananas with a fork. Stir in oil, beaten eggs and finally the dissolved yeast mixture.

Combine liquid and dry ingredients and pour into oiled 9x9-inch pan. Let cornbread rise for 30 minutes or until it is doubled in the pan.

Preheat oven to 350°F. and bake bread for 30 to 35 minutes until it is golden brown on top. Serve warm.

Yield: 6 to 8 servings

- 4 *teaspoons dry yeast*
- ½ *cup lukewarm water*
- 2 *tablespoons honey*
- 1 *cup cornmeal*
- ¾ *cup oat flour*
- ¼ *cup soy flour*
- ¾ *teaspoon salt*
- 1 *cup bananas (approximately 2 bananas)*
- 3 *tablespoons oil*
- 2 *eggs, beaten*

Cornmeal and Rye Pancakes

Sprinkle dry yeast over lukewarm water. Add honey. Let soak for 10 minutes.

Combine beaten eggs and oil. Stir in cornmeal, rye flour and salt. Add yeast mixture. Leave in a warm place for 30 minutes.

Lightly oil an iron skillet and heat to medium-high heat. Spoon pancake batter into skillet in desired amount. When bubbles appear on the surface of the pancakes, turn them. Remove when brown on underside. Serve immediately.

Yield: 20 4-inch pancakes

- 6 *teaspoons dry yeast*
- 1½ *cups lukewarm water*
- 1 *tablespoon honey*
- 2 *eggs, beaten*
- 2 *tablespoons oil*
- 1 *cup cornmeal*
- ½ *cup rye flour*
- ½ *teaspoon salt*

Cornmeal Puff

1½ cups milk
3 tablespoons butter
⅓ cup yellow cornmeal
½ teaspoon salt
1 cup shredded sharp
    cheddar cheese
5 egg yolks
2 tablespoons chopped
    green onion
5 egg whites

Preheat oven to 350°F.

In the top of a double boiler, cook the milk, butter, cornmeal and salt, stirring occasionally, until thick and steaming (approximately 7 minutes). Remove from heat; stir in cheese, egg yolks and green onion. Beat egg whites until stiff. Gently fold into cornmeal mixture. Turn into a well-greased 2-quart casserole. Place dish in a pan of hot water and bake in preheated oven for 35 minutes.

Yield: 6 to 8 servings

Gnocchi

2 cups milk
½ cup yellow cornmeal
1½ teaspoons honey
1 teaspoon salt
½ cup grated Swiss cheese
1 tablespoon soft butter
2 eggs, beaten
½ cup grated Swiss cheese
1 tablespoon soft butter

Combine milk and cornmeal, then add honey and salt, and cook in a double boiler for 30 minutes or until cornmeal is soft and has absorbed most of the milk. Remove from heat and add ½ cup cheese, 1 tablespoon butter, and the beaten eggs, stirring each in to blend well. Spread at least ½ inch thick in an oiled, shallow casserole. Cool and chill several hours or overnight.

Preheat oven to 375°F. Before baking, top with ½ cup cheese and 1 tablespoon butter. Bake 30 minutes in preheated oven. Cut into 1-inch squares and serve in Tomato Sauce. (See Index.)

Yield: 6 servings

Indian Pudding

3 cups milk
¼ cup butter
⅔ cup molasses
3 tablespoons honey
⅔ cup cornmeal
1 teaspoon salt
¾ teaspoon cinnamon
¾ teaspoon nutmeg
1 cup milk

Heat 3 cups milk. Stir in butter, molasses and honey. Combine cornmeal, salt and spices and stir gradually into warm milk mixture, using a wire whisk to avoid lumps. Cook over low heat, stirring constantly, approximately 10 minutes or until thick. *Preheat oven to 300°F.* Turn into oiled casserole, pour 1 cup milk over pudding (do not stir), and bake in preheated oven for 3 hours.

Yield: 6 to 8 servings

Beat egg yolks, add yogurt, salt and cornmeal. Beat egg whites stiff and fold them into cornmeal mixture. Heat 10-inch cast-iron skillet medium-hot, melt butter in it and pour in cornbread batter. Cover skillet and keep over medium-hot fire or burner for 10 minutes.

Carefully loosen cornbread around the outside, cut into wedges and turn each wedge over. Cover skillet and let cook another 2 minutes or so, until top of cornbread has browned. Remove from skillet and serve hot.

Yield: 8 servings

Skillet Cornbread
(Cooked over a campfire or on top of the stove)

4 *egg yolks*
2 *cups yogurt*
1 *teaspoon salt*
2 *cups cornmeal*
4 *egg whites*
¼ *cup butter*

Preheat oven to 375°F.

Mix ingredients thoroughly, place in oiled, uncovered casserole and bake 50 minutes in preheated oven.

Yield: 6 to 8 servings

*If you prefer a very light dish, separate the eggs, adding the yolks first and then carefully folding in the stiffly beaten whites.

Baked Pennsylvania Dutch Dried Corn

1 *cup dried corn*
3 *cups cold milk*
2 *tablespoons oil*
1 *teaspoon salt*
1 *teaspoon honey (optional)*
2 *eggs, well beaten**

Millet

Millet comes in whole kernels or as flour. You cook it like rice or any other cereal and use it in many of the same ways. It has a pleasant nutty flavor and the addition of fresh, canned or dried fruit, or maple syrup, results in a most appetizing hot breakfast food. It can also be served as a luncheon or dinner course—cooked in bouillon it makes a tasty side dish.

Millet is highly adaptable to almost any recipe. It can be used by itself, or in combination with other grains, in casseroles, breads, crackers, stews, souffles, stuffings, granola or it can be served plain with butter, gravy or a vegetable sauce.

To bring out the unique flavor of millet, toast it first in a heavy, dry skillet, for one or two minutes, stirring constantly. Then use it as you would any grain.

Millet Bread

2 teaspoons honey
2½ cups lukewarm water
2 tablespoons dry yeast
2 eggs
2 tablespoons oil
2 teaspoons salt
1 cup millet flour
2 cups cornmeal
2 cups oat flour

Add honey to lukewarm water and sprinkle yeast over the surface. Leave to soak.

Combine eggs and oil. Combine salt, millet flour, cornmeal and oat flour. When yeast mixture is activated, add it to egg mixture, then stir this into the dry mixture, blending well.

Pour batter into oiled 9x9-inch pan. Leave in a warm place for 30 to 40 minutes or until batter has risen, increasing its volume by at least half as much. *Preheat oven to 350°F.* and bake 30 minutes or until bread is brown on top.

Yield: 8 to 10 servings

Millet Lentil Loaf

½ cup millet
1 cup lentils
2 green onions, thinly sliced
¼ cup oil
2 cups fresh, coarsely chopped spinach
2 eggs, beaten
2 apples, grated
1 tablespoon ground coriander
salt to taste
1 tablespoon lemon juice

Cook millet and lentils according to preferred methods. (See "Cooking with Cereal Grains" and "Basic Methods for Cooking Beans and Other Legumes.") Drain lentils if necessary.

Preheat oven to 350°F. Saute green onions in oil for a minute, then add spinach and toss lightly to steam for another minute or two. Combine cooked millet, lentils, sauteed vegetables, and remaining ingredients. Turn into oiled loaf pan and bake in preheated oven for 30 to 40 minutes or until firm and golden brown on top. Serve warm.

Yield: 4 to 6 servings

Bring salted water to a boil, stir in millet, turn heat down and simmer over direct heat or transfer to top of double boiler, place over boiling water and cook, covered, for 25 to 30 minutes until millet is soft. Turn into oiled loaf pan and cool. Refrigerate overnight or for several hours.

Remove from pan, slice loaf into ½-inch slices. Dust slices with flour and fry in a little oil until they are golden and crisp on both sides. Serve hot with maple syrup or honey.

Yield: 4 to 6 servings

Millet Mush

salt to taste
4 *cups water*
1 *cup millet*
flour
oil

Cook millet according to preferred method. (See "Cooking with Cereal Grains.")

Steam peppers for 5 minutes. Saute onion and beef in oil for approximately 5 minutes, stirring to brown meat evenly. *Preheat oven to 350°F.*

Combine millet with meat mixture, add seasonings and stuff into pepper halves. Top with wheat germ and Parmesan cheese and bake in preheated oven for 20 minutes. Serve with Tomato Sauce. (See Index.)

Yield: 4 to 6 servings

Millet-Stuffed Peppers

½ *cup millet*
4 *green peppers, halved, cored and seeded*
1 *medium-size onion, minced*
½ *lb. ground beef*
1 *tablespoon oil*
2 *tablespoons chopped parsley*
1 *teaspoon oregano*
2 *tablespoons wheat germ*
1 *tablespoon Parmesan cheese*

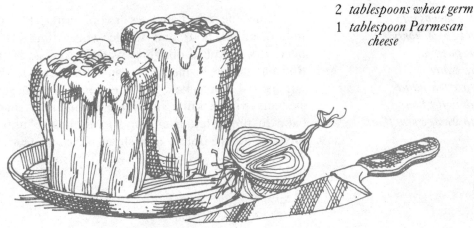

Millet-Wheat Bread

2 *tablespoons dry yeast*
¼ *cup lukewarm water*
2 *cups milk*
2 *tablespoons oil*
⅔ *cup honey*
1 *tablespoon salt*
3 *cups millet ("cracked" in electric blender)*
½ *cup soy flour*
4 *to 5 cups whole wheat flour*

Soften the yeast in water. Scald milk; add oil, honey, and salt. Pour this mixture over cracked millet, and allow it to cool, stirring occasionally. When mixture has cooled, add the softened yeast, soy flour, and 3 cups whole wheat flour. Blend well. Keep adding more flour until the dough is thick and fairly dry.

Knead for approximately 10 minutes until the dough seems moist and stretches without tearing. Shape the dough into a ball, place in a greased bowl, and turn over once. Cover bowl with a clean towel and set it in a warm place to allow dough to rise.

When dough has doubled in volume (in approximately 1½ hours) punch it down, place it on floured board, and shape it into loaves. Score top of each loaf with a sharp knife and place in well-greased loaf pans. Or, shape into round or oblong loaves and place on a cookie sheet sprinkled generously with cornmeal. Cover loaves and set them in a warm place to rise for 45 minutes. *Preheat oven to 375°F.* and bake approximately 50 minutes until done.

Yield: 2 loaves

Whole Millet Crackers

5 *tablespoons oil*
1 *tablespoon honey*
½ *teaspoon salt*
½ *cup water*
¼ *cup whole millet*
½ *cup millet flour*
1 *cup whole wheat flour*

Preheat oven to 350°F.

Combine oil, honey, salt and water. Stir in whole millet, millet flour and whole wheat flour. It may be necessary to knead dough to work in the last of the flour. Roll out dough ⅛ inch thick on *buttered* cookie sheet. Do not use oil as crackers may be difficult to loosen. Score crackers with a knife in square or diamond shapes, and bake in preheated oven for 20 minutes or until golden brown. Remove from cookie sheet and cool on rack.

Yield: 4 dozen crackers

Oats

Once you get away from the idea that oats is primarily a hot breakfast cereal, you are in for a lot of pleasant surprises. You can make terrific pastry, crackers and cookies with oats; it can be used as thickening for soups. Oats gives a distinct flavor and a lot of nutrition to granola, and oat flour can be added to make bread doughs better.

Scotland has given us many fine foods made from oats. There are scones, bannocks, buns, baps and parkins. Scones and bannocks are first cousins, made of the same dough, but scones are small and bannocks are plate-size. A bap is a small loaf or roll. Parkins are large cookies made of oatmeal and syrup. Many of these appear on the Scottish breakfast table together with fresh whole meal bread, all of them full of nutrition and easy to make.

Say No to Instant Oatmeal

Don't fall for the pretty packages of speedy cooking oats, ready porridge, instant oatmeal breakfast and the like. They usually contain additives and artificial flavorings and, in the case of the breakfast envelopes, lots of salt. If you really can't afford the time to cook your breakfast oatmeal for a few more minutes, soak the oats the evening before and just bring it to a boil the next morning. That's homemade instant oatmeal, cheap and additive free.

Oats is also a main ingredient in *muesli*, a high vitamin-protein food used by the famous physician Bircher-Benner, who held that a nutritious diet often has more healing power than pills. In making *muesli*, the oats (highest in protein of all the grains) are soaked, mixed with fruits and some milk, yogurt or other milk product, and eaten raw. It is similar to granola, but not toasted.

Oat Crepes

Combine all ingredients in electric blender and process until batter is smooth. Let rest for 2 hours to allow particles of flour to expand in liquid, resulting in a tender crepe. Just before baking crepes, process again briefly to blend ingredients.

Follow standard method for cooking crepes. (See Index.)

4 *eggs*
1 *tablespoon honey (optional)*
2 *tablespoons oil or butter*
2 *cups milk*
1½ *cups oat flour*
½ *teaspoon salt*

Yield: 16 8-inch crepes

Oat and Rice Flaky Pastry

¾ *cup oat flour*
¾ *cup brown rice flour*
½ *teaspoon salt*
6 *tablespoons butter*
1 *tablespoon oil*
2 *tablespoons ice water*

Preheat oven to 400°F.

Sprinkle a 9-inch pie pan lightly with flour.

Combine flours and salt in a bowl. Cut butter in with knives or a grater. Add oil gradually, working it in with fingers, then the ice water. Knead dough briefly until water is distributed evenly.

Press into prepared pie pan or roll out between well-floured sheets of wax paper and place in pie pan, making a high fluted edge around the outside. If baking shell without filling, prick it well with a fork. Bake in preheated oven for 10 to 12 minutes.

Yield: 1 9-inch pie shell

Oat and Wheat Pastry

1 *cup rolled oats*
1 *cup whole wheat pastry flour*
¼ *teaspoon salt*
¼ *cup unhulled sesame seeds*
½ *cup oil*
1 *tablespoon apple juice*

Preheat oven to 375°F.

Combine oats, flour and salt. Mix in sesame seeds and oil. Moisten with apple juice and press evenly into lightly oiled pie pan to ⅛-inch thickness. Bake in preheated oven for 20 minutes.

Yield: 1 9-inch pie shell

Oat Candy

2 *to 3 cardamom seed pods*
2 *cups oatmeal*
½ *cup almonds*
1 *medium-size apple*
¼ *cup honey*

Remove seeds from cardamom seed pods and crush them. "Grind" oatmeal and then almonds to a meal in electric blender. Peel, core and grate the apple. Combine all ingredients and stir in honey. Mix well with a spoon until thoroughly blended.

Pat out onto ungreased cookie sheet to a depth of ¼ inch. Refrigerate uncovered for several hours to allow to dry. Cut into squares, then turn over and let dry on bottom. When completely dry, store in airtight container.

Yield: approximately 3 dozen pieces

In a bowl, combine wet ingredients. In another bowl, combine dry ingredients. Stir wet mixture into dry mixture. Allow to stand for 30 minutes until oatmeal has absorbed some of the liquid. *Preheat oven to 325°F.*

Drop mixture by teaspoons onto greased baking sheet. Bake in preheated oven for 12 minutes.

Yield: 50 cookies

NOTE: For variations, add to recipe ½ cup peanut butter or ¼ cup carob and omit spices.

Preheat oven to 350°F.

Combine dry ingredients. Combine water, oil and honey. Stir dry ingredients into wet ones, to make a cohesive ball. Butter cookie sheet and pat out dough in shape of pan. Roll to thickness of ⅛ inch, using rolling pin. Score with knife in desired shapes and bake 12 minutes in preheated oven. Cool 5 minutes before removing crackers from baking sheet.

Yield: 4 dozen crackers—2 inches square

In an iron skillet or heavy-bottom saucepan, toast oatmeal over medium-high heat, stirring constantly to keep it from burning, until it is light brown. Remove oatmeal from pan and set aside.

Saute onion and garlic in oil or butter until tender. Combine with tomato, stock, soy grits and toasted oatmeal and cook over low heat for approximately 5 minutes. Season with tamari soy sauce and salt and serve.

Yield: approximately 4 cups

Oatmeal Cookies

    2 *eggs, beaten*
    ½ *cup oil*
    ½ *cup honey*
    ½ *cup non-fat dry milk*
 1¾ *cups oatmeal*
    ½ *cup wheat germ*
    ½ *teaspoon salt*
    ¼ *teaspoon ground cloves*
    1 *teaspoon cinnamon*
    ½ *cup sunflower seeds (optional)*

Oatmeal Crackers

 1½ *cups oatmeal (ground to a coarse flour in electric blender)*
    1 *cup whole wheat flour*
    ½ *teaspoon salt*
    ½ *cup water*
    5 *tablespoons oil*
    1 *tablespoon honey*

Oatmeal Soup

    ½ *cup oatmeal*
    ½ *small onion, finely chopped*
    1 *large clove garlic, minced*
    1 *tablespoon oil or melted butter*
    ¾ *cup chopped tomato, fresh or canned*
    4 *cups any soup stock*
    2 *tablespoons soy grits*
    2 *teaspoons tamari soy sauce*
    ¼ *teaspoon salt*

Scottish Scones or Bannocks

2 *tablespoons dry yeast*
6 *tablespoons lukewarm water*
2 *teaspoons honey*
2 *cups oatmeal (ground to a coarse flour in electric blender)*
2 *tablespoons lukewarm milk or light cream*
4 *teaspoons honey*
2 *eggs, beaten*
½ *teaspoon salt*
2 *tablespoons melted butter*

Dissolve yeast in the lukewarm water to which 2 teaspoons honey have been added. Add yeast mixture to oat flour along with milk or cream and 4 teaspoons honey. Mix well, cover and set aside in a warm place for 1 hour. Combine beaten eggs, salt and melted butter and stir into batter. Cover again and set aside for 1 more hour.

For scones, drop by tablespoon into oiled iron skillet and bake in preheated 400°F. oven for 10 minutes. For bannocks, pour batter all at once into large oiled skillet (approximately 10-inch), and bake as for scones. Cut into wedges before serving. Serve hot with butter and honey.

Yield: 6 servings (approximately 24 scones or 1 large bannock)

("Yankee Haymaker's Drink")

6 *tablespoons molasses*
6 *tablespoons honey*
½ *cup cider vinegar*
1½ *teaspoons ginger*
1 *egg, beaten (optional)*
½ *cup oatmeal*

In a 2-quart jar, combine all ingredients. Fill jar with water and refrigerate. Excellent thirst quencher.

Yield: 2 quarts

Rice

Brown rice is taking its place right up there, with wheat germ and yogurt, as a symbol of foods that build health. It's hard to imagine anyone who knows about food values and food flavor serving the white, quick-cooking variety when hearty brown rice is available. Brown rice is so easy to prepare and has so much character that anyone who has used it once will never again be satisfied with mushy, flat-tasting white rice.

Rice polish (the part of the rice that is removed from the kernel in making white rice) is sold in most health food stores as a rich source of important minerals and B vitamins. You can sprinkle rice polish on the children's cereal in the morning or use it to enrich bread and cookie doughs.

Brown rice flour is a necessary ingredient in authentic Scottish shortbread and gives an interesting texture to pastry or cookies made with it.

Never-Fail Cooked Rice

Rice is a typical example of convenience food marketing. TV commercials, for example, hammer away at how much time is saved by using instant this or that. Nonsense. All you need do to make delicious natural rice is—

Rinse 1 cup of rice (enough for serving three to four). Combine rice with 2 cups of water, cover and bring to a boil, turn heat down and simmer for 30 to 35 minutes. Do not stir during cooking.

The rice remains fluffy and each kernel is distinct.

Both short-grain and long-grain rice are available at natural food stores. Food cooperatives make a specialty of having wide selections of all grains, including organically grown rice. Use airtight containers and store the rice in a dry, cool location.

Rice is an excellent change from the potatoes which accompany so many American meals. This versatile grain can be the base of pilafs, salads, grainburgers, crackers and bread.

Cook rice according to preferred method. (See "Cooking with Cereal Grains.")

Combine cooked rice, vegetables, egg and grains. Season. Mold into patties. Dust with flour and wheat germ mixture. In hot skillet, brown in oil on both sides.

NOTE: As an extra touch, add a slice of cheese after you have turned the pattie to brown on the second side.

Yield: 6 to 8 patties

Grainburgers

1 *cup brown rice*
⅓ *cup chopped green pepper*
⅓ *cup chopped onion*
⅓ *cup chopped celery*
1 *egg, beaten*
⅓ *cup cornmeal*
⅓ *cup oatmeal*
⅓ *cup wheat germ*
1 *tablespoon tamari soy sauce*
 salt, pepper to taste
2 *tablespoons rye flour*
2 *tablespoons wheat germ*
2 *tablespoons oil*

Hot Cream of Rice

1 *cup brown rice*
4 *cups milk*
1 *teaspoon salt*

In a dry frying pan over medium heat, toast or "pop" the grains of rice for approximately 10 minutes, shaking the pan gently to prevent scorching. The grains should be slightly brown and smell nutty. Grind the grains in electric blender to the desired degree of coarseness.

Bring milk and salt to a boil, then stir in ground grain. Cover the pan, lower the heat and simmer for 5 to 10 minutes. If you wish, sweeten to taste with honey, molasses or maple syrup. Serve plain or with milk.

Yield: 4 servings

NOTE: If cereal is left over, mold in a square pan and cool. When set, slice and fry in oil. Serve as "mush" with molasses or maple syrup.

Kedgeree

1 *cup brown rice*
1 *lb. fish filet*
3 *tablespoons butter*
2 *hard-cooked eggs, chopped*
½ *teaspoon salt*
   pinch of pepper

Cook rice according to preferred method. (See "Cooking with Cereal Grains.")

Simmer fish filet in a little water until fish flakes easily (approximately 5 to 10 minutes). Drain and set aside.

Melt butter in saucepan. Add cooked rice, fish, eggs, salt and pepper. Stir gently over moderate heat until hot. Serve as entree.

Yield: 4 servings

Mexican Dry Rice Soup

1 *lb. fresh sausage*
1 *small onion, chopped*
1 *clove garlic, minced*
2 *tablespoons oil*
1 *cup brown rice*
¼ *cup tomato puree*
3 *cups chicken stock or water*
   salt, pepper to taste

Cook sausage, drain off fat and cut into pieces.

Saute onion and garlic in oil for a few minutes until onion is tender. Stir in rice. Add tomato puree, chicken stock or water and sausage. Cover, bring to a boil, then turn heat down and simmer for 30 to 40 minutes, until rice is cooked and liquid is absorbed. Do not stir during cooking. Season to taste and serve.

Yield: 6 servings

Combine all ingredients in electric blender and process until batter is smooth. Let rest for 2 hours to allow particles of flour to expand in liquid, resulting in a tender crepe. Just before baking crepes, process again briefly to blend ingredients.

Follow standard method for cooking crepes. (See Index.)

Yield: 12 8-inch crepes

Rice and Soy Crepes

4 *eggs*
2 *tablespoons sesame oil*
2 *cups water*
1 *cup brown rice flour*
½ *cup soy flour*
½ *teaspoon salt*

Preheat oven to 400°F.

Combine all ingredients except egg whites. Mix thoroughly and beat with whisk until light (approximately 2 minutes). Fold in egg whites. Pour into oiled muffin tins and bake in preheated oven for 20 minutes, or until done.

Yield: 12 muffins

Rice Flour Muffins

2 *cups brown rice flour*
1 *teaspoon salt*
3 *egg yolks, slightly beaten*
2 *tablespoons maple syrup or honey*
1 *cup milk*
2 *tablespoons oil*
3 *egg whites, stiffly beaten*

Cook brown rice in water to the "mushy" stage (approximately 1 hour). Combine carrot and rice mixture in electric blender. Process briefly to a puree consistency. There should be approximately 2 cups of this mixture.

Add oil, salt and flour. Knead at least 5 minutes to develop gluten in the flour, using more flour as required. Shape into a round loaf, lightly oil surface of loaf, and place on oiled cookie sheet. Score top of loaf by cutting shallow, horizontal lines across it before baking to prevent cracks and make it easier to cut slices.

Place in cold oven, turn oven to approximately 150°F. and leave for 1 hour; turn oven to 250°F. for another hour and then turn oven to 375°F. for a third hour. Bread will be done when inserted toothpick comes out clean. Cool on wire rack.

Yield: 1 small loaf

Unyeasted Rice Bread

1 *cup brown rice*
3 *cups water*
1 *raw medium-size carrot, cut into chunks*
1 *tablespoon oil*
½ *teaspoon salt*
3 *to 3½ cups whole wheat flour*

Rye

After more than 2,000 years of star status among breads, good, nutritional rye has been reduced to playing a bit part in this country. Why are we willing to pass up the lusty, sensual feeling that comes with biting into the hard crust of a good, homemade rye bread? Surely one answer lies in the pale imitation that is labeled and sold as rye bread in our supermarkets. It's like comparing fresh strawberries with strawberry Jello.

When a European orders rye bread in an American restaurant, he is probably surprised at what the waiter brings. Chances are that it won't look like or taste like the product he's used to. More than most breads, rye bread has varying shapes and ways of being made in different countries.

In the Scandinavian countries people eat a lot of rye crisp bread. It is called *Knacke* and baked from unsifted whole rye flour which contains all parts of the grain. Usually it comes in the shape of a large disc with a hole in the center. This shape originated long ago, when the week's supply was baked for the farmer's household. When the large rounds of bread came out of the oven, a stick was passed through the center and the bread was hoisted to the rafters of the house to keep the bread dry and crisp. At the table, diners help themselves by breaking off the size they want.

The dark, heavy rye of Russia has a hard and snappy crust. It is served at almost every meal. Eaten with sweet butter, cottage cheese, herring, or as is, this bread is almost a meal in itself.

Those Dark Ryes of Germany

Equally tasty and nutritious are the dark rye breads of Germany. There is the *Hamburger Schwarzbrot* or *Vollkornbrot* (whole grain bread) which contains a lot of completely unbroken kernels. Then there is the internationally famous pumpernickel, a leavened bread baked at a rather low temperature for as long as 12 hours, during which the oven must contain steam (a pan of water set on a rack will supply it). This bread really is more cooked than baked and it has no crust. It is very dark and not crisp so it can be sliced very thin. This is quite different from the so-called pumpernickels we find in our supermarkets, mostly darkened with caramel coloring and fluffed up with chemicals.

The rye grains are long and slender and can be sprouted easily. They can be cooked whole, like wheat berries or triticale, and combined with lentils or split peas for a pilaf. The flour made from rye is grayer in color than whole wheat flour and some millers not only refine it, but bleach it as well. When you buy rye flour, get it from a reliable source where you are assured it is the whole grain flour.

When using rye flour for bread, include some wheat flour, because rye contains less gluten than wheat and an all rye loaf will be too heavy. Often, rye flour is used to make sourdough bread. The flavor of rye seems to be enhanced by the sour taste which the starter imparts to the bread.

Try using rye flour to bread liver, kidneys or stewing beef and you will discover that it gives the dish a very special flavor. Rye flour can also be used to thicken sauces, but it's best to mix it with a little cornstarch for this. To use rye flour for soups, brown it in butter or oil before the liquid is added.

Rye sticks or soft pretzels are dark, tasty and nourishing. When you bake them, try putting a little onion on top, or caraway seeds, unhulled sesame seeds or poppy seeds. The pretzels make a welcome and unusual snack.

Hot Rye and Peanut Cereal

Bring water to boil in a 2-quart saucepan. Stir rye into boiling water. Add peanut flour, salt and raisins and cook for 10 to 15 minutes, until the rye is tender. Add honey, molasses, wheat germ and sesame seeds. Serve warm, with milk.

Yield: 4 servings

2½   *cups water*
1   *cup whole rye (toasted in dry skillet and "cracked" in electric blender)*
½   *cup peanut flour**
¼   *teaspoon salt*
¼   *cup raisins*
1   *tablespoon honey*
1   *tablespoon molasses*
2   *tablespoons wheat germ*
2   *tablespoons unhulled sesame seeds*

*Peanut flour may be ordered from Walnut Acres, Penns Creek, Pennsylvania 17862, or raw peanuts may be chopped, ½ cup at a time, in electric blender.

No-Knead Rye Bread

(electric mixer)

*(amazingly light, wheatless bread—
takes 4 hours from start to finish)*

4 *cups lukewarm water*
2 *tablespoons honey or
     molasses*
8 *teaspoons dry yeast*
6 *cups rye flour*
2 *cups oat flour*
2 *teaspoons salt*
4 *tablespoons oil*
butter
*unhulled sesame seeds
     (optional)*

Put lukewarm water into mixer bowl. Add honey or molasses. Sprinkle yeast over top and leave for 30 minutes in a warm place until yeast is activated. Warm rye flour in low (150° to 250°F.) oven for 15 minutes or so.

Add rye flour to yeast mixture and beat for 10 minutes, on low speed, using the flat beater attachment if you have one. Meanwhile, warm oat flour in low oven during the 10-minute beating of the rye mixture.

Stir salt into oat flour. Add oil to rye mixture and then add the oat flour and salt. Beat just until ingredients are well combined.

Put mixer bowl into a larger bowl of hot water and place in oven which is turned off but still warm. Leave it rise until dough reaches top of mixer bowl (approximately 45 minutes to 1 hour).

Turn dough out into two bread pans (9x5x3-inch) which have been well buttered. (Be generous with the butter and never use oil or margarine because whole grain breads have a tendency to stick to the pan.) The dough will be sticky. Smooth the surface of each loaf by letting cold water run over your spatula. Sprinkle sesame seeds over top, if desired.

Set pans in oven, but do not turn oven on until loaves have risen to top of pan. Then turn oven on to 350°F. and bake 1 hour until loaves are firm and crusty. Loosen loaves by banging sides of pans down hard on table, use a knife if necessary, but be careful not to cut into loaf. Turn loaves out onto rack to cool.

Yield: 2 loaves

Simple Rye Bread

1½ *cups milk, scalded*
 ½ *teaspoon honey*
 2 *tablespoons dry yeast*
2½ *tablespoons honey*
 ½ *tablespoon salt*
 1 *cup rye flour*
2½ *cups whole wheat flour*
 ⅓ *cup whole wheat flour
      (for kneading)*

Cool ¼ cup hot milk and stir ½ teaspoon honey into it. Soften yeast in this milk and honey mixture.

Combine remaining hot milk, honey and salt. When this mixture is lukewarm, stir in yeast mixture and add both flours, reserving ⅓ cup whole wheat flour for kneading. Knead for at least 5 minutes to develop gluten.

Place in oiled bowl, turning dough to coat surface. Cover with damp towel and set in warm, draft-free place to rise for approximately 2 hours.

Punch down, knead briefly, shape into a round loaf, lightly oil surface of loaf and place on oiled cookie sheet. Allow to rise almost double (approximately 1 hour).

Place in a cold oven, turn oven to 325°F. and bake for 1 to 1¼ hours or until inserted toothpick comes out clean. Cool on wire rack.

Yield: 1 loaf

Old Country Soft Pretzel Sticks
(rye)

Soften yeast in lukewarm water. Add honey and set mixture aside for 5 minutes. Combine 4 cups rye flour with salt. Stir in yeast mixture.

Turn dough onto lightly floured board and knead with ½ cup rye flour until smooth. Divide dough into 48 pieces and roll each into a rope about ½ inch in diameter and 5 inches long. Place on a buttered baking sheet.

Brush with egg and water glaze and sprinkle with onion. Let rise for 20 to 30 minutes. *Preheat oven to 425°F.* and bake for 15 to 20 minutes. Cool on rack.

Yield: 48 sticks

- 1 *tablespoon dry yeast*
- 1¼ *cups lukewarm water*
- 1 *tablespoon honey*
- 4 *cups rye flour*
- 1 *teaspoon salt*
- ½ *cup rye flour*
- 1 *egg, beaten with ½ teaspoon water*
- 1 *medium-size onion,* * *chopped, sauteed and drained on paper towel*

*Caraway seeds, unhulled sesame seeds or poppy seeds may be substituted for the onion.

Rye Bread Berry Pudding

Preheat oven to 325°F.

Beat egg yolks and honey together. Add soft butter and beat in to blend. Add apple juice, bread crumbs, cinnamon and berries. Carefully fold in stiffly beaten egg whites. Pour into ungreased casserole dish and bake in preheated oven for 45 minutes or until set. Cool slightly and serve pudding warm with cream or yogurt.

Yield: 4 servings

- 2 *egg yolks*
- ¼ *cup honey*
- 2 *tablespoons soft butter*
- 1 *cup apple juice*
- 1½ *cups soft rye bread crumbs or ¾ cup dry crumbs*
- ¼ *teaspoon cinnamon*
- 1 *cup fresh raspberries, blueberries or other berries*
- 2 *egg whites, stiffly beaten*

Rye and Lentil Pilaf

(This recipe can be cooked in a crockery pot. See marker 🍲 *for method below.)*

½ *cup rye*
½ *cup lentils*
1 *small onion, minced*
½ *cup diced carrot*
½ *cup diced celery*
1 *tablespoon oil*
1 *teaspoon caraway seeds (optional)*
¼ *teaspoon thyme*
¼ *teaspoon sage*
3 *cups chicken stock*
salt, pepper to taste

🍲 (If using crockery pot, omit the following steps and continue with method below.)

Cook rye and lentils according to preferred method. (See "Cooking with Cereal Grains" and "Basic Methods for Cooking Beans and Other Legumes.") Drain and reserve liquids for soup.

Saute onion, carrot and celery in oil until tender. Combine with cooked rye and lentils, add herbs and chicken stock. Season to taste, cover and steam for 10 minutes or until hot.

Yield: 4 servings

🍲 Soak lentils for at least 4 hours in water to cover. Drain. Omit oil. Combine soaked lentils with remaining ingredients. Cook on low for 8 to 10 hours.

Sourdough Starter

¾ *cup water*
¼ *cup non-fat dry milk*
¾ *cup rye or whole wheat flour*

Using glass or stainless steel bowl, reconstitute milk by combining water and non-fat dry milk. Cover loosely with a cloth and leave at room temperature for 2 or 3 days until it smells sour. It is not necessary to leave it until it is thick or clabbered.

When the milk smells sour, stir in ¾ cup rye or whole wheat flour. Leave again, at room temperature for 3 or 4 days until there seems to be some "action" in it. Look for small holes, evidence of gas forming and being given off.

When the starter seems to be "working," it should be "doubled" by adding 1 cup reconstituted milk (as above) and ¾ cup rye or whole wheat flour, just as you did the first time.

Leave this "doubled" starter at room temperature for a few hours and then refrigerate it in a glass or plastic container, large enough so there is no danger of it overflowing. It can also be frozen.

Remove starter from refrigerator or freezer the night before you plan to use it for baking. Double it as above and leave it at room temperature overnight. Don't forget to return some of it to the refrigerator or freezer in the morning for the next time. Most recipes call for at least 1 cup of starter.

Sourdough Pumpernickel Bread

½ *cup cornmeal*
1 *cup cracked wheat*
2 *cups cracked rye (rye can be "cracked" in electric blender)*
3½ *cups boiling water*
1 *cup sourdough starter (see above)*
½ *cup lukewarm water*
½ *cup molasses*
2 *teaspoons dry yeast*
2 *teaspoons salt*
2¾ *cups rye flour*
3 *cups whole wheat flour*

Combine cornmeal, cracked wheat and cracked rye and pour boiling water over them, stirring briskly to avoid lumping. Cool to lukewarm and add sourdough starter, stirring it in until dough is smooth. This is the "sponge." Leave overnight in a warm place (a turned off oven is a good spot). Next day remove 1 cup of sponge, combine it with 1 cup lukewarm water and refrigerate for future use.

Combine ½ cup lukewarm water and 1 tablespoon of the molasses. Sprinkle dry yeast over surface and set aside for 5 minutes until yeast is softened. Add yeast mixture and remaining molasses to sponge, then add salt, rye flour and whole wheat flour, reserving some for kneading. Knead dough until no longer sticky. Place dough in large oiled bowl, first putting it upside down to coat surface with oil, and then placing it right side up. Cover with a cloth and set in turned off oven for 2½ hours to rise.

Punch dough down, form into one large loaf or two smaller loaves. Place each in oiled casserole. Cover again with a towel and let rise for 1 hour. *Preheat oven to 200°F.* Cover casserole tightly with foil and/or lid and bake in preheated oven for 3 to 4 hours. Place a pan of water on the lowest shelf of the oven and leave it there throughout the baking process. When bread is done (inserted toothpick comes out clean), remove it from casserole and cool before slicing.

Yield: 1 loaf approximately 3½ lbs. or
2 loaves approximately 1¾ lbs.

Sourdough Rye Bread

1 *cup sourdough starter*
(see above)
1½ *cups water*
2 *cups rye flour*
1 *tablespoon molasses*
½ *cup lukewarm water*
1 *tablespoon dry yeast*
2 *tablespoons oil*
2 *teaspoons salt*
4 *cups brown rice flour*
2 *cups rye flour*
⅓ *cup (approximately) oat*
flour (oatmeal coarsely
ground in electric
blender)

To make the "sponge" mixture, combine first three ingredients in a large bowl, cover and set in a warm, draft-free place overnight. (A cold oven is a good place.) Next morning, dissolve molasses in lukewarm water and sprinkle yeast over the surface. Set aside for 5 minutes to activate.

Stir down the sponge, add oil, salt, activated yeast mixture, and all of the rice flour. Mix in as much of the remaining rye flour by hand as possible, then turn out dough onto board or counter which has been well floured with the rye flour. Knead dough briefly, to incorporate all the flour and finish with the oat flour to reduce stickiness of dough. Place in oiled bowl, turning dough to oil surface. Cover and put in warm place to rise for approximately 1 hour, or until double in bulk.

Form dough into one large loaf and one small loaf, place in well-buttered bread pans and leave to rise to the top of the pan (approximately 1½ hours). *Preheat oven to 375°F.* and bake for 35 minutes or until done. Remove loaves from pans and cool on racks.

Yield: 1 large and 1 small loaf

Tiny Cream Puffs

1 *cup water*
½ *cup butter*
¼ *teaspoon salt*
1 *cup rye or whole wheat flour*
4 *eggs*

Preheat oven to 400°F.

Bring water, butter and salt to a boil in a medium-size saucepan. Remove pan from heat. Add flour all at once, stirring hard with a wooden spoon. Lower heat and continue to cook dough, stirring constantly, for a minute or two to make sure flour is cooked. Transfer dough to bowl of electric mixer.

Add eggs, one at a time, beating well after each addition.

Drop dough by teaspoon onto a lightly buttered cookie sheet, leaving 1 inch between each puff. Bake in preheated oven for 25 to 30 minutes or until they are quite firm. Loosen carefully with spatula and cool on wire rack. Store in a cool dry place until time to split and fill them. Filling should be done just before serving to prevent them from getting soggy.

Yield: approximately 6 dozen 1½-inch puffs

Triticale

Triticale (trit-i—kay-lee) is a cereal grain developed by cross breeding wheat (*Triticum*) and rye (*Secale*). It can bring a decided lift to any menu and will provide extra protein for the family without hurting the budget one bit.

The triticale grain is twice as large and heavy as wheat, and in some field tests the triticale plant has yielded almost twice as much grain. In contrast to most hybrid offspring, triticale is not sterile, having the ability to reproduce itself generation after generation.

Commonly available wheat and/or rye flour contains 12 percent protein. Dr. S. P. Yang, chairman of the Department of Food and Nutrition at Texas Tech University, says the rye-wheat combination grain contains 16.4 percent more protein than most other cereal grains. And it is high-quality protein—rich in lysine and methionine, amino acids which are low in most grains and which consequently limit the biological value of those grains. With this improved amino acid balance, triticale has a biological value close to that of eggs and meat; closer than either rye or wheat.

How do you use triticale? If you can get the grain, by all means sprout it. It sprouts quickly and easily and has a chewy texture. Add the sprouts to salads, casseroles, brown rice dishes, soups or just use the sprouts as snacks. The sprouts are best if they don't get any longer than the grain itself. They will continue to grow in the refrigerator, so use them quickly. Start a new sprouting every night and you will always have a supply of "fresh" vegetables.

Triticale flour can be used in breads, cookies and pancakes, either by itself or mixed with other flour. It gives a pleasing nutty flavor to bread and you can use it in your favorite bread recipe. If you prefer a lighter loaf of bread, stick to a 50—50 ratio of mixing it with whole wheat flour.

Triticale is available in many health food stores and co-ops. If your retailer has difficulty obtaining it, he or she can write to:

Golden Sun Triticales, Inc.
Box 502
Devils Lake, North Dakota 58301

Frank Ford
Arrowhead Mills
Hereford, Texas 79045

Letoba Farms
Route 3, Box 100
Lyons, Kansas 67554

Triticale Food Corporation
Muleshoe, Texas 79347

Herbed Triticale Casserole Bread

4 *teaspoons dry yeast*
1 *cup lukewarm water*
1 *tablespoon honey*
2 *tablespoons minced onion*
2 *tablespoons butter*
2 *cups triticale flour*
1 *cup yogurt*
2 *teaspoons basil*
1 *teaspoon oregano*
2 *teaspoons dill*
1½ *teaspoons salt*
½ *cup triticale flour*
2 *cups whole wheat flour*

In bowl of electric mixer, soften yeast in lukewarm water to which honey has been added. Saute onion in butter until tender. Set aside to cool. When yeast mixture is active, add 2 cups triticale flour to it, stirring to blend. Add yogurt and then the sauteed onion, herbs and salt. Beat on medium speed for 2 minutes, scraping sides of bowl once during this time. Beat in ½ cup triticale flour and whole wheat flour.

Cover bowl with a clean, dampened towel, and set in a warm place to rise for 1 hour—until almost double in size. Punch down dough, turn into a well-oiled 2-quart casserole and let rise for 30 minutes. *Preheat oven to 375°F.* Place casserole in preheated oven and bake for 50 minutes. Turn loaf out onto wire rack and cool.

Yield: 1 loaf

No-Knead Triticale Bread

4 *teaspoons dry yeast*
⅔ *cup lukewarm water*
2 *teaspoons honey*
2 *cups triticale flour*
3 *cups whole wheat flour*
3 *tablespoons unsulfured*
    molasses
⅔ *cup lukewarm water*
½ *tablespoon salt*
⅓ *cup wheat germ*
1⅓ *cups lukewarm water*
½ *tablespoon butter*
1 *tablespoon unhulled sesame*
    seeds

Sprinkle yeast over lukewarm water and add honey. Leave to "work" while preparing the dough. Warm flours by placing them in a 250°F. oven for approximately 20 minutes. Combine molasses with ⅔ cup lukewarm water. Combine yeast mixture with molasses mixture. Stir this into the warmed flour, then add salt and wheat germ and finally 1⅓ cups lukewarm water. The dough will be sticky.

Butter loaf pan (9¼x5¼x2¼-inch), taking care to grease the corners of the pan well. Turn the dough into the pan. No kneading is necessary. Smooth dough in pan with spatula which has been held under cold water to prevent stickiness. Sprinkle sesame seeds over top of loaf. Leave to rise to top of pan in warm, draft-free place. Meanwhile *preheat oven to 400°F.*

Bake in preheated oven for 30 to 40 minutes or until crust is brown and sides of loaf are firm and crusty. Set pan on rack to cool for 10 minutes, then remove loaf from pan and cool completely on rack before slicing.

Yield: 1 loaf

Triticale Buns

Soften yeast and diastatic malt in warm water to which ginger has been added. Set aside until it becomes foamy. Combine coffee, molasses, cornmeal and salt. Add yeast mixture to coffee mixture and stir flour in gradually. Knead dough until smooth, adding more flour if necessary to keep it from sticking. Put dough into oiled bowl, turning dough to oil surface. Cover with damp towel and leave in a warm place until doubled.

Knead down, pinch off pieces of dough the size of a large egg, and form into oval buns. Place on oiled cookie sheet, brush with egg and water mixture, and sprinkle with seeds. Leave to rise for 1 hour in a warm place. *Preheat oven to 375°F.* and bake for 25 to 30 minutes.

Yield: approximately 18 buns

- 1 *tablespoon dry yeast*
- 1 *tablespoon diastatic malt (see Index)*
- ½ *cup warm water (100° to 110°F.)*
- ½ *teaspoon ginger*
- 1½ *cups coffee*
- ¼ *cup molasses*
- 1 *cup cornmeal*
- 1 *tablespoon salt*
- 4¼ *cups (approximately) triticale flour*
- 1 *egg, beaten with 2 tablespoons water*
- ¼ *cup caraway seeds or dill seeds*

Triticale Egg Bread

Dissolve honey in lukewarm water. Sprinkle yeast over surface and set aside for 5 minutes to activate. Add vinegar to milk, heat just to lukewarm temperature, stirring constantly, until the milk curdles. Remove from heat and pour into large bowl. Add salt, oil, eggs and triticale flour to soured milk. Add yeast mixture, stirring in well, then add 3 cups whole wheat flour, reserving approximately 1 cup for kneading.

Turn dough out onto board or counter which has been well floured, and knead for a full 5 minutes. Place dough in oiled bowl, turning it to oil surface. Cover and put in warm place to rise for approximately 1¼ hours or until double in

- 2 *tablespoons honey*
- ½ *cup lukewarm water*
- 2 *tablespoons dry yeast*
- 2 *teaspoons vinegar*
- 1 *cup milk*
- 2 *teaspoons salt*
- 2 *tablespoons oil*
- 3 *eggs, beaten*
- 2 *cups triticale flour*
- 3 *cups whole wheat flour*
- 1 *cup whole wheat flour (for kneading)*

bulk. Punch down dough. Let rise again for 30 minutes or so.

Form into one large loaf and one small loaf, place in buttered bread pans and let rise for another 30 minutes or until dough is slightly rounded over the top of the pan. *Preheat oven to 350°F.* and bake for 30 to 35 minutes or until done. Remove loaves from pans and cool on racks.

Yield: 1 large and 1 small loaf

Triticale Nut Drops

2 *eggs, beaten*
½ *cup oil*
½ *cup honey*
½ *teaspoon vanilla*
2½ *cups triticale flour*
½ *teaspoon salt*
1 *teaspoon cinnamon*
¼ *teaspoon crushed anise seeds*
½ *cup chopped walnuts*

Preheat oven to 375°F.

Combine eggs, oil, honey and vanilla. Combine flour, salt, spices and nuts, and add to liquid ingredients. Drop by teaspoon onto buttered cookie sheet, press flat with the bottom of a glass which has been dipped in water, and top with a walnut piece if desired. Bake in preheated oven for 12 to 15 minutes or until golden brown. Cool on rack.

Yield: 4 dozen cookies

Triticale Sourdough Pancakes

1 *cup sourdough starter (see Index)*
¾ *cup triticale flour*
½ *cup water*
3 *teaspoons dry yeast*
½ *cup lukewarm water*
1 *tablespoon honey*
2 *eggs, beaten*
2 *tablespoons oil*
½ *cup cornmeal*
¼ *cup triticale flour*
½ *teaspoon salt*

Combine first three ingredients and leave in warm place overnight.

Next morning, sprinkle dry yeast over lukewarm water. Add honey. Let soak for 10 minutes. Combine beaten eggs and oil. Add to sourdough mixture. Stir in cornmeal, ¼ cup triticale flour and salt. Add yeast mixture. Leave in a warm place for 30 minutes.

Lightly oil an iron skillet and heat to medium-high heat. Spoon pancake batter into skillet in desired amount. When bubbles appear on the surface of the pancakes, turn them. Remove when brown on underside. Serve immediately.

Yield: 20 4-inch pancakes

Wheat

When treated right, wheat, like all cereals, plays a valuable role in a balanced diet, and it is so versatile that one never gets tired of it.

Perhaps you've been lucky enough to stroll through the country along the fields, pulling a blade of wheat grass here and there, chewing the berries. Sweet. Wheat berries carry their share of protein, carbohydrates, minerals and—most important—vitamins B_1 and E. If the berry is ground up as is, the whole wheat flour you get contains all of that.

There are two kinds of wheat flour—bread flour, ground from hard wheat (13 percent protein), and pastry flour, ground from soft wheat (8 to 10 percent protein). Don't use the low-protein flour when baking bread. It won't rise as well.

For breakfast or a main dish, you also can cook the whole wheat berries, but they are slow cooking. Therefore it helps to use the pressure cooker method. If you don't have a pressure cooker, there are two ways to cut down on the cooking time. If you sprout the berries first, they will cook in half the time. Or you can use the thermos method: Bring the berries to a boil in the evening, put in a thermos container and in the morning they will be ready.

The Secret behind the Tastiest Breads

If you have ever wondered why even the professionally baked breads taste so good in Europe—the secret is diastatic malt which is contained in the wheat berry. Generally unfamiliar in the United States, diastatic malt can occasionally be found in health food stores. But you can make it at home. Using diastatic malt, you can bake yeast bread without sugar, honey or molasses.

Most recipes for yeast breads—even for those breads which are not supposed to taste sweet—call for some sugar. The sugar feeds the yeast and also makes the crust brown and crunchy. People who know about the drawbacks of sugar try to replace it with either honey or molasses. But both are high in calories and forbidden in certain diets. Diastatic malt does all of sugar's jobs and has none of these shortcomings. It is rich in enzymes and vitamins, so when the malt is added to the dough, the bread's nutritional value increases. The action of the enzymes on the yeast and flour improves the flavor and appearance of a loaf of bread, and, in addition, gives it a finer texture and helps the bread stay fresh longer.

This ingredient is made from sprouted grain. Beer brewers have known about it for generations. They use barley sprouts which are roasted and ground.

But it is quite difficult for the average consumer to get unhulled barley (the only kind that will sprout) so it is easier for most of us to use wheat berries for making diastatic malt at home. The enzyme action is the same as in the barley product.

Make Your Own Diastatic Malt

For a batch of dough yielding three or four loaves of bread, one tablespoon of diastatic malt is enough. Too much will make your bread too sweet, dark and sticky.

Here's how to make your own diastatic malt, according to Jane Nordstrom in *Barmy Bread Book* (Sante Fe: Lightning Tree Books, copyright 1974 by Jane Nordstrom):

Place one cup of wheat berries in a glass jar and sprout them the way you sprout any other grain (see Index). Wheat sprouts relatively fast and you will see little shoots, about the same length as the grain, appear after about two days. At this point, drain them well and spread them out evenly in thin layers on two large baking sheets. You can dry the sprouts in an oven in about eight hours at a maximum temperature of 150°F. You also can dry them by placing the baking sheets in the sun; it will take several days if you use this method. Grind the dried sprouts into a fine meal one cup at a time in a blender or an electric grinder.

The result, which is enough diastatic malt for about 150 loaves of bread, can be stored indefinitely in a tightly closed glass jar in the refrigerator or freezer.

100% Whole Wheat Bread

(Reprinted with permission of Lightning Tree Books and the author, from Barmy Bread Book. *Copyright 1974 by Jane Nordstrom.)*

2 *cups warm water (100° to 110°F.)*	2 *tablespoons vegetable oil*
1 *teaspoon diastatic malt*	2 *teaspoons salt*
2 *tablespoons or 2 packages yeast*	5 *cups whole wheat bread flour (approximately)*

Combine first three ingredients and let sit until bubbly. Add oil and salt and enough flour to make a firm dough. Knead until smooth and elastic. Place in a warm place to rise until double in volume.

Punch down dough, knead briefly and let rise a second time. Punch down and divide dough into two pieces and let rest 10 minutes. Then form into loaves and place in two medium-size greased loaf pans. Let rise until dough is approximately 1½ times the original volume.

Bake in a preheated oven at 350°F. for 35 to 40 minutes or until loaf sounds hollow when rapped with knuckles. Cool on racks.

Yield: 2 medium loaves

Black Bread

(Reprinted with permission of Lightning Tree Books and the author, from Barmy Bread Book. Copyright 1974 by Jane Nordstrom.)

1 *tablespoon or*	1½ *cups coffee (or water)*
1 *package yeast*	¼ *cup dark molasses*
½ *teaspoon ground ginger*	1 *tablespoon salt*
1 *tablespoon diastatic malt*	2 *cups whole wheat*
½ *cup warm water (100° to*	*bread flour*
110°F.)	2 *cups rye meal*
1 *cup cornmeal*	*(approximately)*

Combine first four ingredients and let sit until bubbly. Mix cornmeal with warm coffee and add molasses, salt, yeast mixture and whole wheat flour. Stir well and add enough rye meal to make a firm dough. Knead on a board sprinkled with rye meal, using more as needed to keep the dough from sticking. Knead until smooth and let rise in a warm place for 1 hour.

Punch down and divide dough into three pieces. Let them rest for 10 minutes and form into balls. Coat lightly with rye meal and place on buttered baking sheets. Let rise approximately 45 minutes.

Bake at 375°F. for 50 minutes or until loaves sound hollow when tapped on bottom. Cool on racks.

Yield: 3 round loaves

Apple Pie with Whole Wheat and Rice Pastry

1 *cup whole wheat pastry flour*
1 *cup brown rice flour*
½ *teaspoon salt*
3 *tablespoons oil*
4 *tablespoons butter*
5 *tablespoons ice water*
½ *cup honey*
1 *teaspoon cinnamon*
2 *tablespoons whole wheat flour (not pastry flour)*
1 *teaspoon grated lemon rind*
6 *cups peeled and sliced apples*

Sift flours and salt together. Using fingertips, work in oil and then butter until mixture resembles coarse crumbs. Add ice water gradually, kneading slightly to form a ball of dough. Roll out one-half of dough between sheets of wax paper and press into 9-inch pie plate.

Combine honey, cinnamon, whole wheat flour and lemon rind and drizzle one-third of mixture onto bottom of pie shell. Pack apple slices into shell and drizzle remaining honey mixture over the top. *Preheat oven to 425°F.* Roll out top crust between sheets of wax paper and cover apples, joining top and bottom crusts and fluting the edges. Cut several slits in top crust for steam to escape.

Bake in preheated oven for 50 minutes or until apples are tender. Cool and serve.

Yield: 1 9-inch pie

Basic Gravy

2 *tablespoons poultry or meat drippings, or butter*
6 *tablespoons whole wheat flour*
   or 2 tablespoons cornstarch
   or 3 tablespoons whole wheat flour and
      1 tablespoon cornstarch
2 *cups meat or vegetable stock*
salt to taste

In a saucepan, melt fat. Remove pan from heat, stir in flour or cornstarch or a mixture of both, to make a smooth paste. While pan is still off the heat, add stock slowly, stirring with a whisk to avoid lumps. Cook over high heat, stirring constantly, until gravy boils. Turn heat down, and simmer gravy for a few minutes until it is thickened. Season to taste.

Yield: 2 cups

Basic White Sauce

Combine flour and cornstarch. In a saucepan, melt butter, stir in flour mixture, and add milk gradually, stirring with a wire whisk to prevent lumps. Cook until thickened. Salt to taste.

Yield: 2 cups

3 *tablespoons whole wheat flour*
1 *or 1½ tablespoons cornstarch (use 1 tablespoon for thin sauce; use 1½ tablespoons for thick sauce)*
2 *tablespoons butter*
2 *cups milk*
salt to taste

Chive Wafers

Preheat oven to 400°F.

Place wheat germ, flour and salt in a bowl. With the fingertips or a pastry blender cut in the butter until the mixture resembles coarse oatmeal. Stir in chives, egg and enough milk to make a very stiff dough.

Roll out the dough on a lightly floured board to ⅛-inch thickness. Cut into 1-inch rounds or fancy shapes and place on a lightly greased baking sheet. Bake in preheated oven 10 minutes or until lightly browned. Cool on a rack and store in an airtight container.

Yield: 48 wafers

½ *cup wheat germ*
1 *cup whole wheat flour*
¼ *teaspoon salt*
¼ *cup butter*
4 *tablespoons chopped chives*
1 *egg*
milk

Crepes Suzette

Crepes

    4 *eggs*
    1 *tablespoon honey*
    2 *tablespoons melted butter*
    1 *cup milk*
    1 *cup water*
 1¾ *cups whole wheat*
        pastry flour
    ½ *teaspoon salt*

Sauce

    ¾ *cup butter*
    ¾ *cup honey*
    ¾ *cup orange juice*
    ½ *cup cognac (optional)*

Make Crepes

Combine first seven ingredients in electric blender and process until batter is smooth. Let rest for 2 hours to allow particles of flour to expand in liquid, resulting in a tender crepe. Just before baking crepes, process batter again briefly to blend ingredients.

Standard Method for Cooking Crepes

Heat heavy skillet or crepe pan to medium-high heat. The pan is ready when a drop of water "dances" on it. Oil pan well, stir batter, then pour it into pan (¼ cup batter will make about the right size crepe). Add more liquid, if necessary, to make a thin crepe. Let crepe cook approximately 2 minutes. It should be golden brown underneath and dry on top. Flip crepe over, using fingers, and let second side brown for approximately 1 minute. Slide crepe onto heatproof plate and keep warm in low oven until ready to fill and serve. Crepes may be stacked on top of each other.

Make Sauce

Heat butter, honey and orange juice together, just until they blend well. When ready to serve dessert, dip both sides of each crepe in the orange sauce, fold in half and then in half again and arrange on individual plates. If desired, warm ½ cup cognac over a low flame, pour over crepes and ignite at once. (The alcohol will evaporate.) Foamy Sauce (see Index) or Apricot Sauce (see Index) may be used in place of cognac. Serve immediately.

Yield: 16 8-inch crepes

Herb and Onion Bread

Soften yeast in ½ cup lukewarm water. Cook onion in oil until golden.

Combine milk and water. Add onion mixture, honey, salt and herbs. Stir in yeast mixture. Beat in cornmeal. Beat in approximately 2 cups whole wheat flour. Stir in remaining flour by hand to make moderately soft dough. Turn out on lightly floured surface. Knead 3 to 5 minutes. Place in oiled bowl, turning once to oil surface. Cover bowl with clean towel and let rise in warm, draft-free place until double in bulk, approximately 1 hour.

Punch down dough. Divide in half. Place in 2 well-greased 1-pound coffee cans. Cover and let rise till double (30 to 45 minutes). *Preheat oven to 350°F.* and bake for 45 minutes, covering loosely with foil the last 15 minutes. Remove immediately from cans and cool loaves.

Yield: 2 loaves

5	*teaspoons dry yeast*
½	*cup lukewarm water*
½	*cup chopped onion*
3	*tablespoons oil*
½	*cup non-fat dry milk*
1¾	*cups water*
1½	*tablespoons honey*
1	*teaspoon salt*
½	*cup chopped parsley*
2	*teaspoons dill*
1	*teaspoon oregano*
¾	*cup cornmeal*
3½ to 4	*cups whole wheat flour*

Honey Spice Cake

Preheat oven to 375°F.

Set mixing bowl in skillet which has water to the depth of about 1 inch in it. Heat water to simmering and keep this temperature throughout the mixing process.

Pour honey into the warmed bowl, add eggs and vanilla. Heat electric mixer beaters a few minutes in the oven. Beat egg mixture at medium speed until very thick and high (approximately 18 minutes). The eggs will form soft peaks when beaters are lifted.

While eggs are beating, warm flour in oven, then combine with spices. Add flour mixture to egg mixture a little at a time, folding in gently with a rubber spatula. Add the melted butter (still warm) and fold in thoroughly.

Pour batter into buttered spring mold or two 9-inch cake pans, and bake in preheated over for 35 minutes, or until cake is golden brown and the sides begin to pull away from the pan. Allow cake to cool in pan for 20 minutes, then turn out.

Yield: 1 high cake or 2 cake layers

⅔	*cup honey*
6	*large eggs, warmed in hot tap water*
1	*teaspoon vanilla*
1¼	*cups whole wheat pastry flour*
½	*teaspoon cinnamon*
½	*teaspoon ginger*
½	*cup butter, melted and warm*

Noodle Kugel

10 *ounces medium-wide, whole wheat noodles*
3 *quarts boiling water*
1 *tablespoon oil*
4 *eggs, beaten*
⅓ *cup melted butter*
1 *apple, chopped*
½ *cup chopped nuts*
⅔ *cup chopped raisins or other dried fruit*
⅓ *cup honey*
½ *teaspoon salt*
2 *tablespoons strawberry preserves*
grated rind of 1 *lemon*
4 *tablespoons lemon juice*
1 *teaspoon cinnamon*

Preheat oven to 325°F.

Cook noodles in 3 quarts boiling water to which 1 tablespoon oil has been added. Drain and rinse with cold water. Combine with remaining ingredients and turn into lightly oiled baking dish. Bake in preheated oven for 1 hour. Serve warm or cold.

Yield: 6 servings

Wheat Berry and Beef Casserole

1 *cup wheat berries*
3 *cups water*
½ *teaspoon salt*
4 *medium-size potatoes*
1 *lb. ground beef*
1 *onion, chopped*
5 *tablespoons oil*
⅓ *cup whole wheat flour*
2 *teaspoons chopped parsley*
½ *teaspoon sweet basil*
½ *teaspoon salt*

In a saucepan which has a very tight-fitting lid, combine wheat berries, water and salt. Bring to a boil, cover, and remove from heat. Wrap pot in newspapers or a heavy woolen blanket and allow to stand overnight in a warm place. Drain and reserve liquid.

Cook and mash potatoes. Saute the beef and onion in 2 tablespoons oil and set aside. Drain and discard excess fat. Heat remaining 3 tablespoons oil in skillet, stir in whole wheat flour and cook for a minute or so. Then add 1½ cups reserved wheat berry liquid and cook, stirring constantly, until mixture is thick and smooth. Add herbs and salt. *Preheat oven to 350°F.*

Butter a 2½-quart casserole and put the wheat berries in the bottom, then a layer of meat covered with half of the sauce. Top casserole with mashed potatoes and pour remaining sauce over them. Bake in preheated oven for approximately 30 minutes or until casserole is hot and bubbling.

Yield: 8 servings

Have eggs and flour at room temperature.

Combine honey and lukewarm water and sprinkle yeast on the surface. Set aside to soften. Combine scalded milk, currants (if using them), butter and salt.

Mix cinnamon and walnuts (if using them) into flour. Using an electric mixer, beat egg yolks briefly, add ½ cup honey and beat until fluffy. Beat in yeast and milk mixture. Gradually add the flour mixture and beat hard for 3 minutes. Beat egg whites until stiff. Fold one-fourth of the egg whites thoroughly into batter, then gently fold in remaining egg whites.

Gently turn batter into two well-buttered bread pans or one well-buttered 9-inch tube pan. Set pans or pan into a larger pan of warm water and leave to rise in a warm, draft-free place for approximately 1 hour. Carefully lift pans or pan out of water and into a cold oven. Turn oven to 400°F. After 15 minutes, turn oven to 325°F. and continue to bake for 25 to 30 minutes or until an inserted toothpick comes out clean. Remove pans or pan from oven and cool for 5 minutes on wire rack. Gently loosen bread from sides of pan and carefully turn out bread. Cool on rack.

Yield: 1 9-inch cakelike bread or 2 loaves

Sally Lunn

1 *teaspoon honey*
¼ *cup lukewarm water*
2 *teaspoons dry yeast*
1¾ *cups milk, scalded*
1 *cup currants (optional)*
½ *cup butter*
1 *teaspoon salt*
2 *teaspoons cinnamon*
1 *cup chopped walnuts (optional)*
3 *cups whole wheat flour*
4 *egg yolks*
½ *cup honey*
4 *egg whites*

Soak wheat berries in water for at least 12 hours. Soak oatmeal in water for 30 minutes. Drain wheat and oatmeal, reserving liquid for soup or gravy.

In a large bowl, combine yogurt, honey and lemon juice. Grate apple quarters, including the peel, and slice bananas into yogurt mixture, stirring often to mix in the fruit and keep it from discoloring.

Stir drained wheat and oatmeal into the fruit mixture, add berries or grapes and serve immediately.

Yield: approximately 3 cups

Wheat Berry *Muesli*

¼ *cup wheat berries*
½ *cup water*
¼ *cup oatmeal*
½ *cup water*
1 *cup yogurt*
3 *tablespoons honey*
1 *teaspoon lemon juice*
2 *medium-size eating apples, quartered and cored*
1 *banana*
1 *cup berries or seedless grapes*

Wheat Soybean Casserole

½ *cup soybeans*
1 *cup wheat berries*
2 *cups whole corn, fresh
    or frozen*
2 *cups canned tomatoes,
    drained*
1 *cup chopped onion*
1 *clove garlic, crushed*
½ *teaspoon thyme*
1 *teaspoon salt*
pinch of cayenne
¼ *cup tomato paste*
3 *tablespoons brewer's yeast
    (optional)*
½ *cup chicken, beef or
    vegetable stock*
⅓ *cup grated cheese*

Cook soybeans and wheat berries according to pre-ferred methods. (See "Basic Methods for Cooking Beans and Other Legumes" and "Cooking with Cereal Grains.") Drain and reserve liquid for soup or gravy.

Combine cooked soybeans, corn, tomatoes, onion, garlic, thyme, salt and cayenne. Set aside. *Preheat oven to 350°F.*

Combine tomato paste, brewer's yeast, if using it, and stock. Set aside.

Place half the cooked wheat berries on the bottom of an oiled 4-quart casserole. Cover this layer with the soy-bean mixture. Spread the tomato paste mixture over the soybean layer and top casserole with remainder of wheat berries. Sprinkle with grated cheese. Bake uncovered for 30 minutes in preheated oven.

Yield: 6 to 8 servings

Whole Wheat Flaky Pastry

1 *cup whole wheat pastry
    flour*
1 *cup brown rice flour*
½ *teaspoon salt*
6 *tablespoons butter*
2 *tablespoons oil*
2 *tablespoons ice water*

Preheat oven to 400°F.

Sprinkle a 9-inch pie pan lightly with flour.

Combine flours and salt in a bowl. Cut butter in with knives or a grater. Add oil gradually, working it in with fin-gers, then the ice water. Knead dough briefly until water is distributed evenly.

Press into prepared pie pan or roll out between well-floured sheets of wax paper and place in pie pan, making a high fluted edge around the outside. If baking shell without filling, prick it well with a fork. Bake in preheated oven for 10 to 12 minutes.

Yield: 1 9-inch pie shell

Cook macaroni in plenty of boiling water to which 1 tablespoon oil has been added. Drain and rinse with cold water. Cook green beans and carrots according to preferred method. Drain if necessary.

Combine the macaroni, beans, carrots and seasonings. Process cottage cheese and ricotta in electric blender. Add mustard and lemon juice and blend until smooth. Toss macaroni mixture with cheese dressing until ingredients are well coated. Chill and serve.

Yield: *6 servings*

Whole Wheat Macaroni Salad with Cheese Dressing

2 *cups whole wheat macaroni*
   boiling water
1 *tablespoon oil*
1 *lb. fresh green beans, cut*
   into 1-inch pieces
   (approximately
   2 cups)
2 *cups diced carrots*
2 *tablespoons chopped parsley*
½ *cup chopped green onions*
½ *teaspoon dill*
½ *teaspoon basil*
1 *teaspoon salt*
½ *teaspoon black pepper*
1 *cup cottage cheese*
1 *cup ricotta cheese*
2 *teaspoons prepared*
   mustard
2 *tablespoons lemon juice*

Preheat oven to 450°F.

Combine milk, oil, pastry flour and salt. Beat until smooth, then add the eggs one at a time, beating only until batter is smooth.

Fill well-greased muffin or popover tins three-quarters full. Bake at 450°F. for 15 minutes, then lower heat to 350°F. and bake approximately 20 minutes longer.

Yield: *1 dozen popovers*

Whole Wheat Popovers

1⅓ *cups milk*
1½ *tablespoons oil*
1½ *cups whole wheat*
   pastry flour
¼ *teaspoon salt*
3 *eggs*

Bran

Although old-timers have traditionally preached the virtues of roughage (fiber-rich foods like bran) for regularity, only in recent years has serious medical research into fibrous foods been done. And, sure enough, doctors find that such foods help to prevent the so-called diseases of civilization—constipation, hemorrhoids, cancer, diverticulosis and heart disease.

Large quantities of bran are available as the by-products of flour milling. Unprocessed bran is more effective than the processed breakfast cereals and much less expensive. Unprocessed bran can be purchased at most natural food stores and is distributed nationally by at least two companies:

Shiloh Farms
White Oak Road
Martindale, Pennsylvania 17549

Shiloh Farms
Route 59
Sulphur Springs, Arkansas 72768

Pure and Simple
Box 13
Boyertown, Pennsylvania 19512

(The above companies will supply in quantities of five pounds or more.)

Bran is a concentrated source of B vitamins and minerals. As a rich source of food fiber, bran is particularly effective against constipation because, in addition to containing lots of fiber, it has the ability to absorb large amounts of water. The combination of these two properties makes bran a better regulator of the bowels than other fibrous foods.

There is also evidence that food fiber speeds the metabolism of cholesterol into bile acids, helping in this way to guard against diseases like atherosclerosis and various types of venous disorders.

To be effective, bran need only be taken in small amounts. One teaspoon to several tablespoons daily, depending on individual needs, will provide full benefits to most people. If you like cereal for breakfast, sprinkle some bran on top; if you enjoy baking, include bran in your homemade bread and muffins. You can also add bran to cookies, crackers, casseroles and meat loaves.

Bran Cookies

Preheat oven to 350°F.

Combine dry ingredients in a large bowl. Beat eggs in separate bowl, then add oil, honey and milk to them and blend together. Stir wet ingredients into dry, add raisins and nuts, if using them. Drop by teaspoon, 2 inches apart, on a greased cookie sheet. Bake in preheated oven for 8 to 10 minutes. Watch cookies carefully as these tend to brown quickly on the bottom.

Yield: 4 dozen cookies

1½ *cups whole wheat flour*
 3 *cups bran*
 ½ *teaspoon salt*
 1 *teaspoon ginger*
 1 *teaspoon cinnamon*
 ½ *teaspoon cloves*
 2 *eggs*
 ½ *cup oil*
 ½ *cup honey*
 ½ *cup milk*
 ½ *cup raisins (other chopped dried fruit may be substituted)*
 ½ *cup chopped nuts (optional)*

Bran Muffins

Preheat oven to 375°F.

Combine bran and flour. Add salt and cinnamon. In another bowl, combine oil, milk, beaten egg yolks and honey or molasses. Add to the dry ingredients. Add the raisins, seeds or nuts or a combination of them—as you like. Beat the egg whites until stiff and fold them into the batter. Bake in oiled muffin pan or Pyrex custard cups in preheated oven for 25 minutes.

Yield: 8 muffins

 1 *cup bran*
 1 *cup whole wheat pastry flour*
 1 *teaspoon salt*
 1 *teaspoon cinnamon*
 2 *tablespoons oil*
 1 *cup milk*
 4 *egg yolks, beaten*
 3 *tablespoons honey or molasses*
 ½ *cup raisins, sunflower seeds or nuts*
 4 *egg whites*

Bran Sesame Crackers

¾ cup oatmeal (ground to
    a coarse flour in
    electric blender)
½ cup bran
1 cup whole wheat flour
½ teaspoon salt
6 tablespoons oil
1 tablespoon honey
½ cup water
¼ cup unhulled
    sesame seeds

Preheat oven to 350°F.

Combine first four ingredients. Combine wet ingredients and stir into dry. Grease a cookie sheet generously. Pat dough out on the cookie sheet and roll it with a rolling pin until it is as thin as possible (⅛ inch). Sprinkle sesame seeds over the surface and roll them into dough with the rolling pin. Score the dough with a knife in square or diamond shapes.

Bake 10 to 12 minutes in preheated oven. Loosen crackers with a spatula as soon as they are removed from the oven. Cool and store in airtight container.

*Yield: 4 dozen crackers
approximately
2 inches square*

Bran Vegetable Meat Loaf

1 cup tomato juice
1 medium-size onion,
    quartered
1 clove garlic
1 stalk celery, cut into
    1-inch pieces
1 carrot, cut into chunks
4 sprigs parsley
1 cup chopped broccoli or
    zucchini
1½ lbs. ground beef
1 teaspoon salt
⅛ teaspoon pepper
1 teaspoon oregano
1 egg
¾ cup bran

Preheat oven to 350°F.

In electric blender, combine tomato juice, onion, garlic, celery, carrot, parsley and green vegetable. Process until completely pureed.

In a large bowl, mix remaining ingredients. Add pureed vegetables, combining well, and put mixture into a 9x5x3-inch loaf pan. Bake in preheated oven for 1 to 1¼ hours. Serve with Basic Gravy (see Index) or Tomato Sauce (see Index).

Yield: 6 servings

Carob Bran Cake

Preheat oven to 350°F.

Combine raisins and hot water in a bowl. Add grated carrot, egg yolks, sifted carob, sifted soy flour, whole wheat flour, cinnamon, salt and lemon rind. Finally add the bran, stirring to blend together. Beat egg whites stiff and fold into mixture.

Turn into oiled 9-inch pie pan, or if using a large bread pan, line it first with oiled brown paper. Bake in preheated oven for 35 to 40 minutes. Remove from oven. If bread pan was used, remove cake from pan and after approximately 10 minutes, strip off paper. Cake can remain in pie plate until serving time.

Yield: 6 to 8 servings

½ *cup raisins*
⅔ *cup hot water*
1 *cup finely grated carrots*
2 *egg yolks*
3 *tablespoons carob, sifted*
¼ *cup soy flour, sifted*
¾ *cup whole wheat flour*
¾ *teaspoon cinnamon*
¼ *teaspoon salt*
grated rind of 1 *lemon*
½ *cup bran*
2 *egg whites*

Cooked Bran Granola

Preheat oven to 250°F.

Combine all dry ingredients except raisins or dried fruit. Combine honey, oil, water and vanilla if using it, and add gradually to dry ingredients stirring to coat grains and nuts evenly.

Bake in lightly oiled baking pan for 1 to 1½ hours in preheated oven, stirring every 15 minutes until granola is dry and lightly browned and crisp. Remove from oven, add fruit if using it, cool and store in airtight container.

Yield: 8 to 12 cups

3 *cups oatmeal*
1 *cup any other flaked or rolled grain*
1 *cup bran*
2 *cups any combination of nuts and seeds*
1 *cup coconut*
½ *cup soy grits (optional)*
brewer's yeast to taste (optional)
non-fat dry milk to taste (optional)
¼ *to* ½ *cup honey*
¼ *cup oil*
½ *cup water*
vanilla to taste (optional)
1 *to* 2 *cups chopped raisins or dried fruit (optional)*

Hot Bran Cereal

5 *cups milk*
1 *teaspoon salt*
1 *cup wheat, brown rice, rye*
    or a mixture of grains
    (toasted in a dry skillet
    and "cracked" in
    electric blender)
¼ *cup bran*
honey or molasses to taste
raisins or other dried fruit
    (optional)
milk (optional)

Bring milk and salt to a boil, stir in cracked grains and bran. Lower heat, cover pan and allow it to simmer for 5 to 10 minutes or until the cereal is as thick as desired. Sweeten to taste, add raisins or other dried fruit and more milk if desired.

Yield: 4 servings

Molasses Bran Candy

½ *cup bran*
½ *cup non-fat dry milk*
4 *tablespoons molasses*
    or honey
1 *teaspoon vanilla or*
    ½ teaspoon cinnamon

Combine all ingredients thoroughly and allow to stand for 15 or 20 minutes. Drop by teaspoon onto plastic wrap, shape into rounds and press flat. Allow to stand for several hours or until dry and no longer sticky.

Yield: 2 dozen 1-inch rounds

Uncooked Bran Granola

2 *cups oatmeal*
1 *cup wheat germ*
1 *cup any other flaked*
    or rolled grain
1 *cup bran*
1 *to 2 cups any combination*
    of nuts and seeds
1 *cup raisins*
1 *cup any other dried or fresh*
    fruit
honey or maple sugar
    to taste

Combine all ingredients. Store in an airtight container. Serve with fresh milk or yogurt or, if preferred, add ⅓ cup non-fat dry milk for every cup of granola and blend in well, before storing.

Yield: 8 to 9 cups

Bulgur

For some people bulgur's fast cooking time is one of its main attractions. But that's the cook talking. Ask the diners why they go for this precooked cracked wheat product and they'll talk about its pleasant nutty flavor and its fluffy consistency, both reminiscent of brown rice. Basically, since bulgur contains some of the wheat germ, it has about the same nutritive value as whole wheat. Though a few nutritionists point out that some B vitamins are lost in the precooking, others say that the loss is balanced by the increased availability of the wheat's protein. In any case, bulgur is far superior to white rice or any refined grain food.

You can use bulgur in any of the ways you would use rice—in pilafs, in salads, in soups or served alone as a side dish. However, bulgur really stars in a classic Middle Eastern dish, *couscous*, a delicately flavored base for a stew, usually of lamb or chicken, that has been simmered with onions and seasoned with herbs. Traditionally, the *couscous* cooks right above the simmering stew picking up all the delicious flavors as they rise with the steam. To do this, simply place the bulgur *couscous* in a steamer or strainer lined with a thick layer of cheesecloth, set inside the tightly covered stewpot. Try this dish and you'll find that it quickly becomes a regular favorite of your family and friends.

Bulgur Soybean Loaf

Cook bulgur and soybeans according to preferred methods. (See "Cooking with Cereal Grains" and "Basic Methods for Cooking Beans and Other Legumes.") Drain and reserve liquids for soup. Put soybeans through meat grinder using fine blade.

Preheat oven to 325°F. Combine all ingredients and turn into oiled loaf pan. Bake in preheated oven for approximately 1 hour or until browned.

Yield: 6 servings

1 *cup bulgur*
¾ *cup soybeans*
½ *cup chopped onion*
2 *eggs, beaten*
1 *cup milk*
1 *teaspoon salt*
1 *tablespoon chopped chives*
½ *teaspoon thyme*
1 *teaspoon chopped parsley*
2 *teaspoons dry mustard*
2 *tablespoons tamari*
    soy sauce

Bulgur *Couscous*

¾ *cup chick-peas*
2 *lbs. lamb, cut into*
    2-inch cubes
2 *tablespoons oil*
1 *clove garlic, minced*
3 *medium-size onions,*
    quartered
3 *carrots, cut into*
    1-inch chunks
¼ *teaspoon ginger*
¼ *teaspoon ground cumin*
⅛ *teaspoon cloves*
½ *teaspoon ground coriander*
1 *teaspoon salt*
water to cover
2 *cups water (approximately)*
2 *cups bulgur (finely ground*
    in electric blender)
2 *small zucchini, cut into*
    1-inch slices and
    lightly steamed

Cook chick-peas according to preferred method. (See "Basic Methods for Cooking Beans and Other Legumes.") Drain and reserve liquid for soup.

Brown lamb in oil, turning to sear all sides. Add garlic, onions, carrots, seasonings and water to cover. Bring to a boil, lower heat and simmer, covered, for approximately 1 hour.

Meanwhile, using your hands, work approximately 1 cup water into bulgur, using enough water to moisten each grain. Put bulgur in cheesecloth-lined strainer which is small enough to fit into pot in which stew is cooking. Place strainer over the stew above the water level so bulgur will steam, not boil. Replace cover and cook for 30 minutes. Remove strainer and turn out bulgur into a bowl. With your fingers, separate the grains and add enough water (approximately 1 cup) to again moisten all particles. Put bulgur back into strainer, replace over stew and continue to steam for another 15 minutes.

Remove bulgur and add cooked chick-peas and zucchini to the stew. Continue to cook just long enough to heat the chick-peas and zucchini.

Serve bulgur *couscous* immediately, topped with lamb stew.

Yield: 6 servings

Bulgur Raisin Custard

¼ *cup bulgur*
2 *cups warm milk*
¼ *teaspoon salt*
½ *cup raisins*
¼ *cup honey*
¼ *teaspoon cinnamon*
3 *egg yolks, beaten*
3 *egg whites, stiffly beaten*

Mix bulgur, milk and salt and let stand, covered, for approximately 1 hour. *Preheat oven to 325°F.* Stir raisins, honey, cinnamon and egg yolks into bulgur mixture. Mix thoroughly then fold in stiffly beaten egg whites. Turn into oiled casserole and set casserole in a pan of hot water to bake. Bake in preheated oven for 1 hour and 15 minutes.

Yield: 4 to 6 servings

Cook navy beans according to preferred method. (See "Basic Methods for Cooking Beans and Other Legumes.") Drain and reserve liquid for soup.

Pour the boiling water over the bulgur and let stand 1 hour until the grain is light and fluffy. Drain and press out excess water. Add cooked navy beans and all remaining ingredients and chill for about 1 hour. Serve on salad greens.

Yield: 8 servings

Tabouli Salad

¼ *cup navy beans*
4 *cups boiling water*
1¼ *cups bulgur*
¾ *cup chopped green onion or onions*
3 *medium-size tomatoes, chopped*
1½ *cups chopped parsley*
1 *cucumber, chopped*
½ *cup lemon juice*
¼ *cup oil*
1 *teaspoon salt*
¼ *teaspoon black pepper*

Wheat Germ

Expert cooks who want to add a fresh, interesting taste and texture to an old favorite like oven-fried chicken or a macaroni and cheese casserole are likely to reach for the wheat germ. It adds a crispness to the dredging flour and a new zip to the melted cheese crust.

Wheat germ flakes come raw or lightly toasted. The toasted variety has a delicious taste and crunchy texture that most people prefer, though it is slightly lower than the raw in some nutrients because of the heat involved in processing. Raw or toasted, wheat germ is a perishable product and should be kept refrigerated.

It's too bad that wheat germ's fabulous reputation as a high-nutrition food overshadows its terrific taste qualities, because it diverts attention from the most pleasant aspect of this product. With the exception of vitamins A, C and B_{12}, just about every nutrient is present in wheat germ. To see just how superior wheat germ is compared with other wheat products look over this chart, compiled from data in the United States Department of Agriculture's Handbook No. 8, *Composition of Foods,* and *Home Economics Research Report No. 36.*

	"Enriched" White Flour	Whole Wheat Flour	Raw Wheat Germ
Nutrients per 100 Grams (about 3½ ounces)			
Protein (grams)	10.5	13.3	26.6
Fiber (grams)	.3	2.3	2.5
Calcium (mg)	16	41	72
Iron (mg)	2.9	3.3	9.4
Potassium (mg)	95	370	827
Magnesium (mg)	25	113	336
Thiamine (mg)	.44	.55	2.01
Riboflavin (mg)	.26	.12	.68
Niacin (mg)	3.5	4.3	4.2
Vitamin B$_6$ (mg)	.06	.34	1.15*
Pantothenic Acid (mg)	.465	1.1	1.2*

*Toasted wheat germ

To get a fix on what wheat germ is, imagine the whole wheat grain as you know it—a seed actually. The outer covering, the bran, is a rough, many-layered shield, rich in crude fiber. Underneath this covering is the bulk of the kernel, a starchy mass of carbohydrate called the endosperm. Deep inside, near the base of the kernel is a dark speck so tiny you could easily overlook it. This is the wheat germ.

Coping with Rancidity

Modern milling methods strip the germ from our flour because the oil in the wheat germ tends to go rancid rapidly, ruining the flour if it is not used within a few days. Of course the nutrients in the wheat germ are then lost to the consumer.

Fortunately not all the wheat germ sifted out of flour is sold as a powerhouse feed supplement for livestock. Some is set aside and reserved for sale through health food stores and supermarkets.

Wheat germ can be used in a thousand ways. It can be eaten by itself as a cold cereal, or added to almost any dish. Those new to it start by sprinkling wheat germ on puddings, yogurt, and fruit salad or adding it to pancakes. The longer you use wheat germ, the more ways you will find to add it to other food.

Use wheat germ as a delicious breading on fish, veal, chicken and liver. Or try mixing a quarter- or half-cup of wheat germ with each pound of ground beef when making meat loaf or hamburgers. A couple of tablespoons of wheat germ will also blend well with other ingredients in tuna or chicken salad.

Wheat Germ Breading Mix

(good coating for chicken, liver, fish and chops)

⅓ cup cornmeal
⅓ cup rye flour
⅓ cup wheat germ
1 teaspoon salt

Combine ingredients in a jar and keep on hand in refrigerator.

Yield: 1 cup

Wheat Germ Giblet Stuffing

1 cup brown rice
4 chicken livers
2 to 4 tablespoons butter
1 onion, chopped
½ cup chopped celery
1 cup wheat germ
½ cup chopped parsley
1 teaspoon salt
⅛ teaspoon black pepper
½ to ¾ cup chicken stock

Cook rice according to preferred method. (See "Cooking with Cereal Grains.")

Meanwhile, in a large skillet, saute chicken livers in butter. Remove them from skillet and chop coarsely. Using same skillet, saute onion and celery using more butter if needed.

Combine cooked rice, chopped chicken livers, wheat germ and sauteed mixture. Add parsley, seasonings and ½ cup stock. Mix well, adding more stock if needed.

Yield: 3½ cups stuffing

Wheat Germ Muffins

 2 *teaspoons dry yeast*
¼ *cup lukewarm water*
1½ *cups wheat germ*
 2 *cups oat flour*
½ *cup non-fat dry milk*
½ *cup unhulled sesame seeds*
½ *cup whole wheat flour*
½ *teaspoon salt*
⅓ *cup oil*
¼ *cup honey*
 2 *cups warm water*
 2 *eggs, beaten*

Soften yeast in lukewarm water. Set aside for 5 minutes. Combine wheat germ, oat flour, non-fat dry milk, sesame seeds, whole wheat flour and salt. Combine oil, honey, water and eggs; then add this mixture to the softened yeast. Combine liquid and dry ingredients.

Let stand 10 minutes. Mix approximately 1 minute and fill well-greased muffin tins with batter. Let stand 10 minutes more. *Preheat oven to 400°F. and bake for 20 minutes, then lower heat to 350°F. and bake 5 minutes more.*

Yield: 12 muffins

Wheat Germ Spread

¼ *cup wheat germ*
½ *cup peanut butter*
¼ *cup cottage cheese or yogurt*
 2 *tablespoons honey*

Combine all ingredients in electric blender and process until thoroughly mixed. Use as a spread in sandwiches or on crackers.

Yield: 1 cup

Milk and

Its Marvelous Products

Is all the enthusiasm about milk as a great food really justified? Much of it is. However, it is clear that milk is better for children than it is for adults. Because children are growing and their bones and teeth are developing, they need more calcium and protein than adults do. Milk's main claim to fame is an uncommonly rich supply of both of these nutrients.

Unfortunately, as we grow older our supply of rennin, an enzyme children have which aids in digesting milk, is depleted. So adults can best take advantage of milk's values by concentrating on the milk products that are, in a sense, predigested. That is, bacteria have been added to, or encouraged to grow in the milk, and as they grow the bacteria perform the function of curdling, or predigesting, the milk. You've probably enjoyed one or more of these wonderful-tasting, helpful milk products many times without being aware of their exceptional values.

We'd like to consider milk in its many forms to provide a clear picture of what each one has to offer in terms of nutrition, flavor and use as a cooking ingredient.

Skim Milk

Whole milk standards are governed by the individual states and so they vary a bit. But 3.25 percent milk fat and 8.25 percent milk solids are just about the minimum that any state allows. If milk falls a little below this it is classified as partially skim and if it is much below it is called skim milk.

There are two types of powdered skim milk, or non-fat dry milk as it is technically called, instant and noninstant. The noninstant has a slight nutritional edge on the instant since it is produced by a low-heat method as opposed to the high heat used for instant. But the nutritional value is not significant enough to rule out the use of instant. And the instant does seem to be easier to use in cooking when milk as a liquid is called for as it dissolves more easily in water. However, if the non-fat dry milk called for in a recipe is as a dry ingredient—to be mixed with the flour of a bread, cookie or cracker recipe—as a protein booster, the noninstant, which is a finer powder, is the one to use, as it blends better.

Buttermilk

Rich, marvelous-tasting real buttermilk is the liquid that is left after butter has been churned. When fresh cream is churned while it is cold, sweet natural buttermilk is produced; if lactic acid-producing bacteria are added to that, the result is sour natural buttermilk. Both of these milks are low in fat and are much easier to digest than regular milk. Real buttermilk is also an excellent source of B vitamins. Unfortunately, real buttermilk is hard to come by these days. A few natural food stores have it and you can make your own by adding a freeze-dried buttermilk culture to skim milk (available from The International Yogurt Company, 628 North Doheny Drive, Los Angeles, California 90069). From then on you can make more using 2 to 3 tablespoons of your homemade buttermilk as a starter for each quart of fresh skim milk.

Unfortunately, buttermilk as it is sold in the supermarkets today is quite remote from real buttermilk. It is a commercially cultured product, often with added bits of butter. It is made either with skim or whole milk that might not be fresh enough to sell as milk. The culture that is added produces a flavor only slightly reminiscent of the old-time buttermilk.

Nondairy "Milks" and "Creams"

What about these nondairy "coffee lighteners" that cholesterol-conscious customers are buying in an effort to avoid milk's drawbacks? These products have little nutritional value and, though they contain no butterfat, they do contain quantities of highly saturated vegetable oil. In fact, virtually all lighteners are made with saturated fats such as coconut oil or hydrogenated vegetable oil. Of course, this makes them poor choices for a fat-controlled diet.

Far from being the nutritional equivalent of milk, the nondairy "milks" are much too low in protein and calcium and provide, along with the undesirable fat, 16 to 23 calories per serving, while a like amount of whole milk contains 17 calories.

Nondairy substitutes present a particular danger to people on milk-free diets who look to them as a safe way to wet their cereal or lighten their coffee.

Although the creamers contain no lactose, they do contain sodium caseinate, a milk protein derivative. Anyone who is allergic to the casein fraction in milk will run into trouble with a nondairy product.

The principal—probably the only—advantage of nondairy "milks" is their keeping quality. The liquid lighteners keep for three weeks in the refrigerator after thawing; the dry lighteners keep for months.

Non-fat dry milk, if stored in a cool, dry place, will keep for months. It comes in packets that can be made up in seconds, is cheaper per serving than the nondairy lighteners—and it's *real* milk, with the protein and calcium intact, minus the cholesterol-rich butterfat.

Cheese

Is there anyone who doesn't like some kind of cheese? With so many varieties, that have such diverse flavors, aromas and textures, surely there is a cheese to suit almost everyone's palate.

Cheese fanciers, also known as turophiles, not only know what tastes good, but, apparently, they know what's good for them. Cheese is an interesting food which is impressively nutritious.

It is a complete protein. Ounce for ounce, cheese contains seven times as much protein as the milk from which it is made. It is also rich in minerals, milk fat and vitamin A. Of course, these nutrients vary greatly, depending on how each cheese is made and what type of milk it is made from.

Yellow cheeses, such as brick, are a superior source of protein to white cheeses. Hard and semisoft cheeses have more calcium than their softer counterparts, but soft cheeses provide more B vitamins. Cheeses made from whole milk have a higher saturated fat and cholesterol content. So if you're on a diet or watching your cholesterol it's best to stick with those made from skim or semiskim milk. Labels usually indicate if skim milk is used.

Processed Cheeses

Most of the cheese sold in this country today is processed cheese. There are several types and none of them is as desirable as natural unprocessed cheese. Natural cheese matures slowly through enzymatic action, while processed cheese is made quickly using heat to speed up the action and air to increase volume. The processed type is apt to contain numerous additives.

Pasteurized process cheese is always labeled as such. It's made by grinding, blending and heating natural cheeses with water and an emulsifier.

Several questionable substances are used to dye commercial cheeses. However, some commercial cheeses are never dyed: Gruyere, Roquefort, Limburger, cook cheese *(kochkase)* and sapsago retain their natural colors. When buying commercial cheeses one safe way to avoid dyes is to choose a cheese which is close to the color of milk.

Storing Cheeses

Most cheeses should be tightly wrapped, in moisture-proof, airtight wrappers, such as plastic wrap. "Moldy" cheeses such as Roquefort or blue cheese are an exception to the tight-wrapping rule. These cheeses need to breathe and should be kept in covered containers with the tops loosened just a bit. All cheese keeps best on the bottom shelf of a refrigerator.

There is no reason not to freeze cheese. It keeps well this way and freezing doesn't destroy the nutritional value. However, it does change the texture of hard cheeses, making them more crumbly. The softer cheeses remain soft or spreadable. Never refreeze cheese once it has been defrosted.

Make Your Own

Why not try making your own cheese? You can do it. There is no mystical art involved. With practice it will seem simple to you.

Start with one of the soft cheeses, like cottage cheese. These are a whole lot easier to make than hard cheeses. Cottage cheese, which is sometimes called pot cheese or *schmierkase,* is made commercially from skim milk or from non-fat dry milk solids. The consistency is more like ricotta (the fine-curd Italian cheese used in many pasta dishes) when you use whole milk.

Cottage Cheese

1 *quart milk (certified, raw;*
   or homogenized, whole;
   or skim; or reconstituted
   non-fat dry milk)
2 *tablespoons buttermilk or*
   lemon juice or vinegar
¼ *teaspoon salt*

In a large pottery, glass or china bowl combine 1 quart of your favorite type of milk and buttermilk, lemon juice or vinegar as "starter." Mix thoroughly, cover with a clean cloth and allow to stand for 18 to 24 hours in a warm place or in a gas oven with only the pilot light burning.

When the milk has clabbered or thickened, place over low heat just until the curds separate from the whey (this only takes a few minutes). Pour into a cheesecloth-lined strainer and allow to drain. When curds are dry, remove them from cheesecloth and stir in salt. Use cottage cheese as desired and use whey as stock for soup or as a drink.

Yield: 1 cup cottage cheese; 3 cups whey

Whey, the liquid that is left when cottage cheese (curds) is produced, is 70 percent lactose which goes directly to the intestines where it establishes an environment favorable to the growth of beneficial bacteria. It also contains lactalbumin, water and most minerals present in milk. So use the whey you get in making cheese.

Whey makes a delicious strawberry drink. Simply blend strawberries and whey in your blender and enjoy. You can also add the whey to soups and sauces.

Making hard cheese takes much longer and is a little more complicated than making cottage cheese. After you have achieved a curd, much the same way as you do for cottage cheese, you must cook it, firm it, drain, salt and press it. *Stocking Up,* revised, (Emmaus, Pennsylvania: Rodale Press, 1977) has a useful section on making hard cheese, and there is an excellent book which takes you through all the steps of making hard cheese, *Cheese Making At Home* by Don Radke (New York: Doubleday & Co. 1974).

There are so many ways to use cheese that you could serve it at every meal for a month and never duplicate a recipe.

But when you use cheese as an ingredient be sure that you do not overcook it. If it is heated for too long cheese becomes stringy. So add cheese to a recipe at the last possible moment and try to avoid cooking it at temperatures exceeding 350°F.

One-fourth pound of cheese equals one cup when grated.

Broccoli Cheese Pie

1 *9-inch unbaked pie shell*
1 *medium-size onion,*
        chopped
1 *tablespoon oil*
2½ *cups sliced broccoli*
        flowerets
1 *cup grated mild cheddar*
        cheese
¼ *cup non-fat dry milk*
¾ *cup water*
2 *eggs, beaten*
½ *teaspoon salt*
¼ *teaspoon dry mustard*
¼ *teaspoon pepper*

Make pie shell according to preferred recipe.

Preheat oven to 375°F. Saute onion in oil until tender and spread over pie shell. Fill pie shell with broccoli and top with grated cheese. Combine non-fat dry milk and water. Add to beaten eggs and add seasonings. Pour into pie shell.

Bake in preheated oven for 45 minutes until lightly brown on top and firm. Remove from oven and allow to cool for 5 minutes before cutting and serving.

Yield: 4 to 6 servings

Preheat oven to 375°F.

Place flour, wheat germ and salt in a bowl and mix well. Work in the butter with the fingertips or a pastry blender until mixture is like coarse oatmeal. Stir in cheese, walnuts, egg yolk and enough water to make a dough. Knead briefly to distribute liquid.

Roll out on a lightly floured board to ⅛-inch thickness and cut into triangles. Place on a lightly greased baking sheet and bake in preheated oven 12 to 15 minutes or until lightly browned. Cool on a rack and store in an airtight container.

Yield: 48 chips

Rub a chafing dish or a heavy casserole which can be put over direct heat, with garlic and pour in the wine or stock. Heat to the boiling point, then add cheese and cook, stirring constantly until the cheese is melted and smooth. Add seasonings. Stir kirsch into cornstarch and add to cheese mixture. Continue to cook for 5 minutes.

Cut bread into 1-inch cubes. Spear one cube of bread at a time on a small fork, dip into fondue and eat.

Yield: 4 servings

In a saucepan, heat butter or oil, stir in flour, then add milk slowly, stirring until sauce is thickened. Add seasonings and cheese. Continue to heat, stirring constantly, until cheese has melted. Salt to taste.

Yield: approximately 3 cups

Cheddar Chips

1   *cup whole wheat flour*
¼   *cup wheat germ*
½   *teaspoon salt*
¼   *cup butter*
1   *cup grated sharp cheddar cheese*
¼   *cup very finely ground walnuts*
1   *egg yolk*
ice water

Cheese Fondue

1   *clove garlic, split*
¾   *cup dry white wine or chicken stock with fat removed*
1   *lb. Gruyere cheese, diced*
¼   *teaspoon salt*
⅛   *teaspoon white pepper*
pinch of nutmeg
2   *ounces kirsch (optional)*
1   *tablespoon cornstarch*
whole grain bread

Cheese Sauce

2   *tablespoons butter or oil*
4   *tablespoons whole wheat flour*
2   *cups milk*
1   *teaspoon dry mustard*
1   *teaspoon tamari soy sauce*
¾   *cup grated cheddar cheese*
salt to taste

Cheese Soup

4 *tablespoons butter*
4 *tablespoons chopped onion*
4 *tablespoons whole*
   wheat flour
5½ *cups milk*
2 *teaspoons chopped chives*
2 *teaspoons chopped parsley*
1 *teaspoon salt*
2 *cups grated cheddar cheese*
chopped parsley
paprika
grated cheese

Melt butter in a large heavy saucepan and saute onion for approximately 5 minutes. Add whole wheat flour and stir until smooth, then add milk and cook for 5 to 8 minutes, stirring constantly as mixture thickens. Add chives, parsley, salt and then cheese. Stir until cheese is melted. Top with parsley, paprika and a little more grated cheese, if desired.

Yield: 4 to 6 servings

Herbed Cheese and Onion Bread

1 *tablespoon dry yeast*
1 *cup lukewarm milk*
2 *tablespoons honey*
1 *egg, beaten*
1 *teaspoon salt*
¼ *teaspoon basil*
¼ *teaspoon tarragon*
1 *teaspoon chopped chives*
1 *cup grated cheddar cheese*
½ *cup chopped green onions*
   or onions
3 *to 3½ cups whole*
   wheat flour

Soften the yeast in lukewarm milk, to which honey has been added. Let stand for approximately 5 minutes. Add the remaining ingredients in the order given, then knead the dough until smooth and elastic, using more flour if necessary. Cover bowl, set in a warm, draft-free place to rise.

When dough has doubled, punch it down, shape into a loaf and place in an oiled bread pan to rise again until double in size. *Preheat oven to 350°F.* and bake for 35 to 45 minutes, or until bread is done. Remove from pan and cool.

Yield: 1 small loaf

Cottage Cheese, Date and Nut Filling

Simmer dates, honey and water together in a saucepan approximately 5 minutes. Add lemon juice, chopped nuts and cinnamon; chill. When chilled, add to cheese and stir until combined. Spread on bread or crackers.

Yield: approximately 2½ cups

½ *cup finely chopped dates*
¼ *cup honey*
¼ *cup water*
 2 *tablespoons lemon juice*
½ *cup finely chopped nuts*
½ *teaspoon cinnamon*
12 *ounces dry cottage cheese or pot cheese*

Cottage Cheese Dressing

Process cottage cheese at medium speed in electric blender until smooth. Add other ingredients and blend just long enough to mix thoroughly. Chill before serving.

Yield: 1⅓ cups

1 *cup cottage cheese*
2 *tablespoons yogurt*
2 *tablespoons lemon juice*
1 *teaspoon prepared mustard*

Cold Whey Soup with Potatoes and Zucchini

In a large saucepan, combine celery, onion, potatoes, and zucchini. Cover with water, add seasonings and simmer for approximately 15 minutes or until vegetables are just tender. Add whey or stock, bring to a boil and simmer for 2 or 3 minutes longer. Cool and then chill in refrigerator for at least an hour. Serve topped with chopped parsley.

Yield: approximately 6 cups

1 *cup chopped celery, including leaves*
1 *cup chopped onion*
2 *cups diced potatoes*
2 *cups diced zucchini*
water to cover
½ *teaspoon dill*
½ *teaspoon basil*
½ *teaspoon salt*
⅛ *teaspoon black pepper*
4 *cups whey or soup stock*
2 *tablespoons chopped parsley*

Messmor
(whey spread)

1 *quart whey*
1 *teaspoon flour (optional)*

Bring 1 quart whey to a boil in a shallow, wide, heavy-bottom pan. Turn heat low and cook whey for 3 to 4 hours, stirring occasionally in the beginning and as it thickens, stirring constantly to prevent it from scorching.

If desired, the thickened whey can be made thicker by adding 1 teaspoon flour dissolved in a little milk or cream, and simmering a bit longer. It may be seasoned to taste and used on bread or crackers.

Yield: approximately 1 cup

Spinach Cheese Blintzes

Blintzes

4 *eggs*
1½ *cups milk*
1½ *cups whole wheat*
        pastry flour
½ *teaspoon salt*
    pinch of nutmeg

Filling

1½ *lbs. fresh spinach*
1 *cup cottage cheese*
1 *cup ricotta cheese*
¾ *cup chopped walnuts*
        or sunflower seeds
½ *teaspoon salt*
⅛ *teaspoon black pepper*
    pinch of nutmeg
    yogurt (optional)

Make Blintzes

Combine first five ingredients in electric blender and process until batter is smooth. Let rest for 2 hours to allow particles of flour to expand in liquid, resulting in a tender blintz. Just before baking blintzes, process batter again briefly to blend ingredients.

Lightly butter a 6-inch frying pan and put it on a medium-high burner to heat. Pour approximately 2 tablespoons of batter into it and rotate it quickly so that batter covers the bottom. Book blintz until the bottom is lightly browned and the top is dry. Turn it out on a towel. Repeat process until batter is all used, stacking blintzes with plastic wrap between each one. Cover with a towel until ready to use. *Preheat oven to 400°F.*

Make Filling

Cook, drain and chop spinach. there should be approximately 2 cups. Combine cottage cheese and ricotta in electric blender and process until smooth. Pour into a bowl and add nuts or seeds, salt, pepper, nutmeg and spinach. Mix thoroughly. Place 2 or 3 tablespoons of filling on browned side of each blintz. Roll up loosely, place side by side in buttered casserole and bake in preheated oven for 10 minutes or until blintzes are nicely browned. Top with yogurt if desired and serve immediately.

*Yield: approximately 24 blintzes
or 6 to 8 servings*

Make pie shell according to recipe. Reserve 2 tablespoons crumb mixture for garnish.

Wash and slice fresh strawberries. Drizzle honey over them. Set aside for an hour or so. Drain. If using frozen strawberries, slice, drizzle honey over them and leave them to thaw. Drain. You should have approximately 1 cup berries and ½ cup juice.

Combine lemon juice with strawberry juice in a small saucepan. Dissolve cornstarch in juice and bring to a boil, stirring constantly. Cook for a minute or so, until thick. Stir in strawberries. Taste and add more honey if needed. Cool. Spread over bottom of pie shell. Refrigerate.

In a small saucepan, soften gelatin in water and then heat slowly, stirring constantly, to melt the gelatin.

Combine milk or light cream with cottage cheese in electric blender and process until smooth. Add honey and melted gelatin and blend to combine.

Spread cheese mixture over the strawberries in the pie shell. Sprinkle with reserved crumb mixture and refrigerate for an hour before serving.

Yield: 1 9-inch pie

Strawberry Cheesecake Pie

1 *9-inch baked pie shell (use Crumb Crust recipe; see Index)*
1 *pint fresh strawberries or ½ 20-ounce package frozen unsweetened strawberries*
2 *to 4 tablespoons honey (depending on sweetness of berries)*
2 *tablespoons lemon juice*
1½ *tablespoons cornstarch*
1 *envelope unflavored gelatin*
2 *tablespoons water*
1 *cup milk or light cream*
1 *cup cottage cheese*
4 *tablespoons honey*

Combine whey, lemon juice and berries or fruit juice in electric blender and process until berries are liquefied. Add nutmeg, mint and honey to taste. Chill several hours before serving.

Yield: approximately 8 cups

Whey Punch

5 *cups whey*
½ *cup lemon juice*
2 *cups berries or 1 cup fruit juice*
¼ *teaspoon nutmeg*
2 *tablespoons fresh mint leaves*
6 *to 8 tablespoons honey to taste*

Kefir

Kefir (kay-feer), a cultured milk product that is virtually unknown in the United States but very popular in many other countries, is one of the oldest of fermented milk drinks. In the Caucasian Mountains kefir is still a part of everyday mealtime. There it is traditionally made in a sealed leather bag of goat's skin. Fermentation is a continuous process, because people add more milk whenever they remove some kefir for their meal.

Kefir is different from yogurt in that it has an added bacillus. It has a very low curd tension, that means the curd breaks up very easily in extremely small particles. This facilitates its digestion because it presents a large surface for the digestive agent to work on. Kefir stimulates the flow of saliva and of the digestive juices. It often can be tolerated by persons who are allergic to milk.

There are two types of kefir: a lactic type and an alcoholo-lactic type. The latter is used for the manufacturing of kefir beverages which are extremely popular in eastern Europe, the Middle East and Russia.

The lactic type of culture resembles yogurt, but is sweeter and less compact, more like a very delicate custard, and is the kind of kefir most commonly used. Its taste is much milder, and it is easy to make. No need for a thermometer, the long incubating period, or other prerequisites. Simply heat the milk, cool it to room temperature, add the culture, put the mixture in containers and let it set for about 12 to 24 hours at room temperature.

To keep on making the lactic type kefir one can use a few spoonfuls of the previous batch.

It's very easy to make ricotta or cottage cheese from kefir.

If you have access to raw milk, the kefir you make from it resembles the old-fashioned clabber with its golden layer of cream on top. Serve it with a slice of very dark bread, for a most refreshing treat. Or blend the kefir together with fresh fruit into a milk shake-like drink.

If you wish to make kefir, a freeze-dried culture may be ordered from:	Fresh kefir grains may be ordered from:
The International Yogurt Company 628 North Doheny Drive Los Angeles, California 90069	R.A.J. Biological Labs 35 Park Avenue Blue Point, New York 11715

Piima

Piima (pronounced pee-ma) is a popular cultured milk in the Scandinavian countries and originated in Finland. Like kefir and cheeses it was discovered by accident. It was found that the milk of the cows grazing on a northern European wild herb, butterwort, at its peak growth, clabbered easily at room temperature.

Just as with yogurt or kefir, once you have the first batch made from a freeze-dried culture, you can go on indefinitely, making each new batch with the help of a few spoonfuls of the previous batch.

Piima's great advantage is that it can be made from milk at room temperature—about 70°F.—no previous heating needed. It may take from eight to twenty-four hours to set depending on how much below or above 70°F. your room temperature is. Piima is milder than kefir therefore it can be used as a direct substitute in any recipe that calls for milk. Blend it with egg and gelatin for a delicious quick custard dessert. Or serve it on baked potatoes. It mixes well with mayonnaise, enhances salad dressings and toppings. Mixed with fruit juice or concentrate, it makes a delicious shake.

A custard from piima not only tastes superb, it also is tolerated by people who are allergic to milk. The menu for such persons can be enlarged considerably by substituting piima in many recipes. As it is not tart, but very mild, it will barely alter the taste of the end product.

If your food store does not carry piima, the owner can order it from PIIMA, Box 2614, La Mesa, California 92041.

Comparing yogurt, kefir and piima, you'll find that they get milder tasting in that order.

Piima Eggnog

Blend on low just long enough to mix.

Yield: approximately 3 cups

NOTE: For variety, add any of the following:

2 *tablespoons carob, or*
2 *tablespoons brewer's yeast, or*
½ *cup raw fruit or juice, or*
½ *cup fresh berries.*

4 *eggs*
2 *cups piima*
1 *tablespoon ground almonds*
1 *teaspoon vanilla*
4 *tablespoons honey*

Yogurt

Yogurt's popularity is an American success story in the finest tradition. It has come up from virtual obscurity—an exotic dish eaten by a select few—to a table favorite and a satisfying snack, familiar to everybody and sold by the case in stores all over the country. But it's not surprising that this marvelous food has finally made it. It tastes great, it's very nutritious and it's remarkably economical, especially if you make your own. Homemade yogurt is not only cheaper, but it's better. And it's easy.

First of all, there are a number of kits on the market which turn yogurt making into a real snap. These yogurt makers are simple, inexpensive appliances that don't use much power. All come complete and ready to use. Because they are designed to produce low-level heat for hours at a time, yogurt makers are very inexpensive to operate—much cheaper to run, in fact, than just about any other appliance in the kitchen.

The yogurt you can make at home is considerably less expensive than the commercial product. At home you can prepare eight 8-ounce portions of yogurt from a half-gallon of milk, using only a few cents worth of electricity. The price for eight of the customary 8-ounce cups sold in stores would be nearly triple what these ingredients cost.

You Have Control over the End Product

Another advantage to making your own yogurt is that you have full control over the end product. You can leave out chemical preservatives, artificial flavors and colors, sugar and all the other ingredients that lessen the value of many commercial yogurts. (Some commercial yogurts are pasteurized, which inactivates the healthful bacteria.) At the same time, by carefully selecting your starter culture, you can include whatever particular strains of beneficial bacteria you desire. *Lactobacillus acidophilus,* for example, is frequently cited in clinical studies for its highly desirable effects on the intestinal tract. Most store-bought brands however don't include the *L. acidophilus* strain in their formulations.

The beneficial bacteria which yogurt contains in abundance have been shown to have a normalizing effect on the lower digestive tract. Middle Eastern countries, where refrigeration was not always available, long ago developed the custom of having yogurt as an appetizer to prepare the stomach for the onslaught of food to be digested.

Homemade yogurt is fresher. Unlike most commercial varieties with their preservatives and stamped expiration dates, your own yogurt won't be sitting on some store shelf for a week or two before your family eats it. You simply make a fresh batch as you need it. And freshly made yogurt tastes sweeter than commercial unsweetened yogurt because the culture hasn't had much time to acidify and turn sour. Your children will probably appreciate the difference. In fact, many grown-ups who thought they didn't like yogurt have changed their minds after being introduced to the homemade variety. Properly made yogurt should be creamy, rich and custardlike with a slightly tart taste.

Finally, with your own yogurt maker in the kitchen, you and your family will probably eat this health-giving food more often, and that's the best advantage of all. For in addition to being a dependable source of calcium and protein, yogurt contains respectable amounts of the B vitamins (particularly riboflavin), as well as some potassium.

It Practically Makes Itself!

Actually, there's no special knack involved in making good yogurt. Unlike cheese or ice cream, yogurt practically makes itself. The bacteria do all the work. All you have to do is provide a warm place so the bacteria can thrive and multiply—you can use the back of a coal stove, an oven with a pilot light, or even the warmth of a tea cozy. This way of making yogurt takes a little more attention than if you use an appliance especially made for this purpose. For one thing, the yogurt maker will maintain a constant temperature of approximately 100°F. This is important. If the mixture gets too cool, the growth of bacteria will be retarded; if it gets too hot, the bacteria may be killed off.

Any kind of milk—whole, skim or powdered—can be used to make yogurt. If you're using a yogurt maker, directions may vary slightly from manufacturer to manufacturer, but basically the procedure goes like this:

Simply pour the milk into a saucepan and heat until just below boiling. Allow to cool to room temperature, then stir in the starter culture (or two tablespoons of yogurt left over from your last batch), pour into containers and let the yogurt maker do the rest.

But with or without the appliance, at the properly maintained temperature, the milk proteins will begin to curdle and coagulate. When a thickened, custardlike consistency is achieved, your yogurt is ready. This may take from three to nine hours, depending on the heat source and individual eating preferences. (Yogurt gets thicker and tarter the longer it incubates.) You can experiment until you find the most satisfying time period and technique for your taste. Finished yogurt should be refrigerated immediately to prevent further souring.

Once you've made your yogurt at home, the real fun begins in finding new and mouth-watering ways to enjoy it. You can eat yogurt plain, of course. Freshlymade, plain yogurt has an agreeable and unexpected natural sweetness.

If you prefer, you can mix fresh or frozen fruit into your homemade yogurt. That way you can duplicate the tempting flavors found at the supermarket. For added sweetness, try adding honey or blackstrap molasses.

Soft Frozen Yogurt

Now an entirely different life has fanned out for yogurt. The soft frozen kind. Yogurt Huts are proliferating alongside the soft ice cream stands and people who wouldn't think of stopping for a soft ice cream cone are likely to stop by for a cone of frozen yogurt without any guilt pangs. If nothing else, whole soft frozen yogurt provides one-half to one-third fewer calories than a comparable portion of ice cream. Unfortunately, frozen yogurt is not likely to be yogurt and only that. Dannon adds a natural stabilizer and a small amount of kosher

gelatin to its mixture to obtain the proper texture. Other brands do it their own way. If you want to try it at home, try this recipe from the Rodale experimental kitchen:

Strawberry Soft Yogurt Ice Cream

1 *envelope unflavored gelatin*
¼ *cup cold water*
¼ *cup honey*
6 *tablespoons non-fat dry milk*

¼ *cup water*
2 *cups yogurt*
1 *cup frozen or fresh strawberries, sliced (approximately ½ lb.)*

In a small saucepan soften gelatin in cold water. Add honey and warm over low heat until gelatin is dissolved. Mix non-fat dry milk with water. Process reconstituted milk with yogurt and fruit in electric blender.

While machine is working, add gelatin mixture, pouring it in a steady stream into center of vortex, so as to incorporate the gelatin evenly throughout the mixture.

Freeze until desired consistency is reached.

Yield: approximately 1 quart

One good reason for making your own frozen yogurt is that some of the commercial brands are literally riddled with chemical additives. As Mimi Sheraton of the *New York Times* wrote, ". . . considering the chemical additives used as stabilizers, emulsifiers, flavorings and colorings found in three of the four frozen yogurt mixes sold around town, this product may well go down in history as the world's first bona fide junk health food. . . ." To prove her point she lists some of the additives in one of the most popular brands: sugar syrup, corn sweetener, sodium citrate, locust bean gum, sodium carboxymethal, mono and diglycerides, polysorbate 80, artificial flavor and artificial color.

Clearly, the surest way to have a frozen yogurt that does more for you than it does to you is to make your own. If you're not willing to go that far, at least give a careful look at the ingredients listed on the side of the frozen yogurt package and choose the one with the least number of objectionable additives.

Blueberry Yogurt

3 *small oranges
(approximately 1 lb.)
peeled, seeded and cut
into chunks*
1 *cup fresh or frozen blueberries, thawed and
drained*
1 *tablespoon honey*
10 *tablespoons yogurt*

Put oranges in electric blender and process to a liquid. Then add blueberries and blend to a liquid. Add honey and yogurt and process to combine. Pour into serving dishes and chill.

Yield: approximately 3 cups

Coconut Yogurt Cheese Pie

1 *9-inch baked pie shell*
1 *cup Yogurt Cheese
(see Index)*
⅔ *cup yogurt*
2 *tablespoons honey*
1 *teaspoon vanilla*
1¼ *cups shredded coconut*

Make pie shell according to preferred recipe.

In electric blender combine Yogurt Cheese, yogurt, honey and vanilla. Process until smooth. Fold in coconut, saving 1 tablespoon for topping. Pour mixture into baked pie shell, top with remaining coconut and chill until set.

Yield: 6 servings

Cranberry Yogurt Sauce

¼ *cup softened butter*
¼ *cup honey*
½ *cup yogurt*
¼ *cup cranberry puree*

Combine all ingredients. Using electric blender, make a puree. Serve with pancakes or steamed pudding.

Yield: 1¼ cups

Fitness House Spread

1 *cup butter*
1 *cup mayonnaise*
1 *cup yogurt*

Soften butter at room temperature. In electric mixer, beat butter until fluffy. Add mayonnaise and beat until it is blended in. Add yogurt, and beat briefly, just until blended in. Store in airtight container in refrigerator. Remove to room temperature 15 minutes before serving. Use on bread or crackers.

Yield: approximately 4 cups

Combine all ingredients and mix well. Allow to stand in refrigerator for at least 15 minutes before serving.

Yield: approximately 1¼ cups

Savory Yogurt Salad Dressing

¾ *cup yogurt*
2 *tablespoons lemon juice*
1 *teaspoon prepared mustard*
½ *teaspoon kelp powder*
1 *teaspoon basil*
½ *teaspoon salt*
⅛ *teaspoon pepper*
1 *clove garlic, minced*
1 *onion, grated*

Mix all ingredients thoroughly and chill until ready to use.

Yield: 1¼ cups

Spicy Yogurt Dressing for Fruit Salad

1 *cup yogurt*
3 *tablespoons apple juice*
¼ *teaspoon cinnamon*
  pinch of nutmeg
¼ *teaspoon finely grated lemon rind*
1 *tablespoon honey*

Bring milk to a boil, then cool to lukewarm. Make a paste with the yogurt and a little lukewarm milk. Soften gelatin in some of the lukewarm milk and warm it over low heat to dissolve gelatin. Add honey, vanilla, then stir in remaining milk and then (when mixture is cooled to lukewarm) stir in yogurt paste. Place in a yogurt maker or use your preferred method for making yogurt.

Yield: 1 quart

Thick Vanilla Yogurt

4 *cups milk*
2 *tablespoons yogurt*
1 *envelope unflavored gelatin*
2 *to 4 tablespoons honey (according to taste)*
2 *teaspoons vanilla extract*

Yogurt Cheese

Place 2 cups yogurt in a cheesecloth-lined strainer in the refrigerator. Let drain for approximately 8 hours until yogurt is the consistency of cream cheese. Don't stir or press at all. Use just as you would use cream cheese. Save the liquid or whey for a soup stock or beverage. (See recipe for Cold Whey Soup with Potatoes and Zucchini.)

Yield: approximately 1 cup

Yogurt-Cumin Drink

1½ *cups yogurt*
½ *cup water*
¼ *teaspoon ground cumin*
1 *teaspoon honey*
¼ *teaspoon ground dried mint*
pinch of ginger

Combine all ingredients in electric blender and process until smooth. Chill.

Yield: 1 pint

Making the Most of Eggs

"Two eggs any style" can mean much more than poached, fried, or scrambled. Think about an omelet, for instance. It can be filled with cheese, jelly, mushrooms, meat, spinach, mixed vegetables, sprouts, chopped herbs, or with fruit of any kind. Then think of souffles and hollandaise sauce, of meringues and mousses—of Easter eggs! The mellow taste of egg is a treat by itself and it blends well with almost any other kind of food.

The secret to cooking eggs is to cook them very gently over a low heat. Eggs that have been cooked too fast or too long are rubbery. If they are boiled too long they get a greenish-gray coloring around the yolk.

It is easier to peel hard-cooked eggs if they have been allowed to cool completely in cold water. But remember, the fresher they are, the harder they are to peel. Save your older eggs for hard boiling.

When making an omelet it is important not to beat the eggs too hard—just until the yolks and white are combined. Too much beating will make the omelet tough. For a basic omelet recipe figure on one to two tablespoons of water for each egg (never use milk) and enough oil or butter to coat the bottom of the frying pan or cast-iron skillet well. If you make an omelet with nuts or seeds or fresh fruits such as blueberries or strawberries, they can be mixed in with the beaten egg.

The white of an egg contains 10 percent and the yolk 16 percent protein. Except for vitamin C, an egg holds about every nutrient a person needs. It can be combined with fruit juices, bouillon, coffee, milk shakes and many other things.

Buckwheat-Groat Souffle

2½ *cups milk*
 ½ *cup buckwheat groats*
 1 *teaspoon salt*
 ⅓ *cup grated sharp cheddar cheese*
 4 *egg yolks, beaten*
1½ *teaspoons prepared mustard*
 1 *tablespoon tamari soy sauce*
 4 *egg whites*

Heat milk in a medium-size saucepan. Add groats and salt and bring to a boil, stirring constantly. Cover, lower heat and simmer for approximately 20 minutes. Add cheese and stir until cheese is melted. Remove from heat and gradually pour over egg yolks, stirring until well blended. Add mustard and soy sauce. Cool. *Preheat oven to 350°F.*

Beat egg whites until stiff and gently fold them into buckwheat mixture. Turn into ungreased 1½-quart souffle dish. Bake for 40 to 45 minutes in preheated oven, or until souffle is firm to the touch. Serve immediately.

Yield: 4 to 6 servings

Cold Berry Souffle

 2 *envelopes unflavored gelatin*
 ½ *cup lemon juice*
 8 *egg yolks*
 ½ *cup honey*
 1 *cup strained, pureed strawberries or raspberries, sweetened to your taste with honey or your favorite sweet liqueur (Grand Marnier, cassis, apricot, etc.)*
 2 *cups heavy cream*
 8 *egg whites*
fresh berries

Oil a 1-quart souffle dish. Tie around the outside of the dish a strip of brown paper or parchment paper, which extends about 2 inches above the side of the dish making a "collar." Oil this "collar" on the inside.

In a small saucepan, soften gelatin in lemon juice. Warm over low heat, stirring, until gelatin is dissolved. In a bowl, beat egg yolks with honey until thick and lemon colored. Add gelatin mixture, and then the sweetened berry puree, beating after each addition. Transfer this mixture to the top of a double boiler and cook over simmering, not boiling, water, stirring constantly until mixture is thick. Lift top of double boiler out of bottom and cool, stirring to prevent eggs from overcooking. Whip cream. Beat egg whites until stiff and fold them and then the whipped cream gently into cooked mixture. Pour into prepared souffle dish and chill until souffle is set.

Just before serving, remove oiled paper "collar" and garnish with fresh whole berries.

Yield: 6 to 8 servings

Preheat oven to 350°F.

Melt butter and add flour, stirring for a minute or so. Gradually add milk, stirring, and cook until thick. Add egg yolks, then corn and seasonings.

Beat egg whites until stiff but not dry and fold into corn mixture. Pour into ungreased baking dish. Bake 30 minutes in preheated oven. Serve immediately.

Yield: 4 to 6 servings

Corn Souffle

1 *tablespoon butter*
2 *tablespoons whole*
   wheat flour
1 *cup milk*
2 *egg yolks, beaten*
2 *cups freshly grated corn*
1 *teaspoon salt*
pinch of nutmeg
2 *egg whites*

Beat eggs. Add remaining ingredients, combining well. Heat oil in skillet to a medium-high temperature. Ladle 2 tablespoons of the mixture into skillet for each pancake. When pancakes are set, and brown underneath, turn them over and brown the other side. Serve immediately.

*Yield: approximately 15 pancakes
or 4 to 6 servings*

Egg Foo Yung

6 *eggs*
4 *green onions, thinly sliced*
¾ *cup frozen green peas*
1 *cup fresh or ½ cup canned*
   (drained) chopped
   mushrooms
1½ *cups mung bean sprouts*
1 *tablespoon tamari soy sauce*

Cook rice according to preferred method. (See "Cooking with Cereal Grains.")

Pack cooked rice firmly into a buttered baking dish. Make four little wells, evenly spaced, about 1 inch deep, on the surface of the rice. Melt butter in a saucepan, add flour, stirring, and then add beef stock, stirring constantly. Cook until thickened. Add seasoning.

Spoon approximately 1 cup of the sauce over the rice into the wells. Break a raw egg into each well, gently spoon the remaining sauce over the entire surface and bake in preheated oven for 25 minutes or until eggs are firm. Garnish with chopped parsley and serve.

Yield: 4 servings

Eggs on Curried Rice

1½ *cups brown rice*
2 *tablespoons butter*
2 *tablespoons whole*
   wheat flour
2¼ *cups beef stock*
1 *teaspoon chopped chives*
½ *teaspoon thyme*
2 *teaspoons curry powder*
salt, pepper to taste
4 *eggs*
2 *tablespoons chopped parsley*

Foamy Sauce

4 *tablespoons butter*
4 *tablespoons honey*
2 *egg yolks, beaten*
pinch of salt
1 *tablespoon brandy,*
    rum or sherry
2 *egg whites*

In the top of a double boiler, over simmering, not boiling water, mix butter and honey. Add egg yolks and salt, stirring until mixture is smooth and thick.

Lift top of double boiler out of bottom and cool sauce, stirring to prevent eggs from overcooking. Add brandy, rum or sherry. Beat egg whites stiff and gently fold them into sauce. Use immediately, or egg whites will begin to break down. Can be used as an alternate to cognac in Crepes Suzette recipe or as a topping for cake or puddings.

Yield: 1½ cups

Fresh Herb Omelet

1 *cup slivered fresh spinach,*
    beet greens or Swiss
    chard
½ *cup coarsely chopped*
    parsley
2 *tablespoons snipped*
    fresh dill
2 *tablespoons snipped*
    fresh chives
2 *tablespoons snipped*
    fresh basil
¼ *cup minced radishes*
2 *tablespoons minced onion*
6 *eggs, beaten*
6 *tablespoons water*
salt to taste
oil

Combine greens, herbs, radishes and onion. Combine eggs and water, and add to greens mixture. Season to taste.

Heat cast-iron skillet or omelet pan to medium-high heat. Add just enough oil to pan to coat the bottom. Pour in omelet mixture, pushing cooked edges of omelet toward center of the pan, with a metal spatula, and tipping the pan so the liquid will run to the outside rim and cook. When the omelet is almost set, and the bottom is a golden brown color, lift up one side and fold it over the other side. Serve immediately.

Yield: 4 servings

Jelly Roll

Preheat oven to 350°F.

Prepare pan. Oil a baking sheet (approximately 10½x15½x1-inch). Cut parchment or brown paper (from a grocery bag) to fit the pan, lay it in and oil it also, being sure to do so evenly.

Beat egg yolks with honey until thick and light in color. Add flour and vanilla, beating to combine. Beat egg whites until stiff but not dry. Fold egg yolk mixture gently into beaten egg whites, combining thoroughly.

Pour batter into prepared pan, being sure to fill corners and to spread it evenly. Bake on middle shelf of preheated oven for 12 minutes until surface is a golden brown. Be careful not to overbake.

Lay out a clean tea towel which is larger than the cake. Remove cake from oven, loosen sides with knife and turn upside down onto towel. Slowly peel paper from bottom of cake, using a knife to loosen it as you go. Roll up cake immediately, starting with the narrow end, tucking the edge of the towel inside the cake, and rolling it along with the cake. Let the roll cool, making sure the "seam" is directly underneath it. When it is cool, unroll it and spread with jelly. Reroll cake, without towel, slice and serve topped with whipped cream.

Yield: 4 to 6 servings

NOTE: This may be made ahead and frozen, if desired.

5 *egg yolks*
2 *tablespoons honey*
4 *tablespoons whole wheat or rye flour*
1 *teaspoon vanilla*
5 *egg whites*
½ *cup currant jelly, softened, if necessary, for spreading*
whipped cream

Scottish Egg Sauce

Peel eggs and separate yolks from whites. Chop whites fine and mash yolks with a fork. In a small saucepan, over low heat, melt butter and add flour, stirring for a minute or so. Gradually add milk or cream and stir until smooth. Add seasonings and cook slowly for 15 minutes. Add chopped egg whites. When ready to serve, spoon sauce over crepes, broiled fish or any vegetarian loaf and garnish with mashed egg yolks.

Yield: 2 cups

4 *hard-cooked eggs*
2 *tablespoons butter*
2 *tablespoons whole wheat flour*
2 *cups milk or light cream*
½ *teaspoon salt*
⅛ *teaspoon white pepper*
1 *teaspoon prepared mustard or tamari soy sauce (optional)*

Pfannkuchen

(a large German omelet)

  4 *egg yolks*
  ½ *cup water*
1½ *teaspoons honey*
  ¼ *cup soy flour*
  1 *tablespoon cornstarch*
  2 *tablespoons wheat germ*
  ½ *teaspoon salt*
     grated rind of 1 *lemon*
  4 *egg whites, stiffly beaten*
  2 *tablespoons butter*

Combine, all ingredients except egg whites and butter in electric blender and process until smooth. Gradually pour egg yolk mixture into beaten egg whites, folding to blend thoroughly. Melt butter in a 10-inch skillet, over medium-low heat, then pour in omelet mixture. Cover skillet and let cook for 5 minutes until brown on the bottom and dry and set on top. Cut into portions and serve from the skillet, as soon as *Pfannkuchen* is done, or it will begin to fall. Serve as a main dish with Cranberry-Applesauce (see Index) or as a dessert with Apricot Sauce or Carob Syrup (see Index).

Yield: 2 servings as a main dish;
4 servings as a dessert

Thick Custard

2½ *tablespoons cornstarch*
  1 *cup milk*
  2-*inch piece vanilla bean*
       or ½ *teaspoon*
       vanilla extract
  2 *egg yolks*
  2 *tablespoons honey*

Dissolve cornstarch in a little of the cold milk. Heat remaining milk in top of double boiler, with vanilla bean if using it. Remove bean, slit pod open and using the tip of the knife, scrape inside of pod into milk. Discard bean. Stir dissolved cornstarch into hot milk and cook until thickened, stirring constantly. Beat egg yolks with honey. Stir a little of the hot milk into the egg mixture, then stir this into the remaining hot milk. Cook for approximately 1 minute, stirring constantly. Add vanilla extract, if using it. Pour into container and chill.

Yield: approximately 1¼ cups

Get
the Best

in Meat

Muscle Meats

For primitive man, meat was a rare treat, because then, as now, meat was, in a sense, an expensive food. The effort and time spent hunting for meat far surpassed that involved in plant gathering. Our ancestors ate the meat raw so they never ran the risk of ruining their prize in cooking. But we do. The idea, of course, is to minimize the dangers by keeping some basics in mind.

The secret to good meat cookery is to keep the external and internal temperatures the same. If you don't, you might get a burned shell with tough insides. It is a myth that quick searing of a piece of meat keeps the juices sealed in. Cook it slowly and the meat will get brown nicely, with the juices bubbling inside. But don't overcook. Meats served rare are more nutritious than meats served well done.

Tender meat cuts contain little connective tissue and can be cooked relatively fast.

If the beef comes from a reliable supplier, try Steak Tartare sometime. This favorite—raw chopped beef, often with capers and anchovies, plus herbs and spices—is quick, easy and makes a great *hors d'oeuvre* or luncheon dish. (See Index.)

In addition to protein, muscle meats are rich in almost all B vitamins and minerals. However, many nutrients escape into the water when meat is boiled or stewed. Therefore, never discard any fluid in which meat has been cooked. If the meat is roasted, the vitamins and minerals seep into the juice. So serve it with meat, either as is *(au jus)* or make gravy with it.

A little wine, vinegar, lemon, tomato, sour cream or other acid food cooked with a roast not only enhances its taste, it actually increases the nutritional value of a roast cooked with the bones in it. The acid helps dissolve some of the calcium from the bones and disperse it into the meat. The acid also shortens the cooking time because it softens the meat's connective tissues.

119

How Poultry Measures Up

The nutritional value of the muscle meats from poultry is similar to that of the meats we get from four-legged animals. However, poultry meat is often lower in fat. Chicken, especially the white meat, is easier digested than lamb, pork or beef.

There's one important advantage about poultry. It is fairly easy to find a local farmer or small homesteader who will sell a naturally grown bird to you. If you have a freezer, you can stock up when the time is ripe at his homestead. Of course, if you are a member of a co-op, it is easier to establish a good connection for free-ranging poultry.

If you like turkey, don't reserve it just for holidays; make it an all-year meat. According to Frances Moore Lappe, author of *Diet for a Small Planet* (New York: Ballantine Books, 1971), "Turkey apparently surpasses all other meat and poultry in its ability to complement plant protein." Experiments have shown that, in a meal consisting of one-fifth turkey and four-fifths wheat, peanuts or black-eyed peas, the protein will be the same as if the entire meal had been beef. One hundred grams of turkey (about three slices) contain more grams of protein than half a pound of raw, lean, porterhouse steak. At the same time, these three turkey slices add 200 calories to your diet, while the porterhouse throws 800 calories onto the scale.

Another advantage of turkey is that it usually gives you several meals and that different parts have a different taste. From roast to Newburg, soup or salad, there are many possibilities. If you start with a good-size bird and plan it right, you can eat now and freeze a lot of meals for later use.

Steak Tartare

1 *lb. finely ground lean, raw beef*
½ *cup finely chopped onion*
1 *clove garlic, grated*
1 *tablespoon tamari soy sauce*
⅛ *teaspoon pepper*
1 *egg*
1 *teaspoon prepared mustard*
½ *cup chopped parsley*

Mix all ingredients except parsley. Shape into a mound on a serving platter. Chill for several hours. Top with chopped parsley and surround with thin slices of whole grain or pumpernickel bread; or spread on slices of bread and top with chopped parsley.

Yield: 4 to 6 servings

Beef Stew with Plums

(This recipe can be cooked in a crockery pot. See marker 🍲 for method below.)

Preheat oven to 350°F.

Add honey to plums and cook them in the wine until tender (approximately 5 minutes). Drain, reserving the liquid. When cool, remove pits from plums.

Brown beef chunks in butter and oil. Lift out and place in ovenproof casserole or crockery pot. Using the same pan and adding more oil if necessary, saute onions until tender. Add them to the meat. Using the reserved wine and plum liquid, clean out any brown bits left in pan and pour over meat. Stir in allspice and wine vinegar, blending well. 🍲 (If using crockery pot, omit the following steps and continue with method below.)

Bake casserole, covered, in preheated oven for 1½ hours or until beef is tender. Fifteen minutes before serving, stir in the yogurt or sour cream, thicken gravy with cornstarch dissolved in water if desired, salt to taste and top casserole with plums. Continue to cook, covered, 15 minutes longer.

Yield: 4 to 6 servings

2 tablespoons honey (this can be cut in half or omitted entirely)

2 lbs. (about 12) large firm plums, washed

1 cup dry red wine

2 lbs. beef stew (chuck or round) cut into 1½-inch chunks

2 tablespoons butter

2 to 3 tablespoons oil

3 medium-size onions, sliced

1 teaspoon ground allspice

2 tablespoons wine vinegar

1 cup yogurt or sour cream

1 to 2 tablespoons cornstarch (optional)

¼ cup cold water (optional)

salt to taste

🍲 Cover crockery pot and cook on low for 8 to 10 hours. During last hour, stir in yogurt or sour cream. Thicken gravy, if desired, by pouring off some liquid and adding dissolved cornstarch, returning this to crockery pot and simmering on high for 15 minutes. Before serving, pour gravy over beef and top with plums.

Applesauce Meat Loaf

(This recipe can be cooked in a crockery pot. See marker 🍲 *for method below.)*

2 *lbs. ground beef*
1 *cup applesauce*
1 *onion, finely diced*
1 *green pepper, finely diced*
1 *clove garlic, minced*
6 *slices whole grain bread, grated*
1 *egg*
2 *teaspoons salt*
pepper to taste
½ *cup catsup*

Preheat oven to 350°F.

Combine all ingredients except catsup. Knead mixture with your hands until all ingredients are well blended. 🍲 (If using crockery pot, omit the following steps and continue with method below.)

Pack into loaf pan. Pour catsup over top of loaf. Bake in preheated oven for 2 hours. Turn out of pan, slice and serve.

Yield: 6 to 8 servings

🍲 Pack into bottom of crockery pot. Pour catsup over the top. Cover and cook on high for 1 hour. Then turn to low and cook for 6 to 8 hours. Lift out of pot, slice and serve.

Chicken Breasts in Sour Cream Aspic

4 *whole chicken breasts*
3 *cups chicken stock, plus water if needed to cover chicken*
1 *carrot, sliced*
1 *onion, sliced*
1 *stalk celery, in chunks*
3 *sprigs parsley*
1 *bay leaf*
1 *sprig fresh thyme or ¼ teaspoon dried thyme*
1 *teaspoon salt*
1 *teaspoon lemon juice*
2 *envelopes unflavored gelatin*
⅓ *cup cold water*
1 *cup sour cream (yogurt may be substituted)*
parsley or watercress

Place chicken in a large pot, add chicken stock and enough water to cover. Then add carrot, onion, celery, parsley, bay leaf, thyme, salt and lemon juice. Bring to a boil; skim well. Cover pot and simmer for 30 minutes, or until tender. Remove from heat, lift out chicken and reserve stock. Cool chicken breasts and carefully remove the meat from bones. Skin and split chicken breasts into halves. Chill.

Strain stock and boil to reduce to 1 cup. Soften gelatin in cold water and add to stock. Then add sour cream or yogurt and blend in well. Cool.

While the aspic is still liquid, but at the point of congealing, spoon over each piece of chicken, coating completely. Chill until aspic is firm (10 to 20 minutes), then coat with another layer of aspic. Chill. Keep aspic at room temperature during the coating process. When ready to serve, garnish with parsley or watercress.

Yield: 4 to 6 servings

In a saucepan, heat butter and oil, stir in flours, then add liquid, stirring until sauce is thickened. Stir in meat, poultry or fish, grated onion, herbs and seasonings. Put 2 tablespoons filling on each crepe, roll or fold crepe, and serve with Tomato Sauce or Cheese Sauce.

Yield: 16 8-inch crepes

Convenience Crepes

(an ideal use for leftover meat, poultry or fish)

1 *tablespoon butter*
1 *tablespoon oil*
2 *tablespoons rye or whole wheat flour*
2 *tablespoons brown rice flour*
1 *cup milk or half stock and half milk*
2 *cups ground or minced cooked meat, poultry or fish*
1 *teaspoon grated onion*
1 *tablespoon chopped parsley*
1 *teaspoon basil*
1 *teaspoon dry mustard (optional)*
1 *teaspoon tamari soy sauce*
salt, pepper to taste
1 *recipe Oat Crepes (see Index)*
1 *recipe Tomato Sauce (see Index) or Cheese Sauce (see Index)*

Baked Chicken, Quince and Butternut Squash

1½- *lb. butternut squash*
4 *tablespoons melted butter*
salt, pepper to taste
2 *lbs. chicken breasts and legs*
2 *quinces*
1 *cup water*

Preheat oven to 325°F.

Peel and cube squash. Place in bottom of deep, buttered casserole. Drizzle half the melted butter over squash. Add salt and pepper to taste.

Wash chicken. Lay breasts and legs on top of squash, skin side up. Salt and pepper chicken and drizzle remaining butter over them.

Wash and quarter quinces, remove core and slice approximately ¼ inch thick. It is not necessary to peel them. Lay slices over chicken. Pour water into bottom of casserole. Cover with lid or foil.

Bake in preheated oven for 1½ hours. Remove cover, drain off liquid to thicken if desired. Leave in turned off oven for 10 minutes or so to brown slightly.

Yield: 4 servings

Coq au Vin

(Chicken in Wine)

(This recipe can be cooked in a crockery pot. See marker 🍲 *for method below.)*

3 *tablespoons butter*
1 *roasting chicken (4 lbs.) cut into serving pieces*
1 *tablespoon whole wheat flour*
1 *tablespoon cornmeal*
8 *small, whole onions or shallots*
1 *clove garlic, minced*
¼ *teaspoon thyme*
1 *sprig parsley*
1 *bay leaf*
8 *whole mushrooms*
salt, pepper to taste
1 *cup red wine*

Preheat oven to 275°F.

Melt butter in a large frying pan. Wash chicken pieces and pat dry with towel. Combine flour and cornmeal and dredge chicken in it. Saute chicken in butter until golden brown. 🍲 (If using crockery pot, omit the following steps and continue with method below.)

Put chicken and juices from pan in a large casserole. Add remaining ingredients. Cover and bake in preheated oven until chicken is tender (approximately 2 hours). Remove bay leaf and serve.

Yield: 4 to 6 servings

🍲 Put chicken and juices from pan into crockery pot. Add remaining ingredients and cover. Cook on low 7 to 9 hours. Remove bay leaf and serve.

Wash chicken. Pat dry with paper towels. In a small bowl, combine salt, turmeric and paprika and dust chicken with mixture. ⬜ (If using crockery pot, omit the following steps and continue with method below.) Using Dutch oven or large skillet, brown chicken in oil. Stir in onions, saute briefly, then add chicken stock. Cover, bring to a boil, reduce heat and simmer for approximately 45 minutes. Remove lid and continue to simmer until stock is reduced by half. Chicken should be fork tender. Arrange chicken on a heated platter and keep warm. Dissolve cornstarch in water and add to stock, stirring constantly. Cook until sauce is thickened. Add yogurt to sauce, stirring constantly. Stir in chopped parsley. Spoon sauce over chicken and garnish with additional parsley.

Yield: 8 servings

⬜ Using a large skillet, brown chicken in oil. Transfer chicken to crockery pot. Using same skillet, saute onions briefly. Clean out skillet with chicken stock, using 2 cups instead of 3, and add to chicken. Cover crockery pot and cook on low for 6 to 8 hours or until chicken is fork tender. Transfer chicken to a heated serving platter and keep warm. Dissolve cornstarch in water and stir into liquid in crockery pot. Cook on high for 15 minutes. Stir in yogurt, then chopped parsley. Pour sauce over chicken and garnish with additional parsley.

Chicken Paprika

(This recipe can be cooked in a crockery pot. See marker ⬜ for method below.)

2 *chicken breasts, quartered*
   (8 pieces)
4 *drumsticks*
4 *second joints or thighs*
1 *teaspoon salt*
½ *teaspoon turmeric*
2 *teaspoons paprika*
2 *tablespoons oil*
½ *cup chopped onions*
2 *to 3 cups chicken stock*
1 *tablespoon cornstarch*
2 *tablespoons cold water*
1 *cup yogurt*
2 *tablespoons chopped parsley*
fresh parsley sprigs for
   garnish

Madras Chicken Curry

⅔ cup sliced fresh mushrooms
¾ cup chopped celery
½ cup chopped onion
¼ cup oil
¼ cup whole wheat flour
2 tablespoons cornstarch
2 cups chicken stock
1 teaspoon tamari soy sauce
1 teaspoon salt
1½ teaspoons curry powder
⅛ teaspoon cayenne
3 cups diced cooked chicken
½ cup seedless raisins

Saute mushrooms, celery and onion in oil until tender. Blend flour and cornstarch into sauteed vegetables and stir until thoroughly combined. Gradually add chicken stock, stirring until mixture thickens. Add seasonings and more stock if a thinner sauce is desired. Add diced chicken and raisins. Simmer approximately 20 minutes.

Serve over brown rice with accompanying dishes of chopped peanuts, coconut and chutney.

Yield: 6 to 8 servings

Pennsylvania Dutch Chicken Pot Pie

1 chicken (4 lbs.) cut
   into serving pieces
water to cover
1 teaspoon salt
¼ teaspoon pepper
3 large potatoes, sliced
   ½ inch thick
1 large onion, sliced
4 sprigs parsley
1¾ cups whole wheat flour
½ teaspoon salt
1 tablespoon butter
2 eggs, beaten
1 to 2 tablespoons milk

Place chicken pieces in a large, heavy-bottom pot with a tight-fitting lid. Cover with water, add salt and pepper and simmer slowly until tender.

After chicken is tender, add potatoes, onion and parsley. Bring to a boil and continue to simmer, covered. While vegetables are cooking, make noodle dough.

Sift flour and salt. Cut in butter. Add beaten eggs and enough milk to make a dough. Roll approximately ⅛ inch thick and cut into 2-inch squares.

Before vegetables are quite done, drop noodle squares on top of potatoes and onion in pot, keeping them above the chicken broth if possible. Cover pot again and simmer for approximately 20 minutes longer.

Serve in large tureen or casserole, with noodle squares on top.

Yield: 4 to 6 servings

In a large skillet, heat 3 tablespoons butter or oil and saute onions, carrots, celery and garlic for approximately 10 minutes. Transfer sauteed vegetables from skillet to casserole or crockery pot.

Season the shanks with salt and pepper and roll them in flour. Heat 4 tablespoons oil in the skillet and brown the lamb on all sides. Arrange the browned pieces on top of the vegetables in the casserole or crockery pot.

(If using crockery pot, omit the following steps and continue with method below.) *Preheat oven to 350°F.* Skim most of the fat from juices in the skillet. Add the wine and boil to reduce liquid to ½ cup. Add basil, thyme, parsley, bay leaf and beef stock to skillet. Pour liquid into casserole until it reaches half as high as the meat. Add more stock if needed. Cover casserole tightly and bake for approximately 1¼ hours or until lamb is tender.

Serve lamb shanks on a heated platter with the sauce and vegetables around them.

Yield: 6 servings

Skim most of the fat from juices in the skillet. Add the wine and boil to reduce liquid to ½ cup. Add herbs and add only 2 cups beef stock along with ½ cup liquid from skillet to lamb shanks in crockery pot, cover and cook on low 8 to 10 hours.

Braised Lamb Shanks

(This recipe can be cooked in a crockery pot. See marker for method below.)

- 3   *tablespoons butter or oil*
- 1   *cup finely chopped onions*
- ½   *cup finely chopped carrots*
- ½   *cup finely chopped celery*
- 1   *teaspoon minced garlic*
- 6   *lamb shanks (½ to ¾ lb. each)*
- 1   *teaspoon salt*
- ½   *teaspoon pepper*
- 3   *to 4 tablespoons whole wheat flour*
- 4   *tablespoons oil*
- 1   *cup dry white wine*
- ½   *teaspoon basil*
- ½   *teaspoon thyme*
- 4   *sprigs parsley*
- 1   *bay leaf*
- 2   *to 3 cups beef stock*

Trim excess fat off lamb chops. Brown them in oil. Lay them in shallow ovenproof dish or Dutch oven. Saute green onions until golden and sprinkle them over the chops. Saute quince slices until brown on both sides, adding more oil if necessary. Lay them on top of the chops.

Add stock or water to chops, season to taste, cover and cook over low heat on top of stove, or in preheated 350°F. oven until chops are tender. Thicken juices if desired. Pour sauce over chops before serving.

Yield: 4 servings

Lamb Chop Quince* Saute

- 4   *large shoulder lamb chops*
- 3   *tablespoons oil*
- 6   *green onions, thinly sliced*
- 2   *quinces, cored and sliced ¼ inch thick*
- ¾   *cup vegetable or meat stock or water*
- *salt, pepper to taste*

*Apples or pears may be substituted for quince.

Lamb Cassoulet

(This recipe can be cooked in a crockery pot. See marker  for method below.)

2 *cups dried white beans*

cold water to cover

5 *carrots, cut into*
    2-inch pieces

6 *small onions, whole or*
    cut in half

2 *cloves garlic, minced*

½ *cup chopped celery leaves*

1 *teaspoon salt*

½ *teaspoon pepper*

1 *large bay leaf*

1 *teaspoon thyme*

1 *teaspoon sage*

4 *cups chicken, veal or*
    beef stock

2 *tablespoons butter or oil*

1½ *to 2 lbs. lamb shoulder*
    (stew or chops)

salt, pepper to taste

½ *lb. fresh sausage links*

3 *tablespoons chopped parsley*

(If using crockery pot, omit the following steps and continue with method below.)

In a large 6- to 8-quart pot with cover, soak beans in water to cover for at least 2 hours. Without draining beans, add carrots, onions, garlic, celery leaves, salt, pepper, bay leaf, thyme, sage and stock. Bring to a boil, reduce heat and simmer, covered, for approximately 1 hour.

Meanwhile, heat butter or oil in a large skillet. Brown lamb on all sides. Salt and pepper lightly.

Preheat oven to 350°F. Transfer lamb to an oiled 4-quart casserole. Cover with bean mixture. Make deep, diagonal cuts in top of sausage. Place sausage on top of beans. Cover tightly and bake for approximately 1 hour. Uncover for the last 10 minutes to brown the sausage.

Garnish with chopped parsley and serve from casserole.

Yield: 4 to 6 servings

Pierce sausage all over with a table fork. Simmer in water to cover for 15 minutes. Discard water. Brown lamb, then sausage in butter or oil. Meanwhile put unsoaked white beans in bottom of crockery pot. Add carrots, onions, garlic and celery leaves. Place browned lamb on top of vegetables and add seasonings and herbs. Lay sausage on top of lamb. Bring stock to a boil and pour over mixture in crockery pot, poking a bit with a spoon to distribute stock evenly. Cover and cook on low 8 to 10 hours. Garnish with chopped parsley and serve.

 (If using crockery pot, omit the following steps and continue with method below.)

Heat oil in large skillet. Add lamb cubes and saute, turning frequently, for 20 minutes. Add salt, herbs and onions and cook another 20 minutes. Then add mushrooms and saute 5 minutes. Remove lamb mixture from pan and keep warm.

In the same pan, melt butter, add flour and blend thoroughly. Add stock, stirring until sauce is smooth and has reduced somewhat in quantity (approximately 10 minutes). Add lamb mixture, blending in well. Keep warm over low heat. Just before serving, add egg yolks mixed with yogurt. Do not return to heat. Garnish with parsley and serve.

Yield: 4 to 6 servings

 Using a large skillet, brown lamb cubes in oil. Transfer lamb cubes to crockery pot and add salt and herbs. Saute onions, then mushrooms in skillet. Combine lamb and vegetables in crockery pot.

Using the same skillet, melt butter, add flour and blend thoroughly. Add 2 cups instead of 3 of stock, stirring until sauce is smooth. Add sauce to lamb mixture in crockery pot, cover and cook on low heat 6 to 8 hours. Just before serving, pour liquid from crockery pot into a sauce-pan and keep it heated.

Mix 2 instead of 3 egg yolks with the 1 cup yogurt and stir into hot liquid, until smooth. Pour over lamb, garnish with parsley and serve immediately.

Ragout of Lamb

(This recipe can be cooked in a crockery pot. See marker  for method below.)

3 *tablespoons oil*
2 *lbs. shoulder of lamb, cut into cubes (with or without bone)*
½ *teaspoon salt*
1 *bay leaf, crushed*
½ *teaspoon basil*
¼ *teaspoon thyme*
12 *small whole onions*
½ *lb. small whole mushrooms*
2 *tablespoons butter*
1½ *tablespoons whole wheat flour*
3 *cups veal or beef stock*
3 *egg yolks*
1 *cup yogurt*
chopped parsley

Lamb Korma

(This recipe can be cooked in a crockery pot. See marker 🍲 *for method below.)*

1½ *lbs. boneless leg or shoulder of lamb*
½ *cup yogurt*
½ *teaspoon ground cumin*
½ *teaspoon turmeric*
¼ *teaspoon ground cardamom*
1¼ *cups chopped onions*
1 *clove garlic, finely minced*
2 *to 4 tablespoons oil*
2 *bay leaves*
½ *teaspoon dry mustard*
½ *teaspoon ginger*
¼ *teaspoon cayenne*
¼ *teaspoon black pepper*
⅛ *teaspoon ground cloves*
¼ *teaspoon cinnamon*
1 *cup water*
1 *teaspoon lemon juice*
2 *tablespoons coconut*
salt to taste

Trim excess fat from lamb. Cut into 1-inch cubes. In a large bowl combine yogurt, cumin, turmeric and cardamom. Add lamb cubes; toss to coat well. Allow to marinate 1 hour. Drain lamb cubes well, reserving marinade.

Saute onions and garlic in 2 tablespoons oil for approximately 3 minutes. Add the lamb cubes and brown well on all sides, adding more oil as needed. Stir in bay leaves, dry mustard, ginger, cayenne, black pepper, ground cloves and cinnamon. Cook, stirring until well blended (approximately 2 minutes). 🍲 (If using crockery pot, omit the following steps and continue with method below.) Stir in 1 cup water. Cover skillet and simmer slowly for approximately 1 hour or until lamb is tender. Stir mixture occasionally, adding more water if needed, to prevent sticking. Just before serving, stir in reserved marinade, lemon juice and coconut. Heat briefly and salt to taste. Serve with brown rice.

Yield: 5 to 6 servings

🍲 Transfer lamb to crockery pot. Clean out skillet with 1 cup water and pour into crockery pot. Cover and cook on low 6 to 8 hours. Just before serving, stir in reserved marinade, lemon juice and coconut and salt to taste. Serve with brown rice.

Oven-Baked Sausage

1½ *lbs. country sausage in a casing*
1 *cup water*

Preheat oven to 350°F.

Prick sausage with a sharp table fork all over to allow fat to run out during cooking. Place sausage in water in an oven dish or pan and cover with foil. Bake in preheated oven for 20 minutes. Remove cover, turn sausage over and continue to bake uncovered for another 20 to 25 minutes or until sausage is brown. Discard water and serve sausage.

Yield: 4 servings

Broil or saute sausage until thoroughly cooked. Discard fat and cut sausage into slices ½ inch thick. Saute onions and garlic in oil until tender. Add green pepper, tomatoes, seasonings and sausage. Cover and simmer over low heat for 20 to 30 minutes.

If sauce needs to be thickened, dissolve cornstarch in cold water and stir gradually into boiling sauce, continuing to cook it, stirring briefly, until thick.

Yield: 6 to 8 servings

NOTE: *Lecso* can be served as an appetizer or as a main dish topped with a poached egg.

Lecso

(Austrian Tomato, Sausage, Pepper Ragout)

1 *lb. fresh pork sausage*
1 *cup chopped onions*
1 *clove garlic, minced*
2 *tablespoons oil*
1 *green pepper, seeded and cut into ½-inch strips*
1 *1-lb. 12-ounce can tomatoes*
2 *tablespoons paprika*
½ *teaspoon salt*
  freshly ground black pepper to taste
2 *tablespoons cornstarch (optional)*
¼ *cup cold water*

In a glass, ceramic or stainless steel bowl, combine orange, lemon and lime juices, onion and mustard. Cut slits into the fatty exterior of the pork roast and insert slivers of garlic. Put roast into marinade, turn to coat it and refrigerate for 12 to 24 hours, turning it occasionally.

Using the oil, brown roast on all sides in a Dutch oven on top of the stove. Pour marinade over the roast, cover pot and turn down heat to a low simmer. Cook for 1½ to 2 hours or until pork is done. Meat thermometer should read between 185° and 190°F.

Thicken liquid in pot, if desired, by dissolving cornstarch in cold water and stirring it into boiling liquid. Cook until thickened. Carve the meat, pour some of the gravy over it and serve remainder separately.

Yield: 4 to 6 servings

Orange Marinated Pork Roast

1½ *cups orange juice, fresh or frozen*
2 *tablespoons lemon juice*
¼ *cup lime juice*
1 *medium-size onion, sliced*
2 *tablespoons prepared mustard*
3 to 4 *lb. pork roast (shoulder, loin or fresh ham)*
1 *large clove garlic, slivered*
2 *tablespoons oil*
  cornstarch (allow 2 teaspoons per cup of marinade)
  cold water (double the amount of cornstarch)

Pork Mango Saute

1 *lb. pork (shoulder or fresh ham hock)*
4 *tablespoons lime juice*
1 *teaspoon salt*
freshly ground black pepper to taste
4 *small mangoes (2 lbs. before preparation)*
1 *cup coarsely chopped peanuts*
3 *tablespoons peanut oil*
2 *cloves garlic, minced*
4 *green onions, thinly sliced*

Cut pork into strips approximately ¼ inch thick and ½ inch wide. Add half the lime juice, salt and pepper to pork and marinate for 30 minutes.

Peel and slice mangoes. Add remaining lime juice, salt and pepper and marinate for 30 minutes.

Saute peanuts in peanut oil, lightly, just until golden. Remove from pan and drain on paper towel. In the same pan, saute garlic and green onions for 3 minutes or so, adding more oil if necessary, and stir constantly. Add marinated pork strips and cook until the meat is no longer pink. Layer the marinated mango slices over the cooking pork, cover the pan and turn down heat. Simmer for 5 to 10 minutes or until pork is thoroughly cooked.

Garnish with the peanuts and serve with baked yams or brown rice.

Yield: 4 to 6 servings

Pork Prune Roll-Ups

16 *prunes*
water to cover
1 *apple*
1 *teaspoon salt*
¼ *teaspoon black pepper*
¼ *teaspoon ginger*
8 *thin slices lean pork (approximately 2 lbs. shoulder roast)*
2 *tablespoons oil*
2 *to 4 tablespoons whole wheat or rye flour*
water
½ *cup yogurt*

Simmer prunes in water to cover for 10 to 15 minutes. Reserve liquid. Peel, core and quarter apple and slice thinly. Mix salt, pepper and ginger and sprinkle half of mixture over slices of pork.

Pit prunes and lay 2 prunes and some sliced apple on one end of each slice of pork. Roll up with fruit inside, fastening securely with toothpick. Sprinkle outside of roll-ups with remaining seasoning mixture. In skillet or Dutch oven, brown roll-ups evenly on all sides in oil. Add water from the prunes, cover and simmer for 30 to 35 minutes, or until meat is tender. Watch carefully and add more water as it is needed during the cooking period.

Remove roll-ups and keep them warm. Dissolve flour in a little water and add to broth in skillet. Allow to simmer a few minutes, then stir in yogurt. Remove toothpicks from roll-ups, pour gravy over them and serve hot.

Yield: 4 to 6 servings

Grapes Turkey Mornay

(an aristocratic sandwich)

Make Mornay Sauce

In saucepan, melt butter, stir in flour, add stock and milk, whisking, to avoid lumps. Add cheeses, seasonings and onion. Cook until cheese is melted. Set aside until ready to serve. When ready to assemble sandwiches, reheat sauce and add ½ cup milk if needed to make sauce thin enough to pour over and coat sandwich.

Yield: approximately 2½ cups

Mornay Sauce

- 4 *tablespoons butter*
- 4 *tablespoons whole wheat flour*
- 1 *cup chicken or turkey stock*
- 1 *cup milk*
- 2 *tablespoons grated Parmesan cheese*
- 2 *tablespoons grated cheddar or Swiss cheese*
- ½ *teaspoon salt*
- ¼ *teaspoon paprika*
- ½ *teaspoon grated onion*
- ½ *cup milk*

Make French Toast

Beat eggs, add milk and salt and beat to combine. Put oil in skillet and heat to medium-high temperature. Dip slices of bread in egg and milk mixture and fry them on both sides until they are golden brown. Stack slices of French toast and keep them warm until ready to assemble sandwiches.

Yield: 6 to 8 slices French toast

French Toast

- 2 *eggs*
- ⅔ *cup milk*
- ½ *teaspoon salt*
- 2 *tablespoon oil*
- 6 *to 8 slices whole grain bread*

- ¾ *to 1 lb. cooked turkey breast, sliced (allow 2 ounces per sandwich)*
- 6 *to 8 slices canned unsweetened pineapple, drained*
- 2 *to 2⅔ cups seedless green grapes, washed (allow ⅓ cup per sandwich)*

Assemble Sandwiches

Lay French toast slices in shallow baking dish. Place slices of turkey on each one and a slice of pineapple on top of the turkey. Pile approximately ¼ cup grapes on top of pineapple slice. Reheat Mornay sauce and if necessary, thin it with extra milk. Ladle it generously over each sandwich and top with remaining grapes. Put dish into a low oven (250°F.) for approximately 10 minutes to warm the sandwiches completely. Serve warm.

Yield: 6 to 8 servings

Turkey a la King

1 *cup fresh peas or uncooked*
    frozen peas
½ *cup diced carrots*
1 *cup sliced mushrooms*
2 *tablespoons butter*
4 *tablespoons whole*
    wheat flour
½ *teaspoon salt*
⅛ *teaspoon pepper*
2 *cups chicken stock*
⅔ *cup light cream*
1½ *cups cubed, cooked turkey*
3 *tablespoons chopped parsley*
1 *egg yolk*
2 *tablespoons sherry*

Cook fresh peas, if using them, and and carrots according to preferred method. Drain if necessary. Saute mushrooms in butter, add flour, salt and pepper. Blend well. Add stock slowly, stirring constantly until thick and smooth. Boil 2 minutes, then add cream. Transfer sauce to top of a double boiler and heat over boiling water. Add turkey, vegetables and parsley. Just before serving, beat egg yolk with sherry and stir into turkey vegetable mixture. Serve immediately with brown rice.

Yield: 4 to 6 servings

Turkey Bulgur Casserole

1¼ *cups bulgur*
2 *cups turkey gravy or make*
    sauce of:
    2 *tablespoons butter or*
        turkey fat
    4 *tablespoons whole*
        wheat flour
    2 *cups turkey stock*
    salt, pepper to taste
3 *cups cooked turkey*
    in chunks or pieces
    of uniform size
2 *tablespoons chopped parsley*
    or celery tops
1 *teaspoon chopped chives*
1 *tablespoon butter*
1 *cup sliced mushrooms*

Cook bulgur according to preferred method. (See "Cooking with Cereal Grains.")

If making sauce, heat the butter or fat in medium-size pan. Add flour, stirring to blend it in well. Add stock and stir until sauce is thickened and smooth. Season to taste. *Preheat oven to 325°F.*

Place turkey pieces in bottom of an oiled casserole. Top with parsley or celery tops and chives. In a small pan, heat butter and saute mushrooms for 5 minutes. Spread mushrooms over the turkey and cover with gravy or sauce. Top with bulgur and bake in preheated oven for approximately 25 minutes or until heated through.

Yield: 6 servings

Steam broccoli or asparagus until just tender. Keep hot. Melt butter in a saucepan, add flour and blend thoroughly. Gradually add stock and cook, stirring, until sauce is thick and smooth (approximately 10 minutes). Remove from heat.

Fold in whipped cream, sour cream or yogurt. Add sherry. Season to taste.

Heat broiler. Place broccoli or asparagus on a heatproof platter or in a shallow casserole. Pour half the sauce over it. Arrange sliced turkey over the sauce-covered vegetable. Add 4 tablespoons cheese to the remaining sauce and pour it over the turkey. Sprinkle with additional 2 tablespoons cheese and place the platter or casserole under the broiler until heated through and lightly browned. Serve immediately.

Yield: 4 servings

Turkey Divan

4 *stalks broccoli or*
   8 *stalks asparagus*
   (approximately 1 lb.)
2 *tablespoons butter*
4 *tablespoons whole*
   wheat flour
2 *cups turkey stock*
½ *cup heavy cream, whipped,*
   or ½ cup sour cream
   or yogurt
3 *tablespoons sherry*
salt, pepper to taste
8 *slices cooked turkey*
   (approximately
   ¼ inch thick)
6 *tablespoons grated*
   Parmesan cheese

Cook noodles or spaghetti in 3 quarts boiling water to which 1 tablespoon oil has been added. Drain and rinse with cold water. *Preheat oven to 375°F.*

Saute mushrooms in 1 tablespoon butter for 5 minutes. Meanwhile, to the cooked noodles or spaghetti, add butter, cream and grated cheese (reserving 2 tablespoons of cheese for top of casserole). Toss gently until thoroughly mixed, then place half the mixture in a buttered casserole. Place the turkey on this and cover it with the mushrooms and the remaining pasta. Top with the 2 tablespoons of cheese. Bake in preheated oven for 20 to 25 minutes or until nicely browned.

Yield: 6 servings

Turkey Tetrazzini

½ *lb. whole wheat noodles or*
   spaghetti
3 *quarts boiling water*
1 *tablespoon oil*
¼ *lb. mushrooms, sliced*
1 *tablespoon butter*
3 *tablespoons butter*
¼ *cup cream*
½ *cup grated Parmesan cheese*
2 *cups (approximately 1 lb.)*
   cubed, cooked turkey

Curried Apple and Veal

2 *cups sliced onions*
4 *tablespoons oil*
4 *tablespoons butter*
4 *medium-size apples,*
    peeled and sliced
4 *cups cubed cooked veal*
2 *tablespoons whole*
    wheat flour
2 *tablespoons curry powder*
2 *cups chicken stock*
2 *tablespoons lemon juice*
salt to taste

Saute onions in 4 tablespoons each of oil and butter, until they are tender. Remove them from pan. Saute apple slices until tender but still firm. Remove them from pan. Adding more oil and butter to pan if necessary, lightly brown cooked veal. Remove meat from pan.

Stir flour and curry powder into remaining oil and butter and then add chicken stock, stirring to make a smooth sauce. Add veal, onions and apples to sauce. Add lemon juice and salt to taste. Serve with brown rice.

Yield: 6 to 8 servings

Mango-Topped Veal Chops

2 *cloves garlic, minced*
2 *tablespoons butter*
2 *tablespoons oil*
2 *lbs. veal chops*
    (approximately
    8 chops)
2 *tablespoons lime juice*
2 *tablespoons tamari*
    soy sauce
1 *cup chicken stock*
2 *sprigs fresh mint or pinch*
    of dried mint
2 *cups diced ripe mangoes*
    (approximately
    2 average size)
grated rind of 1 *lime*
4 *tablespoons lime juice*
1 *sprig fresh mint or pinch*
    of dried mint

Preheat oven to 350°F.

Saute garlic lightly in butter and oil. Add veal chops and brown them on both sides. Remove chops and place them in an ovenproof casserole. Add lime juice, tamari soy sauce and chicken stock to pan, stirring to dissolve any hardened meat juices. Pour this liquid over chops. Add mint. Cover and bake in preheated oven for 30 minutes or until meat is tender.

Combine mangoes with lime rind and juice in saucepan. When chops are tender, pour off the liquid into the mango mixture and warm through, but do not cook. Serve chops topped with mango sauce and garnished with snipped mint leaves.

Yield: 4 to 6 servings

Saute onion and mushrooms in 2 tablespoons oil for approximately 5 minutes. Remove onion and mushrooms from pan and set aside. Using the same skillet, brown veal cubes on all sides adding more oil as needed. Add salt and paprika. Stir in chicken stock and lemon peel. Cover and simmer for 30 minutes.

Remove lemon peel. Stir in sauteed onion and mushrooms, cover, and continue to simmer for 35 to 45 minutes longer or until veal is fork tender, stirring occasionally. Blend cornstarch with yogurt. Stir into veal mixture. Heat slowly, stirring until the sauce is blended and thickened—do not boil.

Serve with noodles or brown rice. Garnish with chopped parsley and paprika.

Yield: 6 to 8 servings

Veal a la Madelon
(Veal and Mushrooms in Sauce)

½ *cup chopped onion*
2 *cups sliced fresh mushrooms*
4 *tablespoons oil*
2 *lbs. boneless veal, cut into*
    1-inch cubes
1½ *teaspoons salt*
1 *teaspoon paprika*
1 *cup chicken stock*
2 *1-inch strips lemon peel*
2 *teaspoons cornstarch*
1 *cup yogurt*
   chopped parsley
   paprika

Organ Meats

"Since history began, liver has ranked above all other offal as one of man's most prized culinary delights," Jana Allen and Margaret Gin state in their book, *Innards and Other Variety Meats* (San Francisco: 101 Productions, 1974). "Its heritage is illustrious—whether savored by young warriors after a kill or mixed with truffles and cognac for fine *pates de foie gras.* In the *Li-Chi,* a handbook of ritual during China's Han era (202 B.C. to A.D. 220), liver was listed as one of the Eight Delicacies. . . . To this day, practically every cuisine has a liver specialty. . . ." Perhaps this one from Spain will be new to you:

Chanfaina of Liver

3 *large onions, chopped*　　1 *lb. beef liver, cut into*
½ *teaspoon ground cumin*　　　*1-inch-long strips*
½ *teaspoon ground cloves*　　¼ *cup water*
½ *teaspoon cinnamon*　　　½ *cup wheat germ (optional)*
　pinch of turmeric　　　½ *teaspoon salt*
　sprig fresh mint or　　　⅛ *teaspoon black pepper*
　　1 *teaspoon dried mint*　　*sliced pimientos*
1 *tablespoon chopped parsley*　*chopped parsley*
3 *tablespoons olive oil*

Saute onions with spices and herbs in olive oil for approximately 2 minutes in heavy skillet. Add liver and saute, stirring constantly, for another 2 minutes. Add water and simmer, covered, until liver is done. Stir in wheat germ, if desired, then salt and pepper. Serve garnished with sliced pimientos and chopped parsley.

Yield:　3 to 4 servings

NOTE:　This dish is also good served cold on a bed of crisp greens with a bowl of ripe olives.

Traditionally, liver was looked upon as a source of strength and almost magical value. People's instinct somehow told them that liver is, indeed, a super food, with nutrients in almost embarrassingly extravagant abundance.

All meats are superior protein sources, but few pack as much protein into each ounce as liver. Just one serving of four ounces of liver provides half of the *entire* Recommended Daily Allowance of protein for a woman or a child. A five-ounce serving supplies half the full RDA of protein for a man.

Whereas most cuts of meat contain very little or no vitamin A, a pound of raw beef liver supplies four times the amount that a pound of fresh carrots does—and they are usually thought of as vitamin A champs.

A pound of raw beef liver contains 140 mg. of vitamin C, almost, but not quite, as much as there is in a pound of fresh, peeled oranges—and oranges are virtually synonymous with vitamin C in most people's minds.

All the B vitamins are well represented in liver, especially B$_{12}$—that elusive vitamin only present in foods of animal origin.

In addition to all that, liver is a super source of iron which is essential for healthy, red blood. Without adequate amounts of this mineral, our red blood cells can't carry enough life-giving oxygen to every part of the body.

To see how well liver stacks up against some alternative meat dishes which you might serve your family, look closely at the chart we've put together, comparing liver with beef, chicken and frankfurters. All figures are for one pound of food as purchased.

	Vitamin A IU	Iron mg	Thiamine mg	Riboflavin mg	Niacin mg	Vitamin B_{12} mg	Vitamin B_6 mg	Pantothenic Acid mg	Protein grams
Liver, beef	199,130	29.5	1.16	14.79	61.6	362.9	3.81	34.93	90.3
Beef, extra lean	70	14.5	.42	.86	23.2	8.2	1.97	2.81	96.6
Chicken, boned	1,060	6.8	.17	.56	19.7	3.6	1.36	3.86	98.4
Frankfurters	—	8.6	.71	.90	12.2	5.9	.64	1.95	56.7

Other Organ Meats

The other organ meats, such as kidney, brain, sweetbreads, heart and tongue, are extremely nutritious, and good buys as well. All of them have liver's attributes—protein of superior quality and large quantities of vitamins and minerals.

In most cultures organ meats are considered delicacies, and there are virtually hundreds of recipes for them. Brains in Butter is fare fit for a king; dumplings made with calves' brains are the most delicate addition to the finest broth. Sweetbreads (thymus glands) are very important ingredients in gourmet ragouts.

British Steak and Kidney Pie is famous the world over. People who say they are turned off by the strong odor of kidneys probably don't know that it's the ammonia in kidneys they smell. The ammonia is concentrated in the white tissue at the center of the kidney. Just snip this out with a pair of scissors, before washing the kidney, and when you do wash it, add a little vinegar to the water to neutralize any residual ammonia. Kidneys should be cooked at low heat and not for too long. If you follow this method you'll bring out the best in the flavor of kidneys.

Brain Fritters

1 *calf brain (approximately
    1 lb.)*
1 *teaspoon salt*
cold water to cover
2 *eggs*
¼ *cup whole wheat flour*
3 *tablespoons cold water*
salt to taste
3 *tablespoons butter or oil*

Cook brains in salted water for 25 minutes. Drain, remove membrane and slice ¼ inch thick. Beat eggs and stir in flour. Add water and salt. Dip brains in batter and saute in butter or oil until browned on both sides.

Yield: 4 servings

Brain Soup

⅓ *cup chopped onion*
1 *cup chopped mushrooms*
2 *tablespoons oil or butter*
1 *calf brain (approximately
    1 cup after preparation)*
¼ *teaspoon salt*
1' *teaspoon chopped chives*
1 *tablespoon chopped parsley*
2 *tablespoons whole
    wheat flour*
3 *cups milk*

In medium saucepan saute onion and mushrooms in oil or butter for approximately 5 minutes. Rinse brains in cold water and remove veins and membrane. Chop and add to onion-mushroom mixture and continue to saute 10 minutes longer.

Add salt, chives, parsley, then whole wheat flour. Stir until flour has been blended with mixture, then add milk gradually and simmer until slightly thickened, stirring constantly.

Yield: 4 cups

Gizzard Chili

2¾ *cups pinto or kidney beans*
1¼ *lbs. chicken gizzards*
    water to cover
1 *large onion, chopped*
1 *clove garlic, minced*
2 *tablespoons oil*
1 *16-ounce can tomatoes*
⅛ *teaspoon black pepper*
3 *teaspoons chili powder*

Cook beans according to preferred method. (See "Basic Methods for Cooking Beans and Other Legumes.") Drain if desired.

Simmer gizzards in water to cover and cook until tender. Drain and grind. There should be approximately 3 cups.

Saute onion and garlic in oil until soft and lightly browned. Add ground gizzards and saute 5 minutes longer, then add remaining ingredients and simmer for 10 minutes.

Serve immediately or set aside to be reheated. (This dish improves after a day or two when the flavors have blended.)

Yield: 4 to 6 servings

Remove any fat from gizzards and scrape tough skin from the inside surface. Rinse well. Cut into slivers. Heat oil in *wok* or heavy skillet and stir-fry the onions and mushrooms for approximately 1 minute. Add ginger and slivered gizzards and stir-fry on high heat for 2 minutes. Reduce heat to medium, add sherry, soy sauce and salt. Stir for several seconds. Add bamboo shoots, honey and water. Bring to a boil, reduce heat, cover and simmer for 30 minutes.

Yield: 4 servings

Braised Chicken (or Turkey) Gizzards

1 *lb. chicken (or turkey) gizzards*
2 *tablespoons oil*
2 *large onions, sliced*
1 *cup sliced fresh mushrooms*
1 *teaspoon ginger*
2 *tablespoons sherry*
2 *to 3 tablespoons tamari soy sauce*
½ *teaspoon salt*
1 *cup sliced bamboo shoots*
2 *teaspoons honey*
2 *cups water*

Cut off all fat from the heart. Slice vertically into four parts. Cut across the grain horizontally into ⅛-inch-thick pieces. Discard blood vessels and any internal fat. Rinse well.

Combine vinegar, honey, cornstarch, soy sauce and 1½ cups chicken stock; set aside. In a *wok* or heavy skillet which has a lid, stir-fry garlic for a few seconds in oil, then add pieces of heart. Stir-fry, uncovered, until heart loses its uncooked color. Remove meat from pan with slotted spoon. Pour ¾ cup chicken stock into same pan. Add peppers and carrots, bring to a boil and simmer, covered for 5 minutes. Return meat to pan, add vinegar mixture and pineapple and bring slowly to a boil, stirring constantly until sauce thickens. Salt to taste and serve immediately.

Yield: 4 to 6 servings

Sweet-Sour Beef Heart

2 *lbs. beef heart*
¾ *cup vinegar*
½ *to ¾ cup honey*
3 *tablespoons cornstarch*
3 *tablespoons tamari soy sauce*
1½ *cups chicken stock*
1 *clove garlic, minced*
6 *tablespoons oil*
¾ *cup chicken stock*
3 *green peppers, seeded and cut into 1-inch strips*
2 *carrots, sliced*
4 *slices canned unsweetened pineapple*
salt to taste

Stuffed Beef Heart

(This recipe can be cooked in a crockery pot. See marker ⬚ for method below.)

1   *medium-size onion, minced*
4   *stalks celery, chopped*
4   *cups cubed dried bread*
4   *to 6 tablespoons oil*
1   *teaspoon poultry seasoning*
1   *teaspoon oregano*
1   *teaspoon thyme or basil*
salt, pepper to taste
2   *cups beef stock*
1   *beef heart*

Saute onion, celery and then bread cubes in oil, adding as much oil as needed. Add poultry seasoning, herbs, salt and pepper to taste. Gradually stir in 1 cup beef stock. Set aside.

Cut heart open so that it will lie flat. Remove large tubes from inside. Spoon stuffing onto heart then wrap heart around the stuffing, securing it with skewers or toothpicks. Carefully brown outside of stuffed heart in oil. ⬚ Place in Dutch oven or crockery pot with remaining cup stock and cook until heart is tender (in Dutch oven, 1 to 2 hours; in crockery pot, 8 to 10 hours on low heat).

Thicken broth, if desired, to make gravy. Slice heart and serve with gravy.

Yield: 4 to 6 servings

Hearty Hash

1   *cup dried corn*
1   *cup water*
1   *calf heart* (approximately 1 lb.)*
1   *tablespoon wheat germ*
1   *tablespoon rye flour*
2   *tablespoons oil*
1   *cup chopped onion*
½   *teaspoon basil*
½   *teaspoon thyme*
3   *tablespoons chopped parsley*
⅛   *teaspoon black pepper*
½   *teaspoon salt*

Grind dried corn as fine as possible in food mill or electirc blender. Add water and set aside to soak for approximately 30 minutes.

Meanwhile, trim off fat and any arteries from the heart and cut into ½-inch cubes. Dust with wheat germ and flour. Saute in oil (turning to brown all sides) for approximately 5 minutes.

Add onion and continue to saute until tender. Then add soaked corn (with water) and herbs and seasonings. Saute 5 minutes longer and serve.

Yield: 4 to 6 servings

*Kidney or liver may be substituted for the heart, or a combination of all three.

> ### Basic Method for Preparing Kidneys
> *Before washing kidneys, snip out white tissue from center with kitchen scissors. Then wash in water or in a vinegar and water solution if preferred. This will help to remove any strong odor during cooking. Drain. Cut kidneys into cubes as small or large as desired. Cook according to recipe but care must be taken to avoid cooking kidneys too long or at too high a temperature. Heat toughens them and causes them to give off a strong odor during cooking.*

Steak and Kidney Pie

Make pastry dough and set aside.

In a Dutch oven, brown beef and onions in some of the oil. Add water to cover and cook with lid until beef is tender (approximately 1 to 2 hours). Add potatoes for last half-hour of cooking.

Prepare kidney according to basic method (see above). Drain on paper towels. Lightly saute kidney in more of the oil, just until it is no longer pink. Add to the cooked beef and potatoes.

Dissolve flour in water a little at a time and stir into stew. Simmer until thickened. Stir in salt, ginger, allspice and sauterne, and turn into casserole. *Preheat oven to 400°F.*

Roll out flaky pastry dough ¼ inch thick between sheets of plastic. Place ovenproof egg cup or custard cup upside down in center of casserole to hold up pastry. Wet rim of casserole and lay pastry on top, pressing it down over the rim all around to seal it. With a knife, slit the pastry in several places to allow steam to escape.

Bake in preheated oven for 30 minutes, turn heat down to 350°F. and continue to bake 30 minutes longer, or until crust is brown.

Yield: 8 servings

1 *recipe Whole Wheat Flaky Pastry (see Index)*
2 *lbs. beef for stewing*
2 *medium-size onions, chopped*
3 *to 4 tablespoons oil*
water to cover beef
1 *lb. potatoes, peeled and cubed*
1 *beef kidney*
¼ *cup rye or whole wheat flour*
1 *cup water*
salt to taste
½ *teaspoon ginger*
½ *teaspoon allspice*
¼ *cup sauterne wine (optional)*

Kidneys en Brochette

½ cup oil
2 cloves garlic, minced
1 teaspoon oregano
2 tablespoons lemon juice
4 veal or 8 lamb kidneys
16 cherry tomatoes
2 large green peppers,
    seeded and cut
    into 1-inch pieces
16 whole medium-size fresh
    mushrooms
2 bunches small green onions,
    without tops

Make marinade of oil, garlic, oregano and lemon juice. Prepare kidneys using basic method (see above), cut into 1-inch cubes and cover with marinade. Refrigerate them, covered, for 1 to 2 hours, stirring occasionally.

Place marinated kidney pieces, tomatoes, peppers, mushrooms and onions, alternately on skerers. Broil for approximately 15 minutes or until vegetables are tender and kidneys are browned and juicy. Place skewers over brown rice and serve.

Yield: 4 servings

Stir-Fried Kidneys

1½ tablespoons tamari
    soy sauce
1½ tablespoons sherry or
    lemon juice
2 teaspoons cornstarch
½ teaspoon salt
2 lbs. veal, pork or
    lamb kidneys
2 tablespoons oil
4 green onions, including
    tops, sliced into
    1-inch pieces
1 tablespoon unhulled
    sesame seeds

Combine soy sauce, sherry or lemon juice, cornstarch and salt. Prepare kidneys using basic method (see above), then cut into slices. Cover them with soy-cornstarch mixture, cover and refrigerate for 1 to 2 hours, stirring occasionally.

Heat oil in heavy skillet or *wok* until medium hot. Pour in kidney mixture and stir-fry for 1 minute. Add onions and sesame seeds and continue to stir-fry for approximately 5 minutes longer until pinkness of kidneys is completely gone. Serve immediately.

Yield: 3 to 4 servings

Prepare kidneys according to basic method (see above) and cut into slices ¼ inch thick.

Heat butter or oil in a saucepan and saute kidneys until well browned. Remove them from the pan. In the same pan, saute shallots until golden brown, then add mushrooms and saute 3 minutes longer. Add stock, wine, tomato paste and seasonings. Simmer for 5 minutes.

Add the kidneys. Mix cornstarch with water and add slowly to the pan, stirring constantly. Simmer another 5 minutes. Serve immediately garnished with chopped parsley.

Yield: 4 servings

Veal Kidneys Bordelaise

4 *veal kidneys*
3 *tablespoons butter or oil*
½ *cup chopped shallots*
2 *ounces mushrooms, sliced*
1¼ *cups beef or veal stock*
¾ *cup dry white wine*
1 *teaspoon tomato paste (optional)*
salt, pepper to taste
2 *teaspoons cornstarch*
2 *tablespoons water*
chopped parsley

Combine cornmeal and flour and dust liver thoroughly. Heat oil in large skillet and saute liver approximately 15 minutes, until tender and browned on all sides. Remove to heated platter.

To the particles remaining in the pan add red wine, stock, basil, salt and pepper. Bring to a boil, stirring to loosen any brown bits sticking to the pan.

Dissolve cornstarch in cold water and add to the liquid in the pan, stirring constantly. Simmer sauce until clear and thickened. Pour sauce over liver and serve.

Yield: 4 to 6 servings

Beef Liver a la Suisse

1 *tablespoon cornmeal*
2 *tablespoons rye or whole wheat flour*
1½ *lbs. beef liver, cut into strips 3 inches long and ½ inch thick*
3 *tablespoons oil*
½ *cup red wine*
2 *cups beef stock*
½ *teaspoon basil*
½ *teaspoon salt*
⅛ *teaspoon pepper*
1 *tablespoon cornstarch*
2 *tablespoons cold water*

Chinese Chicken Livers

2   *tablespoons tamari*
        soy sauce
1   *tablespoon cornstarch*
1   *teaspoon salt*
1   *teaspoon honey*
1   *lb. chicken livers*
¼   *cup oil*
1   *slice gingerroot, finely*
        chopped
2   *large cloves garlic, minced*
1   *cup snow peas*
½   *cup chopped bamboo shoots*
1   *cup sliced water chestnuts*
4   *large mushrooms, sliced*
2   *tablespoons dry sherry or*
        lemon juice
slivered almonds

Combine tamari soy sauce, cornstarch, salt and honey to make a paste. Saute chicken livers in oil for approximately 5 minutes in *wok* or heavy skillet. Remove chicken livers and set aside. Saute ginger and garlic in same pan, until golden brown. Then add snow peas, bamboo shoots, water chestnuts and mushrooms. Cook for 4 minutes, stirring constantly. Stir in sherry or lemon juice and the paste mixture, then add livers. Cook over medium heat until sauce thickens. Serve over brown rice and garnish with slivered almonds.

Yield: 4 servings

Pennsylvania Dutch Pig's Stomach

(This recipe can be cooked in a crockery pot. See marker   for method below.)

1   *fresh pig's stomach*
salt, freshly ground pepper
1   *lb. fresh sausage, in a*
        casing, or spareribs
4   *to 6 cups diced raw*
        potatoes (according to
        size of stomach)
1   *onion, chopped*
½   *cup chopped celery with tops*
2   *tablespoons chopped parsley*
2   *cups water*

Clean the stomach thoroughly, removing membranes. Rub inside and outside with salt and pepper. Cut sausage into 1½-inch pieces or, if using spareribs, separate into individual ribs. Unless using crockery pot, preheat oven to 325°F. Mix remaining ingredients, except water, to make a dressing. Add sausage or spareribs. Stuff the stomach as tightly as you can and sew it up.   (If using crockery pot, omit the following steps and continue with method below.)

Place in Dutch oven or roasting pan with lid, add water, cover and bake in preheated oven for approximately 3 hours. Uncover and brown for 30 minutes longer, turning several times to brown on all sides. When ready to serve, cut into slices 1½ to 2 inches thick.

Yield: 6 to 8 servings

Place in crockery pot, add water, cover and cook on low for 12 to 16 hours. Remove pig's stomach from crockery pot and brown it in its own juices, turning to brown evenly. When ready to serve, cut into slices 1½ to 2 inches thick.

> ### Basic Method for Cooking Sweetbreads
> *Soak sweetbreads in cold water for a few hours or overnight. Drain and place in saucepan. Add cold water to cover, cover saucepan, bring to a boil, turn heat down and simmer for 5 minutes. Drain and cool under cold, running water. Remove membranes and connective tissue. Cover with paper towels and place between two cutting boards, weighting them down with some heavy object. Let stand for several hours, to firm them. This improves the texture.*

Sweetbread Mushroom Curry

1 *lb. sweetbreads*
1 *tablespoon butter*
1 *tablespoon oil*
½ *cup finely chopped onion*
½ *teaspoon ground cumin*
½ *teaspoon turmeric*
¼ *teaspoon ginger*
½ *teaspoon cardamom seeds, crushed*
1 *teaspoon prepared mustard*
½ *cup finely chopped apple*
1 *cup chicken stock*
salt to taste
1 *tablespoon butter*
1 *tablespoon oil*
¼ *lb. fresh mushrooms, sliced (approximately 1½ cups)*
¼ *teaspoon salt*
⅛ *teaspoon black pepper*

Cook and prepare sweetbreads by the basic method (see above).

Heat butter and oil in skillet. Add onion and cook a few minutes, then add seasonings and apple and cook a few minutes longer. Add chicken stock and continue cooking, stirring constantly, until ingredients are well blended. Salt to taste. Pour sauce into electric blender and process until smooth. Set aside.

Meanwhile, cut prepared sweetbreads into 1-inch cubes and saute butter and oil a few minutes. Add mushrooms and continue to cook for 10 minutes longer. Add salt and pepper, then blended sauce and cook slowly for 15 minutes, stirring occasionally. Serve with brown rice or on whole grain toast.

Yield: 4 servings

Breaded Sweetbreads

1 *lb. sweetbreads*
½ *cup rye or whole wheat flour*
1 *egg*
2 *tablespoons water*
1 *teaspoon oil*
1¼ *cups fresh whole grain*
bread crumbs
2 *tablespoons butter*
2 *tablespoons oil*
salt, pepper to taste
lemon slices
parsley sprigs

Follow basic method for cooking sweetbreads (see above) but before weighting them down, cut into 8 cutlet-like pieces.

Dredge pieces on all sides in flour. Beat the egg, stir in water and oil. Dip sweetbreads in egg mixture, then in bread crumbs. Coat thoroughly and pat to make the crumbs adhere.

In a large skillet, heat butter and oil. Add sweetbreads and saute until golden on both sides. Salt and pepper to taste. Garnish with lemon slices and parsley sprigs.

Yield: 4 to 6 servings

Boiled Fresh Tongue

(This recipe can be cooked in a crockery pot.)

1 *beef tongue or*
   4 *calves' tongues*
cold water to cover
1 *onion, sliced*
2 *bay leaves*
1 *teaspoon salt*
¼ *teaspoon pepper*

Place tongue in large pot, or crockery pot, cover with cold water, add the remaining ingredients and simmer until tender (2 to 4 hours, on top of the stove; 7 to 9 hours on low in the crockery pot, depending on size of tongue).

Drain tongue, cool by dipping in cold water, slit outer skin and peel it off. Remove bones and gristle at the thick end. Return to pot and allow to cool in the stock. Remove tongue and use as desired. Strain stock and use for soup.

Tongue Salad or Sandwich Spread

1 *beef tongue*
2 *hard-cooked eggs, chopped*
1 *stalk celery, chopped*
¼ *cup chopped onion*
2 *tablespoons prepared*
   mustard
2 *tablespoons chopped parsley*
1 *tablespoon vinegar*
3 *tablespoons oil*
¼ *teaspoon thyme*
½ *teaspoon salt*

Cook tongue according to recipe for Boiled Fresh Tongue. Grind in meat grinder. There should be approximately 4 cups. Combine with remaining ingredients and mix thoroughly. Serve as salad on bed of greens or use as a sandwich spread.

Yield: 6 servings

> ## Basic Method for Cooking Tripe
> *Wash tripe in cold water. Cover it with water in a saucepan, add 1 teaspoon salt, bring to the boiling point, and simmer for 3 hours, or until tender. Cool under cold, running water and, with the dull side of a large knife, scrape off all fat. Cut as desired.*

Spanish Tripe

Cook tripe according to basic method (see above). Cut tripe into 2-inch strips approximately ½ inch wide. In *wok* or large skillet, saute onion and garlic in oil for 5 minutes. Add remaining ingredients and cook for several minutes. Add tripe, cover and cook for 30 minutes.

Yield: 4 servings

1 *lb. tripe*
1 *large onion, chopped*
2 *cloves garlic, minced*
3 *tablespoons oil*
2 *cups tomato sauce*
1 *tablespoon tomato paste (optional)*
1 *bay leaf*
1 *teaspoon oregano*
1 *chili pepper, chopped*
½ *teaspoon salt*
⅛ *teaspoon pepper*
½ *teaspoon chopped chives*

Tripe Lyonnaise

Cook tripe according to basic method (see above). Cut tripe into 2-inch strips approximately ½ inch wide. Mix rye flour, salt and pepper and dust tripe with seasoned flour. In *wok* or skillet, saute onions in oil and butter for 5 minutes. Add floured tripe and saute until strips are golden brown. Add sesame seeds and chopped parsley and serve.

Yield: 4 servings

1 *lb. tripe*
2 *tablespoons rye flour*
½ *teaspoon salt*
⅛ *teaspoon pepper*
2 *onions, thinly sliced*
1 *tablespoon oil*
2 *tablespoons butter*
2 *tablespoons unhulled sesame seeds*
1 *tablespoon chopped parsley*

Fish Becomes a Family

Favorite

The trick in cooking fish so that it comes out moist, tender and flaky is to do exactly the opposite of what you do to turn out tender meat. Long slow cooking is recommended for meat to break down the connective tissues; with fish, the idea is to cook it fast so that those tissues do not break down.

The protein in fish starts to firm up at a temperature of about 140°F.; the thin sheets of connective tissue break down at 150°F.—that's when the fish flakes easily. If you cook fish too long, the flavorful, nutritious juices will run out and the fish will be unappetizingly dry.

Never cook fish at boiling temperatures. To prepare a dish of poached fish, just let it cook in barely simmering stock (Court Bouillon) until it has lost its raw appearance and looks white. When poached, fish is at its best and can be served in countless ways—with plain drawn butter, for example, or drawn butter mixed with a good prepared mustard, tahini (sesame seed butter), dill sauce, horseradish sauce or multiherb sauce.

Court Bouillon
(fish stock)

1 *to 2 lbs. fish heads,*
    tails, trimmings
4 *cups cold water*
1 *onion, peeled and cut*
    into quarters
1 *stalk celery, with leaves,*
    cut into chunks
1 *carrot, scrubbed, cut*
    into chunks

2 *sprigs parsley*
2 *tablespoons vinegar*
3 *slices lemon*
1 *bay leaf*
6 *peppercorns*
4 *whole cloves*
  salt, pepper to taste

Combine all ingredients, bring to a boil, turn heat down to a simmer and cook 20 to 30 minutes. Do not cook too long as the stock may become bitter.

Strain and cool. Remove any fish from fish bones and add to stock. Refrigerate or freeze until use.

Yield: approximately 1 quart

If you prefer not to cook the fish in a stock, try steaming it. The moist heat penetrates easily and the fish is ready and delicious in a flash.

If you notice an unpleasant smell when you cook fish, the cooking temperature is probably too high. The substances in fish that create an unpleasant odor start evaporating at 150°F. and that is too high for good-tasting fish.

Most fish contain a good amount of salt, especially ocean fish. Because salt draws out the tasty and healthful juices, you may want to wait until you have tasted the cooked product before adding salt.

What makes fish such a nutritious food? First, there is the protein, almost the same amount as in meat, but with a better balance of amino acids. Then come the vitamins. Fish are active creatures, composed of almost all muscle and little or no fat. Their active life gives evidence of the plenitude of B vitamins.

Not only overcooking but soaking or too much washing can seriously deplete the nutrients in fish. Fish should be washed very quickly and dried immediately. Any remaining cooking liquid should be used in some way. If you buy whole fish, don't discard head and tail; cooked with the fish or by themselves, they help to build up good fish stock for chowders, sauces or aspics.

Fish Chowder

1 *medium-size onion, minced*
½ *cup diced celery*
½ *cup diced carrot*
3 *tablespoons butter*
3 *medium-size potatoes,*
   peeled
1 *cup Court Bouillon*
   (see above)
½ *cup non-fat dry milk*

1 *cup water*
½ *lb. fish filet*
1 *bay leaf*
¼ *teaspoon kelp powder*
   salt, pepper to taste
1 *to 2 tablespoons cider*
   vinegar (optional)
snipped chives

Using a large saucepan, saute onion, celery and carrot in butter for a few minutes.

Cube or grate potatoes and add to sauteed vegetables.

Stir in Bouillon and bring to a boil. Simmer until vegetables are almost done.

Reconstitute milk with water and add to the soup.

Add fish, bay leaf and kelp powder and simmer for 20 to 30 minutes or until fish is tender. Flake fish into bite-size pieces. Season to taste with salt and pepper. Add vinegar if using it. Garnish with snipped chives before serving.

Yield: 4 servings

In addition to its excellent nutrition fish is low in calories. Whatever fat a fish might contain is composed mostly of unsaturated fatty acids. That's why fish appears in almost every reducing diet.

If you can't get fresh fish where you live, the frozen kind is quite good, if you know what to watch for. Caught, frozen and packed quickly, the fish still has its full protein content and most of the vitamins and minerals. If you see ice crystals on the frozen fish, don't buy it. It is a sign that it probably has thawed and been refrozen. If this happens, it loses its good taste together with a good part of the nutrients.

People who think the only way to prepare fish is to fry it, are missing out on a lot of eating pleasure. Try different ways. Steaming, poaching, broiling, baking will make the taste of fish different every time. To broil fish, first brush it with oil, then if using gas heat, set fish on rack one inch away from heat and keep flame very low. If using electricity, set fish about five inches away from heating unit and leave broiler door open. Baked fish can be stuffed with vegetable or grain mixtures.

In the recipes we introduce you to some unusual ways of preparing fish and some unusual kinds of fish which are sometimes neglected. One of the latter is carp. This big brother of the goldfish is a delicacy that Americans rarely have on their menus. Carp can be bought in most fish stores. It might not be available all year round, but you certainly will find it around the Jewish holidays because it is an important ingredient in the delicious dish, *Gefilte* Fish.

Gefilte Fish

(fish balls)

6 *lbs. carp, catfish or whitefish*	1 *egg, beaten*
2 *quarts water*	¼ *cup dry whole grain bread crumbs*
4 *onions, sliced*	½ *cup water*
2 *teaspoons salt*	1 *carrot, cut into thick slices*
¾ *teaspoon pepper*	1 *stalk celery, cut into thirds*
1 *onion, cut in chunks*	

Cut off heads and skin fish. Discard. Fillet fish. Place bones in pot with water, sliced onions, salt and pepper. Bring to a boil over medium heat. Put fish filets and onion chunks through a meat grinder using the fine blade. Add egg, bread crumbs and water to fish-onion mixture, tossing lightly to combine. It will be a soft, wet mixture. Shape into balls approximately 2 inches in diameter. Drop balls carefully into simmering broth, turn heat to low, cover pot and cook slowly for 1½ hours. Add carrot and celery and cook 30 minutes with cover off pot. Allow to cool.

Remove balls carefully to serving dish. If not using all fish balls, strain broth and reserve so that surplus balls may be refrigerated in broth. The fish balls may be served on lettuce and garnished with the cooked carrots. Serve with horseradish or seafood sauce.

Yield: 30 balls or 12 to 15 servings

In other countries, carp is as commonplace as haddock is to us. Polish, Czechoslovakian and German ways of preparing it cover the wide spectrum from simple soup to one-dish meals to gourmet concoctions, cooked with beer, vegetables or spices. Steamed and served with whipped cream mixed with horseradish, carp is the traditional fare for New Year's evening in Germany.

The Rodale experimental kitchen at Fitness House tested several methods for preparing these tender fish so that they could be eaten bones and all. Carp have tiny forked bones throughout the flesh which are impossible to remove along with the backbone in the filleting process. When the fried carp was prepared according to our recipe, these bones were not even noticeable. In another dish, the carp filets were chopped up in the blender, and patties were made from it. Again no bones were detectable. These methods are described with our recipes.

Cook beets in water to cover until tender. Drain, peel and cube.

Combine all ingredients in medium bowl. Chill. Serve on salad greens, topped with more mayonnaise if desired.

Yield: 4 servings

Apple, Beet and Tuna Salad

4 *medium-size beets*
water to cover
1 *7-ounce can tuna, drained*
1 *medium-size tart apple,*
    peeled if desired, cored
    and cubed
1 *stalk celery, chopped*
3 *to 4 tablespoons*
    mayonnaise
2 *tablespoons lemon juice*
1 *tablespoon minced onion*
¼ *teaspoon dill*
salt, pepper to taste

Preheat oven to 400°F.

Place fish in casserole. Sprinkle lemon juice over fish. Dot with butter and season with salt and pepper. Bake, uncovered, for 30 minutes in preheated oven.

Meanwhile, make sauce by combining yogurt, milk, parsley and dill. After fish has baked for 30 minutes, pour sauce over it and continue baking for approximately 30 minutes longer or until fish flakes. Garnish with lemon and parsley.

Yield: 4 servings

Catfish Baked in Dill Sauce

1¼ *lbs. catfish, cleaned*
    and skinned
2 *tablespoons lemon juice*
2 *tablespoons butter*
salt, pepper to taste
¾ *cup yogurt*
¼ *cup milk*
1 *heaping tablespoon*
    chopped parsley
2 *teaspoons dill*
lemon
parsley

Baked Stuffed Whole Fish

Preheat oven to 350°F.

3 *lbs. whole fish (bluefish,
    bass or red snapper)*
2 *cups whole grain soft
    bread crumbs*
2 *tablespoons melted butter*
4 *tablespoons chopped parsley*
2 *tablespoons chopped
    fresh dill*
1 *tablespoon finely chopped
    onion*
3 *tablespoons chopped
    almonds*
salt, pepper to taste
oil
lemon slices
sprigs of dill

Wash fish and drain thoroughly on paper towels.

Mix bread crumbs, butter, parsley, dill, onion and almonds. Add salt and pepper as needed. Fill the cavity of the fish with bread crumb mixture and secure with toothpicks. Brush outside of fish with oil and place in oiled baking pan. Bake, uncovered in preheated oven, for 25 to 35 minutes depending on thickness of fish. Garnish with lemon slices and sprigs of dill and serve.

Yield: 4 servings

Carp Patties

1 *carp (approximately 2 lbs.),
    skinned, cleaned, head
    and tail removed*
¾ *lb. potatoes (approximately
    2 medium-size potatoes)*
3 *eggs*
1 *medium-size onion, peeled
    and cut in chunks*
2 *teaspoons oregano*
1 *teaspoon thyme*
1 *teaspoon sage*
salt, pepper to taste
4 *teaspoons vinegar*
2 *tablespoons butter*
2 *tablespoons oil*

Simmer carp in a little water or milk in a covered, heavy-bottom pot until tender (15 to 20 minutes) or bake, covered, in a little water or milk in a preheated 350°F. oven for approximately 30 minutes or until tender. Meanwhile, cook potatoes, drain and keep warm. Lift out fish, cool and reserve liquid for soup.

Remove large bones and any skin and fins from fish and place fish in electric blender along with eggs and onion chunks. Process to a smooth puree. This step is important in order to "grind up" any small bones remaining in the fish, so be sure there are no lumps of unpureed fish.

Mash potatoes and combine them with seasonings, vinegar and pureed fish mixture. In a heavy skillet, heat butter and oil to medium heat and drop in tablespoons of patty mixture. When each patty is "dry" on top and brown underneath, turn it and leave until it is brown on both sides. Serve hot with catsup or stewed tomatoes.

*Yield: 6 to 8 servings or approximately
        18 to 20 small patties*

Simmer catfish in water to cover until fish is white and flakes easily (approximately 15 to 20 minutes). Lift fish out of water and cool. Remove skin and bones, flake fish and set aside.

Saute onion in oil. Add whole wheat flour, stirring, then gradually add milk and cook until thickened. Add cheeses, salt and fish. Cook until cheeses melt. *Preheat oven to 350°F.* Fill crepes with approximately ½ cup of the mixture and roll. Put crepes, side by side, in greased baking dish and place in preheated oven until heated through, approximately 10 to 15 minutes.

Before serving, sprinkle with extra Parmesan cheese and garnish with parsley.

Yield: 8 8-inch crepes

Catfish Crepes

2 *lbs. catfish*
water to cover
1 *onion, minced*
2 *tablespoons oil*
2 *tablespoons whole wheat flour*
2 *cups milk*
½ *cup grated Parmesan cheese*
½ *cup grated mozzarella cheese*
½ *teaspoon salt*
½ *recipe Oat Crepes (see Index)*
grated Parmesan cheese
parsley

Cut fish into 1½-inch squares. Beat eggs in a bowl with salt. Add cornstarch and beat well with a wire whisk. Add fish to egg mixture, turning to coat fish thoroughly. Heat oil in a large, heavy skillet. Remove fish from egg mixture with a slotted spoon and saute fish, without stirring, until lightly browned. Turn fish with a spatula and cook for 1 minute.

While fish is cooking, add onions, water chestnuts, sherry or lemon juice, water and salt to the leftover egg mixture. Pour this mixture over fish, cover with lid, turn heat to medium and cook until egg is set and fish is tender.

Yield: 3 or 4 servings

Fish Filets Sauteed in Egg

1 *lb. fresh flounder or sole filets*
2 *eggs*
¼ *teaspoon salt*
1½ *tablespoons cornstarch*
2 *to 3 tablespoons oil*
2 *green onions, including tops, thinly sliced*
½ *cup coarsely chopped water chestnuts*
2 *teaspoons sherry or lemon juice*
1½ *tablespoons water*
¼ *teaspoon salt*

Fish Kebabs

¼ cup lemon juice
2 tablespoons oil
½ teaspoon salt
⅛ teaspoon pepper
¼ teaspoon dill
2 tablespoons chopped parsley
1½ lbs. fresh filets (flounder,
    haddock or any
    white fish)
½ lb. medium-size whole
    mushrooms
    (approximately 3 cups)
1 green pepper, seeded and
    cut into 1-inch pieces
2 onions, cut into wedges or
    quarters (depending
    on size)
1 medium-size zucchini, cut
    into 1-inch chunks

Mix together lemon juice, oil, salt, pepper, dill and parsley. Cut fish into 1½-inch cubes and marinate in lemon juice mixture for approximately 1 hour. Drain and place the fish on four skewers, alternating with mushroom, pepper, onion and zucchini. Brush the kebabs with marinade and broil 3 or 4 inches from the heat for 5 minutes. Then, brush again with marinade and broil 10 minutes longer.

Yield: 4 servings

Fish Salad or Sandwich Filling

1 lb. fish filet (haddock or
    any mild-flavored fish)
2 medium-size onions,
    finely grated
4 tablespoons finely chopped
    chives
4 tablespoons finely chopped
    celery
4 tablespoons finely chopped
    parsley
1 teaspoon dill seeds, crushed
1 teaspoon salt
4 tablespoons lemon juice

Simmer fish filet in a little water until fish flakes easily (approximately 5 to 10 minutes). Drain and combine with remaining ingredients. Chill for approximately an hour until flavors are blended. Serve on salad greens or as a sandwich filling.

Yield: approximately 3 cups

Preheat oven to 350°F.

Florida Baked Catfish

Put catfish in a baking pan. Heat butter in saucepan. Add onion and saute until soft. Add juices, lemon rind and ginger, stirring to blend. Pour over fish. Bake, uncovered, in preheated oven for 1 hour or until fish is flaky.

Garnish with orange and lemon slices and parsley.

Yield: 4 servings

1¼ *lbs. catfish, cleaned and*
       skinned
  2 *tablespoons butter*
  1 *small onion, sliced*
  1 *cup orange juice*
  2 *teaspoons lemon juice*
  1 *teaspoon grated lemon rind*
¼ *teaspoon ginger*
  1 *orange, cut into rings*
  1 *lemon, cut into rings*
    parsley

Fried Carp

Lay filet down on a board, with the fleshy side up. Using a sharp, thin-bladed knife, score the filet lengthwise and crosswise, cutting partway through the flesh with a sawing motion in parallel cuts approximately ¼ inch apart. Do not cut all the way through the filet. Then go back over each cut, but instead of sawing with the knife, press heavily with it, until you hear the cracking of the small bones. Then cut filet into serving-size portions.

Mix eggs with water, and brush filet portions with it, coating them on both sides. Mix flour and seasonings and using a spatula, carefully lift each filet portion, dip it in flour mixture and drop it into oil in skillet which has been heated to medium-high temperature. The oil should be at least ½ inch deep in the skillet. Fry filet portions until they are golden brown on both sides, turning them once during the process. Remove and drain on paper towel. Serve hot with catsup or tartar sauce.

Yield: 4 to 6 servings

  2 *carp (approximately 1½*
       lbs. each), skinned and
       filleted
  2 *eggs, beaten*
  2 *tablespoons water*
¼ *cup whole wheat flour*
¼ *teaspoon each of thyme, sage*
       and oregano
    salt, pepper to taste
    oil

Jellied Avocado Tuna Loaf

1 *envelope unflavored gelatin*
¼ *cup cold water*
1 *cup boiling water*
3 *tablespoons lemon juice*
½ *teaspoon salt*
½ *cup chopped celery*
½ *cup chopped green pepper*
1 *tablespoon minced onion*
1 *7-ounce can tuna, drained and flaked*
1 *envelope unflavored gelatin*
¼ *cup cold water*
½ *cup boiling water*
2 *tablespoons lemon juice*
1 *teaspoon honey*
½ *cup mayonnaise*
¼ *cup yogurt*
¼ *teaspoon salt*
2 *cups mashed avocado*

Sprinkle gelatin over cold water. When it has softened, dissolve it in boiling water. Add lemon juice, salt, celery, green pepper, onion and tuna fish. Pour into 9x5x3-inch loaf pan. Refrigerate until firm.

Sprinkle gelatin over cold water. When it has softened, dissolve it in boiling water. Add lemon juice, honey, mayonnaise, yogurt, salt and avocado. Stir it well to blend together. Pour this mixture over the set tuna mixture and refrigerate until firm. Turn out loaf onto bed of salad greens.

Yield: 8 servings

Stuffed Rolled Flounder

1 *lb. fresh flounder filets*
⅓ *cup oil*
2 *tablespoons finely chopped onion*
½ *teaspoon salt*
2 *tablespoons finely chopped parsley*
1 *teaspoon oregano*
⅛ *teaspoon black pepper*
⅓ *cup grated cheddar cheese*
1 *cup pureed tomatoes*
3 *tablespoons whole grain bread crumbs*

Brush filets with oil. Combine onion, salt, parsley, oregano and pepper. Sprinkle on filets, then top with grated cheese. Roll each filet, starting with the narrow end, fasten with toothpicks and place side by side in an oiled baking dish.

Pour pureed tomatoes over rolls and sprinkle with bread crumbs. Bake for 30 minutes at 350°F. Remove toothpicks and serve.

Yield: 4 servings

Respond to Loving Care

Vegetables need—and deserve—loving care. Treat them right and the rewards they provide in flavor and texture will justify the care you take in preparation. If you soak or boil your vegetables only for four minutes, 20 to 45 percent of the total mineral content slips into the water along with 75 percent of the natural sugar and an important percentage of vitamins. That's one good reason to cook vegetables you don't want to eat raw in as little time as possible.

So store vegetables in the refrigerator immediately (light and heat take away nutrients and crispness) and wash them quickly just before preparing them for the table. The preparation of fresh vegetables for cooking is the same as for raw vegetable salads. If you want to chop or slice any kind of vegetable, do it just before it goes in the pot.

Actually, cooking vegetables properly takes very little time. They should be *al dente*, tender but crisp, not mushy. "Short-order" vegetables not only taste better and have more nutrients, they also look much prettier.

One of the best ways of cooking vegetables is to steam them. You heat some water to a boil and place the vegetables in a basket over the water so that the steam, but not the water, reaches them. Or you put them directly into a pan with just a few drops of water to start the steam, and cover tightly. The vegetable juices will add the extra moisture necessary to avoid burning.

The Chinese saute food in their *woks*, but you can do it in any heavy skillet. You just need a few drops of good oil which really don't penetrate the vegetables but coat them just enough to prevent burning. The vegetables are cut into small pieces to speed cooking and, coincidentally, to preserve taste and color.

Baking or broiling is another way of cooking that can save nutrients. You put vegetables, such as potatoes or winter squash, into a preheated oven to bake in their skins. Summer squash, tomatoes and the like, are very good broiled. Just cut them and brush the surfaces with oil or butter, and take them out when they become fork tender.

If long cooking destroys a lot of nutrients, imagine what warming over does! If you have vegetables left over, either warm them carefully in a double boiler or, even better, just put them, cold, into your mixed salads.

Saving for a Savory Soup Stock

Whatever method you use, never throw away the liquid in which the vegetables were cooked. Use it for sauces, soups, drinks—any way you want, but use it.

Save the skins of vegetables, for in most cases the highest concentration of vitamins and minerals is in the skin or directly under it. Collect the peelings of a few days in the refrigerator—either in a plastic bag or an airtight container—and add to the collection such things as the outer lettuce leaves, tops of turnips, carrots and other members of the root vegetable family, the stems of peppers, eggplants and others.

When you've got a goodly amount together, put everything in a large pot, add some chopped fresh onion, leek, celery tops and stalks, a carrot or two, parsley and, if you like, a chopped garlic clove and other herbs, maybe a bay leaf. Add water to cover. Bring the whole collection to a boil and simmer for an hour or so. Strain. There you have a fine vegetarian soup stock or sauce base. Freeze in small portions what you don't use immediately.

Choosing the Vegetable for the Vitamin

For an idea of the type of nutrition a vegetable offers, consider the color. The darker the green, leafy vegetable, the more vitamins, especially vitamins A, C, E, K and a number of B's, and minerals, especially iron, copper, magnesium and calcium, they contain. It's the same with the yellows and oranges: the stronger and deeper the colors, the more vitamins, especially A.

If you want extra vitamin C, parsley, raw turnip greens and raw kale are on top of the list. (Compared with other vegetables, kale loses the least of its vitamin C when cooked.) The dark green, shiny pepper is also high in vitamin C. In salads, on buttered, dark bread, or out of hand, braised, stuffed, mixed with other vegetables, peppers are good at any time. Actually, the green, bell-shaped pepper we eat is the immature sweet pepper that turns red later on. In Hungary and Germany this kind is called paprika.

For added vitamin A, concentrate on carrots, kale, parsley and especially dandelion greens. The old-timers, such as the Pennsylvania Dutch, had no vitamin charts but they knew about the value of dandelion very well, for they swarmed out in early spring to gather it—and some of their descendents still do.

Dandelion and raw mustard greens are good sources of calcium, as are parsley, kale and turnip greens. For iron, it's raw beet greens, Swiss chard, dandelion, parsley and spinach.

Raw kale and turnip greens also offer potassium which is so important to the nerves.

You will have noticed that parsley is mentioned frequently as one of the most nutritious vegetables. That should be enough to get it off the "herb-or-garnish-only" list. It can be used in many ways—in dumplings, omelets, soups and with scrambled eggs. It's good minced into cottage cheese or sprinkled on buttered bread. Try a sandwich filled with peanut butter mixed with honey, topped with a thick layer of lettuce leaves and parsley. Egg, potato, tuna fish and other salads take kindly to a good amount of parsley. Pizza toppings, boiled or mashed potatoes, sauces—these dishes can really be improved by adding plenty of chopped parsley, not just a timid sprinkling.

In spite of its characteristic taste, parsley rarely dominates or kills other tastes. To the contrary, it enhances them. Also, don't forget the parsley root, a tasty vegetable in itself that can be used in many more ways than in the preparation of stock—by itself, in mixed vegetables, raw in salads, sliced and breaded with wheat germ and quickly pan-fried in a small amount of oil, slivered and stir-fried in a *wok*.

Redefining the Potato

"The lowly potato" is a misnomer if ever there was one. Actually, the potato is a noble vegetable. Its vitamin C and B content is high, and it contains a mineral most of us need more of: potassium. Nonfattening, too. A medium-size potato, boiled or baked, has only 80 to 90 calories. The fattener is the butter we put on it, not the potato itself. Most of the nutrients are located right under the skin. On a baked potato, the skin tastes very good and the connoisseur eats all of it. Small, unpeeled young potatoes, spread over a lightly buttered or oiled baking sheet, caraway seeds strewn over them, the whole thing baked and eaten hot from the oven, make a delightful summer treat.

Whenever you boil potatoes for any purpose—mashed, soup, salad, home-fried—boil them in their skins and pull them off afterwards. In this way, you'll remove a thin, outer layer only, leaving most of the nutrients with the potato.

Potato starch can serve as a substitute for flour in many cake and cookie recipes. It is also a good thickener for soups and sauces. Sometimes, it is hard to buy potato starch, but it is not hard to make it. Here's what you do:

> Peel raw potatoes and grate them. Then put the grated mass into a napkin, bag or double layer of cheesecloth and press the liquid into a bowl. Let it settle for a short while. Then—very slowly and carefully—pour off the water into another container (don't throw it away, it has a lot of good in it). What you'll find on the bottom of the first bowl, is a sort of pressed down white matter—your potato starch.

It can help to thicken vegetable soup or stews.

In Arabic, spinach is called "the king of vegetables." It's full of iron, vitamins A and C and other minerals. If you have a big harvest from your garden and you can't use the spinach immediately, don't squash it into a high container or in a plastic bag—the temperature will rise in the center and fermentation will start, destroying valuable minerals and vitamins. Instead, spread it out, flat, preferably in a cool cellar and give it a once-over with a very fine cool water spray.

Here's another good way to keep spinach or any other leafy greens for awhile: wash them and shake off as much of the water as possible, either in one of the salad "wash and shake" containers or in a clean towel. Then put a napkin or paper towel in the bottom of a plastic bag, heap the greens on top of it (don't press them down) and close. The towel will absorb any moisture that is left and prevent a rise in temperature.

People tend to think of parsnips primarily as a flavoring agent in soups, but they have so much more to offer. Thin slices of raw parsnip are a delightful addition to any salad. Whole or halved, baked or steamed, coated with cornmeal and wheat germ and browned in oil, they are a delicate treat.

If you grow your own parsnips, you don't have to freeze, dry or can them. Just leave them in the ground and harvest what you need when you need it. Frost improves the flavor of the root while it kills the green top. But with each thaw, fresh, dark green crowns of feathery leaves appear and supply a vitamin-rich addition to your winter salad.

The radish is another plant that can be used for more than a garnish or salad. In different cultures, various parts of the radish are used for a variety of dishes. The Chinese value the oil pressed from the seeds, while the Egyptians like the green tops best. In Bavaria radishes are sometimes grated and heaped on buttered rye bread to make blood flow and prevent gallstones. All types of radishes are good when eaten raw, but some, especially the long, white ones, make a tasty vegetable dish. Gently fried or boiled, they need a very short cooking time and are delicious with just a speck of butter or in a cream sauce.

Are you familiar with that knobby tuber called Jerusalem artichoke—which has no connection to Jerusalem and isn't even a distant cousin of the globe artichoke? Crunchy and sweet, low in calories, it is great raw, thinly sliced, in a salad. Cooked or baked whole, it is a low-starch, filling vegetable. Its texture is similar to that of the water chestnut but it is much easier to grow. The English used it as a sweetmeat substitute in pies. The young leaves of the plant may be cooked like spinach. Flour from the Jerusalem artichoke makes low-calorie noodles, rolls or breadsticks that have a pleasing nutlike flavor.

Fennel, a member of the parsley family, resembles a stocky celery with feathery leaves that look like dill. The bulbous stalk can be broken into small pieces for a calorie-controlled snack or as a fine scoop for dips. Fennel can be left whole or halved and braised as a vegetable. The seeds are used in baking or as a seasoning, especially in fish dishes and they make a good tea to combat a cough.

If you only think of pumpkin in connection with pies or jack-o'-lanterns, you're missing a lot. Pumpkin, combined with other squash, mashed and seasoned, is a fine side dish, and pumpkin soup, hot or cold, is an international favorite.

If you harvest an overabundance of pumpkins from your garden, you can make flour from them. Cut the raw pumpkin into large chunks, pare off the skin, slice and dry either in the oven or out in the sun. Then grind the dried pulp in a blender or mill. The flour can replace some whole wheat flour in any recipe. It adds moisture and color to the baked product. Store the flour in an airtight container, away from light.

Add Amaranth to Your Greens List

You might call amaranth one of the most underrated and neglected of all vegetables in the United States. It is among the most cultivated leaf vegetables of the humid tropics and as such, compares with spinach in the temperate regions. But perhaps the best feature of amaranth is the nutritional quality of the seed. It is very high in protein which is more complete than the protein of both soybeans and milk. The amaranth flour which is ground from the seeds, when combined with whole wheat or corn, makes a protein about as nutritious as meat. Amaranth seed also tastes good, and the flour is glutenous so that breads and cakes made from it will be light and have good texture.

Amaranth leaves are used like spinach and should be cooked or steamed before being eaten. They have a much more delicate flavor than spinach, however.

The leaves of the weed amaranth (sometimes called pigweed or redroot), that grows in every state of the United States, taste as good as the leaves of the giant amaranth and may be prepared in the same way.

To use the amaranth as a green, all you have to do is to pick off some of the young leaves, rinse them in water, and then steam them until they are limp. You will want to experiment with different added flavors, too. In India they add spices or coconut. You might want to try onions or meat.

Wild mushroom picking is a mysterious art to most Americans. In European countries whole families spend Sunday afternoon in the woods, mushroom hunting. Their labors pay off in good eating and unexpected nutritional benefits. For example, most mushrooms are rich in vitamin D, the sun vitamin, even though they are grown in the dark! They provide iron, copper and B vitamins. To top all this, they contain only 66 calories per pound.

Don't peel fresh mushrooms, just wash them fast without soaking. Sliced raw mushrooms enhance any salad. Or for an appetizer, just squeeze lemon juice over a plate of halved or sliced mushrooms. Like any vegetable, they are best with minimal cooking.

Gift from the Sea

We are becoming increasingly aware of the versatile sea vegetables from Japan. Many Western countries are researching the cultivation of sea vegetables on a scale large enough to make them a staple food in the Western Hemisphere as well.

The most popular varieties of sea vegetables in America are *nori*, *wakame*, *kombu* and *hijiki*. They can be sauteed with vegetables or added to cooked soybeans, soups or salads. Ground up, they can be sprinkled over casseroles or mixed with beverages as a nutritional supplement. One tablespoon of *hijiki*, for example, contains as much calcium as a glass of milk.

Best known in the West is *kombu* which we call kelp. Powdered, it can be used in place of salt. *Nori* (paper-thin seaweed) can be used as a wrapper for cooked brown rice and chopped fish or meat, in the way grape leaves are used in mid-Eastern countries. *Dashi*, a delicate fish stock which is the basis for most Japanese soups and many vegetable dishes, is made from *kombu* and fish flakes.

Sushi

(rice and fish wrapped in seaweed)

1 *cup brown rice*	¼ *cup bamboo shoots, cut into fine strips*
¼ *cup rice vinegar or white distilled vinegar*	½ *cup carrots, cut into fine strips*
3 *Chinese mushrooms or 6 large white mushrooms*	4 *sheets nori*
water to cover	4 *tablespoons tamari soy sauce*
Dashi (see below)	4 *tablespoons water*
4 *ounces fish (sea trout, bluefish, bass, mackerel, turbot, etc.)*	

Cook rice according to preferred method. (See "Cooking with Cereal Grains.")

Toss rice gently, while it is still hot, with vinegar. Cool to room temperature. Soak mushrooms in hot water to cover, until they are soft. Drain, squeeze water out, and reserve water. Cut out and discard stems; cut tops into strips. Add *Dashi* to mushroom water to make 1 cup liquid, then simmer fish in this until tender (approximately 10 to 15 minutes). Lift fish out and set aside to cool. When cool, skin and bone fish.

Using the same liquid the fish cooked in, simmer mushrooms, bamboo shoots and carrots until tender. Drain. Add vegetables and flaked fish to rice, tossing all ingredients together lightly.

Toast *nori,* by holding one sheet at a time above a burner on high heat, waving it back and forth until it has turned a dark green-brown color and has become more rigid. Combine tamari soy sauce and water and spread some over one side of the sheet of *nori.* Spoon the rice mixture down the center of the sheet of *nori.* Wrap the *nori* around it, pulling over and tucking under first one side then the other, to make a cylinder approximately 1½ inches thick. Cut this cylinder into slices approximately 1 inch thick and serve at room temperature.

Yield: 4 cylinders of 4 or 5 slices each; approximately 4 servings

Dashi

(Japanese fish stock)

5 *1-inch pieces kombu seaweed*	1 *cup dried fish (dried bonito flakes) or substitute dried anchovies*
5 *cups water*	2 *teaspoons tamari soy sauce*

Rinse *kombu* well, place in water and bring to a boil. Remove *kombu* and reserve. While stock is still boiling, add dried bonito flakes. Remove from heat and let stand for approximately 3 minutes. Strain the stock, reserve bonito and add tamari soy sauce to the stock.

Yield: 5 cups

Top 16 Vegetables According to Amounts of Nutrients Listed Below

Vegetable (1 lb)	Calcium mg	Iron mg	Potassium mg	Vitamin A IU*	Vitamin C mg	Magnesium mg
Beans, lima	213	11.3	1,914	1,270	77	218 (frozen)
Beet Greens, raw	540	15.0	2,586	27,670	136	269
Beet Greens, cooked	449	8.6	1,506	23,130	68	—
Broccoli, raw	467	5.0	1,733	11,340	513	85
Broccoli, cooked	399	3.6	1,211	11,340	408	95 (frozen)
Brussels Sprouts, raw	163	6.8	1,769	2,490	463	121
Brussels Sprouts, cooked	145	5.0	1,238	2,360	395	95 (frozen)
Carrots, raw	168	3.2	1,547	49,900	36	86
Carrots, cooked	150	2.7	1,007	47,630	27	—
Chard, Swiss, raw	399	14.5	2,495	29,480	145	271
Chard, Swiss, cooked	331	8.2	1,456	24,490	73	—
Dandelion Greens, raw	848	14.1	1,801	63,500	159	163
Kale, raw	1,129	12.2	(1,715)**	45,360	844	107
Kale, cooked	848	7.3	1,002	37,650	422	141 (frozen)
Mustard Greens, raw	830	13.6	1,710	31,750	440	86
Mustard Greens, cooked	626	8.2	998	26,310	218	104 (frozen)
Parsley, raw	921	28.1	3,298	38,560	780	186
Pepper, Green, raw	41	3.2	966	1,910	581	67
Pumpkin, canned	113	1.8	1,089	29,030	23	—
Spinach, raw	422	14.1	2,132	36,740	231	399
Spinach, cooked	422	10.0	1,470	36,740	127	295 (frozen)
Sweet Potatoes, boiled	122	2.7	926	30,100	65	—
Turnip Greens, raw	1,116	8.2	—	34,470	631	221
Turnip Greens, boiled	835	5.0	—	28,580	313	118 (frozen)
Watercress, raw	662	7.8	1,235	21,455	347	83

Prepare a 12-cup muffin pan (2½-inch size) by brushing bottoms and sides with oil.

Sift together flour and salt into a medium-size bowl. Add yeast and mix together. In a mixing bowl, beat egg yolks until thick. Add honey and oil. Combine skim milk with egg mixture. Stir in flour mixture. Add orange rind, mace and raisins. Beat egg whites until soft peaks form. Gently fold beaten egg whites into batter until well combined. Spoon batter into prepared muffin pan cups, filling two-thirds full. Place in warm area or over a shallow pan of hot water, cover, and allow to rise for 30 minutes. Meanwhile, *preheat oven to 375°F.*

Place raised muffins on middle rack in preheated oven and bake 30 minutes or until nicely browned. Remove from oven and loosen edge of each muffin with a spatula; remove and serve immediately.

Yield: 12 muffins

Orange Amaranthus Muffins

1½ cups amaranthus flour
½ teaspoon salt
2 teaspoons dry yeast
2 egg yolks
3 tablespoons honey
2 tablespoons oil
1 cup skim milk
3 teaspoons grated orange rind
¼ teaspoon ground mace
¼ cup raisins
2 egg whites

Heat oil in heavy skillet. Add garlic, onion, green pepper and stir-fry for a few minutes. Stir in amaranth and sprouts. Mix soy sauce and water and add to vegetables. Cover and cook over medium heat just until amaranth is tender (approximately 3 to 5 minutes). Salt to taste before serving.

Yield: 4 servings

Sauteed Amaranth

1 *tablespoon salad oil*
1 *or 2 cloves garlic*
1 *onion, sliced*
1 *green pepper, chopped*
4 *cups amaranth leaves*
1 *cup mung bean sprouts*
1 *tablespoon tamari soy sauce*
1 *tablespoon water*
salt to taste

*International Units
**Values in parentheses denote imputed values usually from another form of the food or from a similar food
Dashes denote lack of data given

Data taken from *Nutritive Value of American Foods*, Agricultural Handbook No. 456, Agriculture Research Service, USDA

Asparagus and Eggs with Sesame Seeds

1 *lb. fresh asparagus or 1 10-ounce package frozen asparagus (cut spears)*
2 *hard-cooked eggs, sliced*
¼ *cup shredded cheddar cheese*
1 *tablespoon unhulled sesame seeds*
3 *tablespoons dry whole grain bread crumbs*
1 *cup chicken stock*

If using fresh asparagus, trim and cut into 1-inch pieces. Steam until tender. If using frozen asparagus, cook according to instructions on package. Drain.

Butter a casserole and arrange half the asparagus on the bottom, cover with hard-cooked egg slices, then add the remaining asparagus. Combine cheese, sesame seeds and bread crumbs. Spread evenly over the asparagus. Pour the chicken stock over all and place under broiler until cheese is melted.

Yield: 3 servings

Asparagus with Yogurt Dill Sauce

3 *cloves garlic, minced*
2 *tablespoons lemon juice*
1 *teaspoon prepared mustard*
½ *teaspoon salt*
⅛ *teaspoon pepper*
2 *tablespoons minced parsley*
1 *teaspoon minced dill*
1 *cup yogurt*
2 *lbs. fresh asparagus or 2 10-ounce packages frozen asparagus, steamed*

Mix all sauce ingredients together and allow to stand at least an hour before serving. Serve over steamed asparagus.

Yield: 6 servings

Beet Dressing

4 *medium-size beets*
water to cover
¼ *cup beet liquid*
2 *tablespoons cider vinegar*
1 *tablespoon minced onion*
6 *tablespoons mayonnaise*

Cook beets in water to cover until tender. Drain and reserve ¼ cup beet liquid. Peel and quarter beets.

Combine all ingredients in electric blender and process until smooth.

Yield: approximately 2 cups

Bring grated beets to a boil in beef stock which has been seasoned to taste with salt and pepper. Turn down heat and simmer, covered, for 30 minutes. Add tomato juice.

Puree mixture in electric blender, then add orange juice, mixing well to combine. Refrigerate for several hours.

Serve with a dollop of yogurt and chopped chives.

Yield: approximately 10 cups

Orange Borscht

4 *medium-size beets, peeled and coarsely grated*
5 *cups beef stock*
salt, freshly ground black pepper to taste
2 *cups tomato juice*
2½ *cups orange juice, fresh or frozen*
yogurt
chopped chives

Saute onions and garlic in oil for a few minutes, stir in turmeric, coriander and cumin, then add carrots and salt to taste. Cover pan, turn down heat and steam for 5 minutes. Add broccoli, then chili powder and finally add the water. Cover pan again and cook over low heat for another 10 minutes or until vegetables are tender but still firm.

Yield: 4 to 6 servings

Curried Broccoli and Carrots

2 *medium-size onions, sliced*
2 *cloves garlic, minced*
¼ *cup oil*
½ *teaspoon turmeric*
1 *teaspoon ground coriander*
1 *teaspoon ground cumin*
½ *lb. carrots (approximately 2 carrots)*
salt to taste
1 *lb. broccoli (approximately ½ of large bunch)*
⅛ *teaspoon chili powder or crushed dried chili peppers*
½ *cup water, more if needed*

Broccoli Mustard Relish

1 *lb. broccoli (approximately 1 medium-size bunch)*
¼ *teaspoon salt*
1 *cup vinegar*
½ *cup water*
2 *tablespoons prepared mustard*
2 *teaspoons honey*

Cut broccoli into separate stalks and steam for 5 minutes or until just tender. Combine remaining ingredients in a saucepan, bring to a boil and pour over broccoli. Let marinate for 3 to 5 hours before serving.

Yield: 6 to 8 servings

Broccoli Timbales

1½ *lbs. broccoli*
4 *eggs*
1½ *cups milk*
½ *teaspoon salt*
⅛ *teaspoon pepper*
1 *tablespoon chopped parsley*

Preheat oven to 325°F.

Cook broccoli in a little water until tender. Chop broccoli and drain well. Use 2 cups for this recipe.

In a bowl, combine eggs, milk, salt and pepper. Beat with a whisk until well blended. Add broccoli and parsley and pour into buttered 1-quart mold or individual molds, filling them approximately two-thirds full. Place molds in a pan of hot water which reaches halfway up the side of molds. Bake in preheated oven for 25 to 45 minutes depending on the size of the molds. When ready to serve, unmold, if desired, and serve immediately.

Yield: 4 to 6 servings

Brussels Sprouts with Brazil Nut Sauce

2 *10-ounce packages frozen brussels sprouts*
1 *cup raw Brazil nuts (approximately 50 nuts)*
1 *clove garlic, minced*
1 *tablespoon butter*
4 *to 6 tablespoons chicken stock*

Cook brussels sprouts using as little water as possible. Drain. Grind Brazil nuts to a meal in electric blender. Saute garlic in butter lightly, then stir in nuts and enough chicken stock for desired consistency. Serve brussels sprouts topped with sauce.

Yield: 6 servings

Steam brussels sprouts until tender but firm. Drain mushrooms, reserving liquid, and saute them in butter or chicken fat. Add flour, then mushroom liquid and chicken stock. Stir until sauce is blended and thickened. Season to taste. Pour sauce over brussels sprouts and serve.

Yield: 6 to 8 servings

Brussels Sprouts in Mushroom Sauce

2 *lbs. fresh brussels sprouts or 2 10-ounce packages frozen brussels sprouts*

2 *4-ounce cans sliced mushrooms*

2 *teaspoons butter or chicken fat*

2 *tablespoons whole wheat flour*

1 *cup liquid from mushrooms and chicken stock*

salt, pepper to taste

Cook and mash potatoes, adding milk to them. Steam cabbage, drain and chop fine. Combine potatoes and cabbage and season to taste. Using a cast-iron skillet, saute onion in butter and oil, turn potato and cabbage mixture into skillet and flatten with pancake turner.

Leave to brown well on the underside, then lift out onto a plate, invert the plate onto another plate, add more oil to pan, if needed, and slip the hash back into the pan to brown the other side. When crisp and golden brown on both sides, lift out onto platter and serve.

Yield: 4 to 6 servings

"Bubble and Squeak"
(*English cabbage and potato hash*)

4 *medium-size potatoes, peeled and cubed*

3 *tablespoons hot milk*

½ *medium-size head of cabbage, cored and cut into wedges*

salt, pepper to taste

1 *medium-size onion, finely chopped*

2 *tablespoons butter*

2 to 4 *tablespoons oil*

Curried Cabbage

4 *tablespoons oil*

2 *onions, chopped*

1 *teaspoon mustard seeds*

1 *teaspoon cumin*

½ *teaspoon Garam Masala (optional; see Index)*

2 *teaspoons coriander*

2 *large carrots, sliced ½ inch thick*

2 *stalks celery, sliced ½ inch thick*

½ *lb. cabbage (approximately ½ small head), cored and shredded*

1 *cup tomato juice*

1 *teaspoon basil*

1 *bay leaf*

salt to taste

In a large skillet, heat oil to a medium-hot temperature and stir-fry onions with spices for a minute or two. Add carrots, then celery and cabbage, tossing and stirring a few more minutes to cook the vegetables evenly with the spices. Add tomato juice, basil, bay leaf and salt to taste. Cover pan and steam for a few minutes until carrots are tender but firm. Keep warm until serving time but do not overcook.

Yield: 6 servings

Stir-Fried Cabbage

2 *tablespoons oil*

1 *medium-size onion, sliced*

8 *cups coarsely shredded cabbage*

1 *teaspoon celery seed*

1 *teaspoon paprika*

1 *teaspoon coriander*

¾ *teaspoon salt*

Heat oil to medium-hot in large skillet or *wok*. Stir-fry onion in oil for a minute or two, then add cabbage and seasonings. Stir-fry for 5 to 10 minutes until cabbage is tender but firm. Pan may be covered briefly toward the end of the cooking process to hasten tenderizing. Serve immediately.

Yield: 4 servings

Dissolve yeast and honey in lukewarm water and set aside to activate for 5 minutes. Put flour into a large bowl, make well in center and pour the yeast mixture into the well. Add melted butter and salt and mix well. Knead for 10 minutes. Cover with a damp cloth and leave to rise for 1 hour.

While dough is rising, mix the sauerkraut, onions and caraway seeds. Fry together in oil for 8 minutes. When the dough has risen, roll it out as thin as you can (¼ to ½ inch thick). Cut the dough into 6-inch squares. Put a heaping tablespoon of the sauerkraut-onion mixture in the middle of each square. Fold into a triangular turnover and pinch edges together. Place on buttered baking sheet and let rise 30 minutes. *Preheat oven to 400°F. and bake for 25 minutes. Serve warm.*

Yield: 8 rolls

Sauerkraut Onion Rolls

1 *teaspoon dry yeast*
½ *teaspoon honey*
½ *cup lukewarm water*
2 *cups whole wheat flour*
2 *tablespoons melted butter*
½ *teaspoon salt*
2 *cups sauerkraut, drained*
2 *cups chopped onions*
¼ *teaspoon caraway seeds*
2 *tablespoons oil*

Toss ingredients together with two forks until well mixed. Chill. Serve on crisp greens.

Yield: 6 servings

Sauerkraut Salad

1 *1-lb. can sauerkraut, chilled*
1 *cup grated carrots*
1 *medium-size onion, chopped*
2 *medium-size apples, chopped*
6 *large ripe olives, pitted and sliced*
2 *tablespoons vinegar*
1 *tablespoon horseradish*
3 *tablespoons oil*

Carrot Confection

1 *lb. carrots, grated*
  (approximately
  7 cups)
¾ *cup milk*
½ *teaspoon nutmeg*
2 *sticks cinnamon*
⅔ *cup honey*
6 *tablespoons butter*
½ *cup raisins*
¼ *cup coconut*
1 *tablespoon slivered*
  almonds

In a heavy saucepan or skillet, combine carrots and milk. Add nutmeg, cinnamon and honey and bring to a boil. Boil over low heat, stirring frequently, until mixture is very thick. Remove cinnamon sticks. Add butter, raisins and coconut and cook for approximately 25 minutes longer. Pour into a buttered, shallow pan, top with almonds and cool. Cut into squares.

Yield: approximately 4 cups or 1 lb.

Carrot Yogurt Sorbet

4 *cups diced carrots*
¼ *cup water*
3 *large oranges, peeled,*
  seeded and sliced
2 *bananas*
2 *tablespoons honey*
1 *cup yogurt*

Combine all ingredients except yogurt in electric blender and process until very smooth. Add yogurt, mix well and pour into refrigerator tray. Freeze. Blend again if smoother consistency is desired and refreeze. Remove from freezer and place in refrigerator an hour before serving. Serve as a side dish with the main course.

Yield: 6 to 8 servings

Cashew Carrot Soup

2 *medium-size onions, sliced*
4 *tablespoons oil*
2 *cups coarsely shredded*
  cabbage, turnip greens
  or Swiss chard
2 *cups grated carrots*
1 *cup chopped apple*
5 *cups beef stock*
2 *tablespoons tomato paste*
⅓ *cup brown rice*
½ *cup coarsely chopped*
  cashew nuts
½ *cup raisins*
  salt, pepper to taste
1 *to 1½ cups yogurt*

Using a Dutch oven or heavy-bottom pot, saute onions in oil, then stir in greens and saute a few minutes; then add the carrots and cook a minute or so longer. Stir in apple, beef stock and tomato paste. Bring mixture to a boil and add rice. Simmer, covered, for 35 to 40 minutes or until carrots are tender and rice is cooked.

Add cashew nuts and raisins and cook until raisins are "plumped." Season to taste. Serve each bowl of soup topped with a generous dollop of yogurt.

Yield: 4 to 6 servings

Combine all ingredients and mix well. Chill, then shape into patties. Saute the patties in oil until nicely browned on both sides. Serve hot or cold with Tomato Sauce if desired. (See Index.)

Yield: *4 to 6 servings*

Sunflower Carrot Patties

2 *carrots, grated*
   (approximately
   2 cups)
2 *small onions, grated*
2 *eggs, well beaten*
2 *tablespoons oil*
¾ *cup sunflower seeds*
   (finely ground in
   electric blender)
½ *teaspoon celery salt*
1 *teaspoon dill*
1 *tablespoon chopped parsley*
  oil (for sauteing)

Steam head of cauliflower whole, using as little water as possible, until it is tender but firm (approximately 20 to 30 minutes). Keep warm. Saute garlic, crumbs and wheat germ in butter until golden brown. Spoon over cauliflower, top with chopped parsley and serve.

Yield: *4 to 6 servings*

Cauliflower with Garlic-Crumb Topping

1 *large head cauliflower*
2 *cloves garlic, minced*
1½ *cups dry whole grain*
   bread crumbs
¼ *cup wheat germ*
½ *cup butter*
1 *tablespoon chopped parsley*

Separate cauliflower into flowerets and cook until just tender but still crisp (approximately 10 minutes). Combine liquid ingredients and seasonings and pour marinade over hot cauliflower. Set aside for several hours, stirring occasionally.

When ready to serve, drain flowerets and arrange in salad bowl. Garnish with thin strips of green pepper and thin slices or wedges of tomato.

Yield: *6 servings*

Cauliflower Salad

1 *medium-size head cauli-*
   flower (approximately
   3 cups flowerets)
½ *cup vinegar*
¾ *cup oil*
1 *teaspoon tamari soy sauce*
½ *teaspoon turmeric*
½ *teaspoon salt*
⅛ *teaspoon black pepper*
⅛ *teaspoon thyme*
  green pepper
  tomato

Cauliflower Vinaigrette

1   *medium-size head cauli-
        flower, separated
        into flowerets
        (approximately 3 cups)*
1   *medium-size green pepper,
        cut into thin strips*
1   *large stalk celery, cut into
        ¼-inch slices*
¼   *teaspoon salt*
½   *cup vinegar*
4   *teaspoons honey*
⅔   *cup water*

Steam cauliflower 10 minutes or so. It should be firm and still on the crisp side. Put cauliflower, green pepper and celery into a bowl. Combine remaining ingredients in a saucepan, bring to a boil and pour over vegetables. Let marinate 3 to 5 hours before serving.

Yield: 6 to 8 servings

Braised Celery Hearts

2   *bunches celery*
2   *cups chicken stock*
2   *tablespoons whole wheat
        flour*
2   *tablespoons water*
*salt to taste (depending on
        saltiness of stock)*
⅛   *teaspoon pepper*
¼   *cup dry whole grain
        bread crumbs*
2   *tablespoons unhulled
        sesame seeds*

If celery is large, peel off several of the outside stalks. Remove some of the tops and leaves. Cut remaining hearts in half lengthwise. Put into a skillet, add the stock, cover tightly and cook until celery is tender (approximately 20 minutes). *Preheat oven to 350°F.*

Take out the celery and place in a buttered shallow baking dish. Make paste of flour and water and stir into the juices in the skillet. Add salt and pepper and cook until sauce is slightly thick. Pour sauce over celery in the casserole, top with crumbs and sesame seeds and bake in preheated oven for 15 minutes.

Yield: 4 servings

Wash celery, cut off tops and, using a potato peeler, remove top layer of strings from outside stalks. Cut crosswise into 1-inch-wide, diagonal slices. Wash and cut green beans into 1-inch lengths. Peel and chop tomatoes.

Using a large skillet (not cast-iron) saute garlic in butter and oil for a minute or so, then add green beans and oregano and saute for 5 minutes. Add celery, saute for 2 minutes, then add tomatoes. Cover pan, turn heat low and continue to steam until vegetables are tender but firm. Season to taste and serve.

Yield: 4 to 6 servings

Celery, Green Bean and Tomato Toss

approximately 8 large outside stalks of celery
1 *lb. green beans*
3 *medium-size tomatoes*
3 *cloves garlic, minced*
1 *tablespoon butter*
2 *tablespoons oil*
2 *teaspoons oregano*
salt, pepper to taste

Drain beets and save liquid. Measure beet liquid and add beef or chicken stock to measure 4 cups. Peel cucumbers and remove any large seeds. Chop beets, cucumbers and onion by hand or puree, in small batches, with some liquid in electric blender. Add yogurt and vinegar, blending in completely. Season to taste, add dill and refrigerate. Serve ice cold.

Yield: 4 to 6 servings

Cold Beet and Cucumber Soup

2 *1-lb. cans beets*
4 *cups beet liquid and beef or chicken stock*
4 *cups chopped cucumbers*
6 *green onions, tops included*
4 *cups yogurt*
4 *teaspoons vinegar*
salt, pepper to taste
2 *teaspoons dill (chopped fresh, if possible)*

Cucumber Vinaigrette

½ cup lemon juice
½ cup cider vinegar
½ cup water
2 tablespoons honey
4 tablespoons chopped
    fresh dill
1 teaspoon salt
4 average-size cucumbers,
    peeled and thinly sliced
4 green onions, thinly sliced

Combine lemon juice, vinegar, water, honey and seasonings and add cucumbers and green onions. Chill for several hours in refrigerator before serving.

Yield: 6 to 8 servings

Cucumber and Walnut Salad

1 large cucumber, sliced
    (approximately 2 cups)
½ cup chopped walnuts
1 teaspoon grated onion
4 radishes, sliced
½ cup diced green pepper
1 tablespoon chopped parsley
1 teaspoon chopped fresh mint
    or ½ teaspoon
    dried mint
½ cup yogurt
  salt, freshly ground black
    pepper to taste

Leave cucumber unpeeled if possible. Run a fork down the outside of the cucumber, so that the tines of the fork make grooves in the cucumber skin. Slice thinly and remove any large seeds from center. Combine all other ingredients with cucumbers and chill in refrigerator before serving.

Yield: 3 servings

Preheat oven to 400°F.

Eggplant Dip or Dressing

Wash eggplant and place whole on pan in preheated oven. Bake for an hour or until skin is charred and wrinkled and flesh is soft. Cool.

Saute onion and garlic in oil, just until tender, not brown. Strip off eggplant skin and mash flesh to a pulp. Combine with sauteed onion and garlic, add pepper, tomatoes and lemon juice. Season to taste and serve as a dip or salad dressing.

Yield: approximately 4 cups

1   *medium-size eggplant*
     (approximately
     1½ lbs.)
1   *onion, chopped*
1   *to 2 cloves garlic, minced*
2   *tablespoons oil*
1   *green pepper, chopped*
2   *tomatoes, skinned and*
     chopped
¼   *cup lemon juice*
     salt, pepper to taste

Eggplant Salad

Steam eggplant in as little water as possible until tender. Combine with other ingredients and chill in refrigerator. Serve on salad greens, garnished with chopped parsley.

Yield: 4 to 6 servings

3   *cups cubed eggplant*
     (approximately 1
     medium-size eggplant)
2   *tablespoons minced onion*
½   *cup chopped pecans*
½   *cup chopped celery*
½   *cup chopped green pepper*
6   *tablespoons oil*
3   *tablespoons vinegar*
     salt, pepper to taste
1   *teaspoon basil*
2   *tablespoons chopped parsley*
     (for garnish)

Eggplant Souffle

3 *medium-size eggplants*
1 *cup water*
6 *to 7 tablespoons oil*
6 *green onions, thinly sliced*
2 *cups sliced fresh mushrooms*
½ *cup whole wheat flour*
2 *cups milk*
6 *egg yolks*
1 *teaspoon salt*
1 *teaspoon basil*
6 *egg whites*
1 *cup water*

Cut eggplants in half lengthwise. Scoop out pulp, leaving a shell ¼ inch thick. Chop pulp and cook it in water until soft. Drain. Mash pulp with fork and set aside.

In a skillet, heat 4 tablespoons oil and saute green onions and mushrooms for 2 or 3 minutes. While retaining as much oil as possible in the skillet, remove onions and mushrooms and add them to eggplant pulp. *Preheat oven to 325°F.*

Stir flour into oil in skillet, adding as much oil as needed to absorb flour, then add milk, stirring to blend smoothly. Cook until sauce is thickened. Beat egg yolks and stir a little of the hot sauce into them, then return this mixture to the pan and stir until sauce is blended and smooth. Combine sauce and eggplant mixture, adding salt and basil. Beat egg whites until stiff and gently fold them into eggplant mixture.

Place eggplant shells in a baking pan and add 1 cup water to the pan to keep the shells from scorching. Pile souffle into the shells and bake in preheated oven for 30 minutes. If eggplant shells won't hold all of the souffle mixture, pile remainder in casserole and bake along with shells. Serve immediately.

Yield: 4 to 6 servings

Garam Masala
(Indian spice mixture)

4 *3-inch pieces stick cinnamon*
¾ *cup cardamom pods*
3 *tablespoons whole cloves*
6 *tablespoons whole cumin*
    seeds
3 *tablespoons whole coriander*
    seeds
3 *tablespoons whole black*
    peppercorns

Preheat oven to 200°F.

Spread out spices in one layer on cookie sheet and roast for 20 minutes in preheated oven. Shake pan every 5 minutes to keep spices from browning. Cool. Break open cardamom pods, remove seeds, discard pods. Crush cinnamon sticks with a rolling pin. Put all spices into electric blender* and grind until spices are powdered. Stop blender every 30 seconds or so to stir spice mixture, then grind again, until mixture is uniformly ground. Store in an airtight jar.

Yield: approximately 1 cup

*A pint canning jar with a standard-size mouth will fit perfectly into most blender bases. For fine grinding, it is best to use a smaller container on the blender. Just put the spices in the jar, place the blade, rubber and screw bottom of blender container onto jar as you would a lid. Turn jar upside down, place in blender base and proceed with grinding.

Rolled Eggplant Italian

Make Filling

Combine mozzarella, Parmesan and ricotta cheeses, 1 egg, 1 tablespoon parsley, salt and pepper to taste in a mixing bowl. Blend to a smooth paste. Chill.

Make Batter

Combine 1 egg, flour, milk and oil. Beat until smooth.

Peel eggplants and cut lengthwise into thin slices. Dip in additional flour and shake off excess. Heat olive oil and butter together. Dip eggplant slices in prepared batter until they are coated. Saute in hot oil until browned on both sides. Drain.

Preheat oven to 375°F. Place 2 tablespoons chilled cheese mixture on each slice. Roll loosely. Arrange rolls seam side down in baking pan. Cover with tomato sauce. Bake in preheated oven for 15 minutes.

Yield: 6 servings

Filling

1   *cup grated mozzarella cheese*
½   *cup grated Parmesan cheese*
⅓   *cup ricotta cheese*
1   *egg*
1   *tablespoon chopped parsley*
salt, pepper to taste

Batter

1   *egg*
2   *tablespoons whole wheat flour*
⅓   *cup milk*
1   *tablespoon oil*

2   *small eggplants*
whole wheat flour
¼   *cup olive oil*
2   *tablespoons butter*
tomato sauce

Green Bean-Sunflower Seed Salad

Wash beans, remove ends and cut into 1-inch lengths. Cook in as little water as possible until tender, but still firm. Combine beans with other ingredients except sunflower seeds. Chill.

Serve chilled green beans on salad greens, topped with toasted sunflower seeds.

Yield: 4 to 6 servings

*Toast sunflower seeds in heavy dry skillet over medium heat, stirring constantly until brown.

1   *lb. fresh green beans*
½   *medium-size onion, minced*
1   *small clove garlic, minced*
2   *tablespoons vinegar*
2   *tablespoons tamari soy sauce*
⅓   *cup toasted sunflower seeds**
freshly ground black pepper

Marinated Green Bean, Celery and Radish Salad

1 *lb. fresh green beans*
1 *small onion, sliced*
1 *cup oil*
½ *cup cider vinegar*
¼ *cup wine or herb vinegar*
1 *teaspoon dry mustard*
1 *tablespoon dry basil*
salt, pepper to taste
2 *stalks celery, finely sliced*
4 *to 6 large radishes, sliced*

Trim and steam green beans for 10 minutes, until they are tender but still very firm.

Add onion to beans. Combine oil, vinegars and seasonings and pour over beans. Chill for several hours, stirring the beans at least once during the marinating process. Just before serving, combine beans with celery and radishes and serve on a bed of salad greens.

Yield: 4 servings

Swiss Cheese, Egg and Green Bean Casserole

1 *lb. fresh green beans or*
   2 10-ounce packages
   frozen cut green beans
2 *tablespoons butter*
3 *tablespoons whole wheat*
   flour
½ *cup milk*
½ *onion, grated*
½ *tablespoon honey*
⅓ *teaspoon salt*
⅛ *teaspoon pepper*
1½ *cups yogurt*
4 *hard-cooked eggs, sliced*
½ *lb. Swiss cheese, slivered or*
   grated
¼ *cup wheat germ*
1 *tablespoon oil*

Cook green beans according to preferred method. Drain if necessary.

In a saucepan, melt butter, add flour, stirring until blended, and then add milk. Continue to cook, stirring until thickened. Add grated onion, honey, seasonings and yogurt. Mix until smooth. Remove from heat.

Preheat oven to 350°F. Make a layer of green beans in a casserole, then a layer of sliced hard-cooked eggs and then a layer of cheese. Pour sauce over top, poking casserole with a fork to be sure sauce seeps down into all the layers. Sprinkle with wheat germ which has been mixed with a little oil. Bake in preheated oven for 10 to 15 minutes, or until sauce is bubbling and cheese is melted. Be careful not to overcook because eggs left too long in the oven can become rubbery. Serve hot.

Yield: 4 to 6 servings

Steam scrubbed whole artichokes in as little water as possible until just tender. Do not overcook. Cool and slice. Fry in oil until browned and crunchy. Sprinkle toasted sesame seeds over the artichokes before serving.

Yield: 4 to 6 servings

*Toast sesame seeds in a heavy dry skillet for 1 or 2 minutes watching them carefully and shaking the pan from time to time so that they do not burn.

Fried Jerusalem Artichokes

4 *to 6 Jerusalem artichokes*
4 *to 6 tablespoons oil*
2 *tablespoons toasted unhulled sesame seeds**

Steam scrubbed whole artichokes in as little water as possible until tender. Cool and cube. Put into casserole and keep warm. In a saucepan, melt butter and pour a little into bread crumbs to moisten them; set aside. Stir flour into remaining butter, then add stock and milk, stirring constantly to avoid lumping. Cook until thickened, then add cheese, stirring until it melts. Pour the sauce over the artichokes, top with buttered bread crumbs and serve.

Yield: 4 to 6 servings

Jerusalem Artichokes au Gratin

4 *to 6 Jerusalem artichokes*
4 *tablespoons butter*
¼ *cup dry whole grain bread crumbs*
4 *tablespoons whole wheat flour*
¾ *cup chicken, beef or vegetable stock*
¾ *cup milk*
4 *tablespoons grated sharp cheddar cheese*

Steam scrubbed whole artichokes in as little water as possible until just tender (approximately 15 minutes). Cool and slice thinly. Combine remaining ingredients, toss with artichokes and serve.

Yield: 4 to 6 servings

Jerusalem Artichoke Salad

4 *to 6 Jerusalem artichokes*
2 *hard-cooked eggs, sliced*
3 *green onions, including tops, thinly sliced*
½ *cup mayonnaise*
¼ *cup yogurt*
1½ *teaspoons lemon juice*
2 *tablespoons chopped parsley*
salt to taste

Dutch Kale with Potatoes and Sausage

1 *lb. fresh kale*

water to cover

3 *medium-size baking potatoes, peeled, scrubbed and cut into 1-inch cubes*

1 *lb. fresh link sausage*

1 *medium-size onion, chopped*

1 *cup milk*

1 *teaspoon salt*

⅛ *teaspoon black pepper*

pinch of tarragon

Wash kale and trim away tough ends and heavy ribs. Chop coarsely and cook in water to cover for 15 minutes. Add potatoes and cook 15 to 20 minutes longer or until kale and potatoes are tender. Meanwhile, cut sausage into ½-inch slices and fry in a heavy skillet until tender and nicely browned. Add onion and saute a few minutes longer. Discard any remaining fat. Add milk, stirring pan to incorporate any of the brown juices from sausage, then add kale and potatoes. Cover and simmer for 5 minutes. Add salt, pepper and tarragon to taste and serve.

Yield: 6 servings

Kale and Kidney Bean Bake

¾ *cup kidney beans*

1 *lb. fresh kale*

water to cover

1 *large onion, chopped*

2 *cloves garlic, minced*

2 *stalks celery, chopped*

4 *sprigs parsley, chopped*

1 *tablespoon tamari soy sauce*

¾ *cup cornmeal*

¼ *cup oil*

¼ *teaspoon thyme*

¼ *teaspoon basil*

1 *teaspoon chopped chives*

Cook kidney beans according to preferred method. (See "Basic Methods for Cooking Beans and Other Legumes.") Drain and reserve liquid for soup.

Wash kale and trim away tough ends and heavy ribs. Chop coarsely and cook in water to cover along with onion, garlic, celery, parsley and soy sauce, until tender (approximately 30 minutes). Drain and set aside. Bring kale cooking liquid to a boil, stir in cornmeal and cook in the top of a double boiler, until soft and all liquid has been absorbed (approximately 20 minutes).

Preheat oven to 350°F. Combine kale, beans, cornmeal, oil and herbs, turn into an oiled loaf tin and bake for 20 minutes in preheated oven.

Yield: 6 servings

Cook kohlrabi in water until tender. Pour off water and reserve for soup. Peel kohlrabi and cut into ½-inch cubes. Add remaining ingredients, warm over low heat and serve.

Yield: 4 servings

Herbed Kohlrabi

5 *kohlrabi*
water to cover
½ *teaspoon salt*
2 *tablespoons butter*
1 *teaspoon chopped chives*
2 *tablespoons chopped parsley*
1 *teaspoon chopped fresh basil*
   (2 leaves)

Cook kohlrabi in water until tender. Drain and reserve liquid for soup. Cool, peel and cut into strips. Combine remaining ingredients, pour over kohlrabi and serve as a salad or side dish.

Yield: 4 servings

Kohlrabi Slaw

5 *kohlrabi*
water to cover
¼ *cup oil*
1 *tablespoon wine vinegar*
⅛ *teaspoon dill seeds*
pinch of pepper
salt to taste
2 *tablespoons yogurt*

Cook kohlrabi in water to cover until tender. Drain and reserve liquid. Peel kohlrabi and cut into chunks.

Saute onions in butter for a few minutes. Place in electric blender, add cooked kohlrabi and liquid and blend well. Add stock and seasonings. Serve hot.

Yield: 4 cups

Kohlrabi Soup

3 *kohlrabi*
water to cover
3 *medium-size onions,*
   chopped
4 *tablespoons butter*
2 *cups beef or chicken stock*
¼ *teaspoon celery salt*
¼ *teaspoon thyme*
pinch of pepper

Lima Bean and Sesame Dip

½ cup unhulled sesame seeds
1 10-ounce package frozen lima beans, cooked
½ small onion, peeled and quartered
3 teaspoons oil
¼ cup mayonnaise
¼ cup yogurt
1 to 2 teaspoons lemon juice
salt to taste

Toast sesame seeds in dry heavy skillet over medium heat, stirring constantly to prevent scorching. Grind toasted sesame seeds to a meal in electric blender.

Combine cooked lima beans with onion and puree in electric blender until smooth, using a little of the cooking liquid if necessary. Add sesame meal and then remaining ingredients to lima bean puree. Stir until well combined. Serve as a dip for crackers or fresh vegetables.

Yield: approximately 2 cups

Mushroomburgers

½ lb. fresh mushrooms (approximately 3 cups), finely chopped
¼ lb. ground beef
1 cup soy pulp (from preparation of Soy Milk; see Index) or ½ cup soy grits and ½ cup water simmered together for 8 minutes
½ teaspoon salt
⅛ teaspoon pepper
1 clove garlic, minced
1 egg

Combine ingredients, form into thick patties and broil on both sides until brown.

Yield: 6 large patties

Pickled Mushrooms

½ lb. small fresh mushrooms (approximately 3 cups)
2 cups boiling water
2 teaspoons salt
⅔ cup cider vinegar
⅛ teaspoon pepper
1 slice onion
1 sprig parsley
1 bay leaf

Wash mushrooms and cut stems even with the caps. Reserve stems for soup. Cover mushroom caps with boiling, salted water. Simmer 5 minutes and drain. Mix remaining ingredients and bring to a boil. Add mushroom caps and simmer a few minutes. Cool and refrigerate at least one day before serving.

Yield: approximately 1 pint

Saute mushrooms in butter and oil. Add flour, stirring, then gradually add 1 cup stock and cook until thickened. Remove from heat. Stir in ½ cup yogurt or sour cream and season to taste. Put 2 tablespoons filling on each crepe and roll or fold crepe. Thin remaining filling, if necessary, with more stock or yogurt, and pour over crepes before serving.

Yield: 8 8-inch crepes

Mushroom Crepes

2 *cups fresh mushrooms or*
   1 8-ounce can mush-
   rooms, drained
   (reserve liquid)

2 *tablespoons butter*

2 *tablespoons oil*

6 *tablespoons whole wheat*
   flour

1 *to 1½ cups meat or*
   vegetable stock (if using
   canned mushrooms,
   use liquid from can)

½ *to ¾ cup yogurt or*
   sour cream

salt, pepper to taste

½ *recipe Buckwheat Crepes*
   (see Index)

Preheat oven to 400°F.

Wash mushrooms and carefully break off stems. Dry caps with paper towel. Chop stems very fine and combine with remaining ingredients. Fill caps with mixture and place in shallow, buttered baking dish. Bake in preheated oven for 20 minutes.

Yield: approximately 1½ dozen

Stuffed Mushrooms

½ *lb. fresh mushrooms*
   (approximately 3 cups)

1 *clove garlic, minced*

1 *small onion, grated*

½ *cup dry whole grain*
   bread crumbs

½ *teaspoon salt*

⅛ *teaspoon pepper*

1 *tablespoon chopped parsley*

½ *cup chopped, cooked meat,*
   chicken or fish

Fried Okra

½ teaspoon salt
⅛ teaspoon black pepper
½ cup cornmeal
1 lb. fresh okra, trimmed and
    cut into ½-inch slices or
    1½ 10-ounce packages
    frozen
2 tablespoons butter or oil

Add salt and pepper to cornmeal and mix thoroughly. Toss okra slices in cornmeal mixture until each piece is well coated. Fry in hot butter or oil for 15 minutes until okra is tender, crisp and golden brown.

Yield: 4 servings

Okra Curry

3 tablespoons oil
1 lb. fresh okra, trimmed and
    cut into 1-inch slices
2 tablespoons oil
1 medium-size onion,
    finely chopped
1 large clove garlic, minced
3 green chilies, seeded
    and chopped
½ teaspoon cumin
¼ teaspoon turmeric
⅛ teaspoon cayenne
½ teaspoon salt
¼ cup water
2 tablespoons lemon juice
1 tablespoon prepared
    mustard
4 tablespoons yogurt

Heat 3 tablespoons oil in a skillet and saute okra about 10 minutes. Remove okra from pan. Add 2 tablespoons oil to pan and saute onion, garlic and chilies with spices for approximately 2 minutes. Add okra, salt and water. Cover and simmer until okra is tender. Stir in lemon juice, mustard, yogurt and serve.

Yield: 4 servings

Heat oil in heavy skillet or saucepan. Add sprouts, okra and chives. Saute for 10 minutes until okra is tender. Add salt, then gradually add flour and stir until well blended with the vegetables. Add stock and stir until mixture is slightly thick. Add red pepper, pimientos and alfalfa sprouts and simmer 5 minutes more before serving.

Yield: 4 cups

Okra Soup

2 *tablespoons oil*
1 *cup mung bean sprouts*
¾ *lb. fresh okra, trimmed and cut into ½-inch pieces or 1 10-ounce package frozen*
2 *tablespoons chopped chives*
½ *teaspoon salt*
2 *tablespoons whole wheat flour*
3 *cups chicken or beef stock*
pinch of red pepper
2 *tablespoons chopped pimientos*
1 *cup alfalfa sprouts*

Preheat oven to 350°F.

Saute onions in butter for a few minutes. Add bulgur, coriander, cinnamon and garlic and saute for several minutes longer. Add stock, raisins, salt and pepper, turn into a buttered casserole and bake in preheated oven for 30 minutes.

Yield: 4 to 6 servings

Baked Onions and Bulgur with Raisins

2 *cups chopped onions*
3 *tablespoons butter*
1 *cup bulgur*
½ *teaspoon ground coriander*
½ *teaspoon cinnamon*
2 *cloves garlic, minced*
3 *cups beef, chicken or vegetable stock*
¼ *cup raisins*
½ *teaspoon salt*
⅛ *teaspoon pepper*

Bavarian Onion
Flat Bread

2 *teaspoons dry yeast*
½ *teaspoon honey*
½ *cup lukewarm water*
2 *cups whole wheat flour*
1 *teaspoon salt*
5 *tablespoons oil*
5 *large onions, chopped*
3 *tablespoons oil*
1 *tablespoon whole wheat*
   flour
½ *cup water*
1 *cup cottage cheese*
½ *teaspoon salt*
½ *cup yogurt*

Dissolve yeast and honey in lukewarm water. Set aside for 10 minutes to activate. Sift flour and salt into a bowl. Pour yeast mixture and oil into flour mixture and knead for 10 minutes to form a soft, elastic dough. Cover with a damp cloth and allow to rise for 1 hour.

Meanwhile, saute onions in oil in a covered skillet over low heat until just tender but not brown. Add flour, stirring, and then water. Cook until thick. In electric blender, combine cottage cheese, salt and yogurt and process until smooth. Combine cottage cheese mixture and onion mixture. *Preheat oven to 400°F.*

Punch down dough and place on a buttered, floured baking sheet. Roll dough evenly over the pan to whatever thickness you prefer (usually ½ to ¼ inch). Spread onion and cheese mixture evenly over dough and bake in preheated oven for 30 minutes. Cut into squares. Serve warm or cold.

Yield: 8 4-inch squares

Parsley Pesto

1½ *lbs. canned chopped clams*
   or 1 cup pignolas
   or walnuts
12 *ounces (approximately)*
   parsley
3 *or 4 cloves garlic*
1 *cup water*
1 *cup olive oil*
¾ *teaspoon salt*
pinch of pepper
1½ *teaspoons rosemary*
3 *teaspoons basil*
1½ *teaspoons oregano*
1½ *teaspoons thyme*
¾ *cup grated Parmesan or*
   Romano cheese

Drain clams, if using them, and set aside. Add water to clam liquid to make 1 cup. If using walnuts, chop and set aside.

Wash parsley and remove stems. There should be approximately 3 cups densely packed leaves. Combine parsley and all ingredients (except clams or nuts and cheese) in electric blender. Process to a smooth puree. Combine with clams or nuts and cheese. Serve over boiled pasta, steamed vegetables or fish.

Yield: 6 servings

Baked Parsnips and Carrots

Preheat oven to 350°F.

Place parsnips, carrots and water in a casserole. Salt and pepper to taste. Cover with lid or aluminum foil and bake in preheated oven for 1 hour or until vegetables are tender but firm. Dot with butter before serving, if desired.

Yield: 4 servings

½ *lb. parsnips, peeled and halved lengthwise*
½ *lb. carrots, peeled and halved lengthwise*
½ *cup water*
salt, pepper to taste
butter (optional)

Glazed Parsnips

Steam parsnips in as little water as possible until they are tender but still firm and the water has cooked away. Add butter and saute them for 5 minutes or so, turning them so as to brown evenly. Season to taste, garnish with parsley and serve.

Yield: 4 to 6 servings

1 *bunch parsnips, peeled if necessary and cut into halves or quarters*
2 *to 4 tablespoons butter*
salt, pepper to taste
2 *tablespoons chopped parsley*

Parsnip Patties

Peel and dice parsnips and cook in salted water approximately 20 minutes or until tender. Mash thoroughly and add egg yolk. Form into patties, dip in egg white, then roll in crumbs and saute in oil and butter until crisp and golden brown.

Yield: 4 servings

4 *medium-size parsnips*
1 *teaspoon salt*
water to cover
1 *egg yolk*
1 *egg white, slightly beaten*
1 *cup soft whole wheat bread crumbs*
1 *tablespoon oil*
2 *tablespoons butter*

Emerald Dressing

1 *cup oil*
⅓ *cup vinegar*
¼ *cup chopped onion*
¼ *cup chopped parsley*
½ *cup chopped green pepper*
½ *teaspoon kelp powder*
   (optional)
½ *teaspoon salt*
1 *teaspoon dill*

Combine all ingredients in electric blender. Process for approximately 3 minutes. Use with seafood or green salads.

Yield: 1½ cups

Green and Red Pepper Casserole

3 *green peppers*
3 *red peppers (sweet, not hot)*
1½ *cups (approximately 4 ounces) sharp cheddar cheese, cut into cubes*
12 *ripe olives, chopped*
6 *eggs*
½ *teaspoon salt*
⅛ *teaspoon black pepper*
2 *cups milk*

Preheat oven to 300°F.

Remove seeds and stems from peppers and cut into ½-inch strips. Place in layers in a buttered casserole, alternating with layers of cheese and a few olives until all the peppers, cheese and olives are used. Beat eggs well, add salt and pepper, then milk. Mix thoroughly and pour over pepper-cheese mixture. Bake in preheated oven for approximately 1 hour, or until firm in center.

Yield: 6 to 8 servings

Cook potatoes in water to cover. Drain and reserve liquid for soup. Peel and cube potatoes.

Saute onion with spices in oil or butter. Add potatoes and salt to taste, mixing lightly. Just before serving, add yogurt and mix carefully so as not to break up the potatoes. Serve warm.

Yield: 4 servings

Curried Potatoes with Yogurt

6 *medium-size potatoes*
water to cover
1 *medium-size onion, chopped*
½ *teaspoon ground cumin*
½ *teaspoon celery salt*
½ *teaspoon turmeric*
½ *teaspoon ground coriander*
pinch of cayenne (optional)
3 *tablespoons oil or butter*
salt to taste
1 *cup yogurt*

Parboil unpeeled potatoes for approximately 5 minutes. Drain, cool partially, peel if necessary and cut into thin slices. Heat oil in a large skillet, add potatoes and onion and brown on both sides. Add olives and cook a few minutes more, then add seasonings. *Preheat oven to 325°F.*

Place potato mixture in a buttered, oblong baking dish. Cover with cheese. With the back of a spoon make six small indentations on the surface of the potatoes. Break an egg into each one. Pour cream over the eggs and potatoes. Bake 10 to 15 minutes or until eggs are set.

Yield: 6 servings

Eggs Moppioli

6 *medium-size potatoes*
¼ *cup oil*
1 *medium-size onion, thinly sliced*
1 *small can ripe olives, pitted and sliced (approximately ⅔ cup).*
salt, pepper to taste
pinch of nutmeg
pinch of paprika
½ *cup grated cheese (Gruyere, Emmentaler or cheddar)*
6 *eggs*
½ *cup light cream*

Kugelis

(Lithuanian potato pudding)

5 *large potatoes (old potatoes*
are best)
1 *medium-size onion*
1 *teaspoon salt*
⅛ *teaspoon pepper*
½ *cup hot milk*
2 *eggs, beaten*
2 *tablespoons melted butter*
yogurt or sour cream

Preheat oven to 400°F.

Peel and grate potatoes and onion. Add salt, pepper, milk, eggs and butter. Pour into a square buttered baking dish, to a depth of at least 2½ inches. Bake in preheated oven for 15 minutes, lower heat to 375°F. and bake 45 minutes longer. Cut into squares and serve hot topped with a dollop of yogurt or sour cream.

Yield: 4 to 6 servings

Baked Pumpkin Ring

2 *lbs. pumpkin*
1 *small onion, minced*
⅔ *cup minced celery*
3 *to 4 tablespoons oil*
1 *cup fresh whole grain*
bread crumbs
2 *eggs, beaten*
¼ *cup milk*
¼ *teaspoon allspice*
salt, pepper to taste

Remove seeds from pumpkin and cut into chunks. Steam in a little water until tender. Scoop pulp from rind; there should be approximately 2 cups. *Preheat oven to 350°F.*

Saute onion and celery in oil until tender. Stir in bread crumbs. Combine eggs, milk and 2 cups pumpkin pulp in electric blender. Process until smooth. Combine with sauteed mixture and add seasonings. Turn into well-oiled mold, set into a pan of water deep enough to reach halfway up the side, and bake in a preheated oven for 45 minutes or until pumpkin ring is set.

Remove from oven, run a knife around the outside and inside of the mold to loosen the pumpkin ring, dip mold briefly in cold water to help loosen bottom of mold and turn out onto warm platter. Serve filled with a steamed green vegetable.

Yield: 6 servings

Pumpkin Pudding

Preheat oven to 325°F.

In electric blender, combine eggs, molasses, milk, melted butter, nutmeg, salt and 1 cup diced pumpkin. Process until smooth. Remove cover while blender is running and slowly add remaining pumpkin. Pour mixture into a buttered baking dish. Add raisins and walnuts if desired. Bake in preheated oven for 1¼ hours or until set. Serve warm.

Yield: 6 servings

3 *eggs*
¾ *cup molasses*
½ *cup milk*
½ *cup melted butter*
½ *teaspoon nutmeg*
½ *teaspoon salt*
3½ *cups diced pumpkin*
½ *cup raisins*
½ *cup chopped walnuts*

Sauteed Pumpkin

Saute onion and pumpkin in butter and oil for 10 minutes, stirring occasionally. Add water, cover pan and steam for another 10 minutes, or until tender. Season to taste and serve.

Yield: 4 servings

1 *onion, minced*
1 *lb. pumpkin, peeled and sliced into pieces approximately 2 to 3 inches long and 1 inch wide*
2 *tablespoons butter*
2 *tablespoons oil*
½ *cup water*
salt, pepper to taste

Radish, Carrot and Apricot Relish

Combine vinegar, honey and salt, bring to boil and pour over remaining ingredients. Cover and let marinate in refrigerator for at least 30 minutes.

Yield: approximately 1 cup

¼ *cup vinegar*
1 *tablespoon honey*
⅛ *teaspoon salt*
⅔ *cup shredded radishes, red or white*
¼ *cup shredded carrot*
3 *dried apricots, cut in strips*

Red and White Radish Relish

1 *bunch white radishes,*
　peeled and grated
　(approximately 1 cup)
1 *bunch red radishes, grated*
　(approximately 1 cup)
½ *cup yogurt*
½ *teaspoon salt*
⅛ *teaspoon pepper*
1 *tablespoon sharp, prepared*
　mustard

Combine all ingredients and chill thoroughly before serving.

Yield:　2½ cups

Garden Soup

1 *bunch green onions*
　(approximately 6)
1¼ *lbs. frozen peas*
2 *cups chicken stock*
　salt, white pepper to taste
½ *large head romaine lettuce*
¼ *lb. fresh spinach, stems*
　removed and washed
2 *cups light cream*

Thinly slice green onions. Set aside one-third of them for garnish. Add the rest to frozen peas and bring to a boil in chicken stock which has been seasoned to taste. Turn heat down and simmer for approximately 10 minutes or until peas are nearly tender.

Add coarsely chopped romaine lettuce and spinach, reserving 8 or 10 leaves of spinach, thinly sliced for garnish. Simmer approximately 5 minutes, stirring to cook the greens evenly, until lettuce is tender, but the rib of the leaves still crunchy. Process mixture in electric blender to a smooth puree. Stir in cream. Refrigerate for several hours. Garnish with reserved sliced spinach and green onions.

Yield:　approximately 8 cups

Combine first five ingredients in a large salad bowl. Add spinach, celery and green onions and toss well. Refrigerate for 1¼ hours before serving.

Yield: 6 servings

Korean Spinach Salad

1 *tablespoon unhulled sesame seeds*
2 *tablespoons oil*
1 *tablespoon tamari soy sauce*
1 *clove garlic, minced*
pinch of cayenne
1 *lb. fresh spinach, washed, drained and coarsely chopped*
4 *stalks celery, sliced on the diagonal, ½ inch wide*
4 *green onions, including tops, thinly sliced*

Combine first four ingredients. Combine remaining ingredients. Just before serving, pour liquid mixture over salad, tossing lightly.

Yield: 6 servings

Spinach and Raw Mushroom Salad

8 *ounces washed and trimmed fresh spinach*
1 *cup ripe olives*
1 *cup broken walnut pieces*
2 *cups sliced fresh mushrooms*
½ *cup oil*
2 *tablespoons cider vinegar*
1 *tablespoon wine vinegar*
1 *clove garlic, minced*
1 *teaspoon dried basil*
salt, pepper to taste

Spinach Lasagna

2 *10-ounce packages frozen*
   spinach or 1 lb.
   fresh spinach
2 *cloves garlic, minced*
1 *tablespoon parsley*
1 *tablespoon basil*
1 *teaspoon oregano*
½ *cup wheat germ*
2 *8-ounce cans tomato sauce*
1 *6-ounce can tomato paste*
9 *whole wheat lasagna*
   noodles
1 *teaspoon oil*
1 *lb. ricotta cheese*
2 *teaspoons salt*
pinch of pepper
2 *tablespoons parsley*
½ *cup grated Parmesan cheese*
½ *lb. mozzarella cheese, sliced*
1 *8-ounce can tomato sauce*

Boil a small amount of water and add spinach. Cover and cook until done. Drain.

Place spinach in electric blender and add garlic, parsley, basil and oregano. Process carefully until mixed but not a liquid. In a bowl, combine wheat germ, tomato sauce and tomato paste and add spinach mixture. Stir to blend.

Cook lasagna noodles according to package directions. Add oil to cooking water so noodles won't stick together. Mix ricotta cheese, salt, pepper and parsley.

Preheat oven to 375°F. Butter the bottom of a 9x13-inch baking pan. Put in 3 lasagna noodles next to each other as a first layer. Then put in a layer of the spinach mixture, a layer of ricotta, shake a little Parmesan over the ricotta and then some slices of mozzarella. Start again with the noodles and keep doing this, ending with the spinach mixture. Cover with remaining cheese and a can of tomato sauce. Bake for 30 minutes in preheated oven.

Yield: 10 to 12 servings

Winter Squash Soup

1 *onion, chopped*
3 *tablespoons butter*
1 *tomato, peeled, seeded*
   and chopped
1 *to 2 teaspoons hot red pep-*
   per, seeded and chopped
   or cayenne to taste
1 *clove garlic, minced*
2 *lbs. winter squash, peeled,*
   seeded and cut
   into ½-inch cubes
   (approximately 4 cups)
4 *cups beef stock*
½ *teaspoon ground cumin*
½ *teaspoon ground coriander*
salt, pepper to taste
chopped parsley

In a large saucepan, saute onion in butter for a few minutes. Add tomato, pepper or cayenne and garlic and saute 5 minutes longer. Then add squash, stock and seasonings. Bring mixture to a boil and simmer, covered, for approximately 20 minutes or until squash is very tender. When ready to serve, garnish with parsley.

Yield: approximately 5 cups

Boil or steam sweet potatoes until they are tender. Peel and puree them. You should have approximately 2¼ cups. *Preheat oven to 350°F.*

Combine pureed sweet potatoes with mashed banana, melted butter, non-fat dry milk and spices. Combine beaten eggs, honey, molasses, water and vanilla and add to sweet potato mixture. Then add raisins.

Turn into buttered 9x5x3-inch loaf pan. Bake in preheated oven for 50 to 60 minutes or until a knife inserted at the center comes out clean.

Yield: 1 loaf

Banana Sweet Potato Cake

2 *lbs. sweet potatoes*
1 *banana, mashed*
¼ *cup melted butter*
½ *cup non-fat dry milk*
¼ *teaspoon nutmeg*
¼ *teaspoon cinnamon*
3 *eggs, beaten*
¼ *cup honey*
¼ *cup molasses*
½ *cup water*
½ *teaspoon vanilla*
¼ *cup raisins*

Make pie shell according to preferred recipe.

Cook potatoes in water to cover until tender. Peel and wash; there should be approximately 2 cups. *Preheat oven to 425°F.*

Mix together 2 cups potatoes, honey, eggs, milk and butter. Add spices, salt, lemon rind and lemon juice. Mix well and pour into unbaked pie shell. Bake in preheated oven for approximately 1 hour, or until the filling is set and lightly browned on top.

Yield: 6 servings

Sweet Potato Pie

1 *9-inch unbaked pie shell*
2 *lbs. sweet potatoes*
⅓ *cup honey*
2 *eggs, slightly beaten*
1½ *cups milk*
3 *tablespoons melted butter*
½ *teaspoon cinnamon*
½ *teaspoon ginger*
¼ *teaspoon nutmeg*
½ *teaspoon salt*
1 *tablespoon grated lemon rind*
1 *tablespoon lemon juice*

Sweet Potato Soup

4 *cups peeled, diced sweet*
    potatoes
4 *cups water*
½ *teaspoon salt*
1 *onion, thinly sliced*
1 *tablespoon oil*
1 *cup yogurt*
chopped parsley
grated orange rind

Cook sweet potatoes in water with salt added until tender. Saute onion in oil for a few minutes. In electric blender, combine onion and cooked sweet potatoes with cooking water. Process until smooth. Return to saucepan, add yogurt and heat but do not boil. Garnish with parsley and orange rind and serve.

Yield: approximately 4 cups

Braised Swiss Chard*

1 *lb. Swiss chard**
1 *medium-size onion, sliced*
1 *large apple, sliced*
2 *tablespoons oil*
½ *teaspoon salt*
⅛ *teaspoon pepper*
2 *to 3 tablespoons cider*
    vinegar (optional)

Chop Swiss chard into 1-inch pieces using the leaves and ribs. There should be approximately 10 cups. Saute onion and apple in oil for a few minutes. Add Swiss chard, salt and pepper and stir-fry slowly for 15 minutes or until ribs of chard are tender. If desired, add vinegar and cook 5 minutes longer.

Yield: 4 servings

**Beet tops or mustard greens may be substituted.*

Swiss Chard Loaf

1 *lb. fresh Swiss chard**
boiling water
salt to taste
2 *unbeaten eggs*
½ *cup milk*
2 *tablespoons butter*
1 *cup fresh whole grain*
    bread crumbs
¼ *teaspoon pepper*
¼ *teaspoon salt*
hard-cooked egg slices
    (for garnish)

Preheat oven to 375°F.

Chop Swiss chard using leaves and ribs into ½-inch pieces (approximately 10 cups) and cook, covered, in as little boiling water as possible, salting to taste, for 15 minutes or until ribs of chard are just tender. Drain. There should be 3 cups. Combine with remaining ingredients and turn into a buttered loaf pan. Set in a pan of hot water and bake in preheated oven for 25 minutes, or until firm. Remove from pan and garnish with hard-cooked egg slices.

Yield: 4 to 6 servings

**Spinach or beet greens may be substituted.*

Saute mushrooms in butter and oil for 5 minutes. Add flour and stir until flour is evenly distributed, then add chicken stock, salt and pepper, and milk. Cook slowly, stirring constantly, until mixture is slightly thickened. Add Swiss chard and simmer for 15 minutes.

Yield: approximately 4 cups

*Spinach or beet greens may be substituted.

Swiss Chard Soup*

¼ lb. fresh mushrooms, sliced (approximately 1½ cups)
1 tablespoon butter
1 tablespoon oil
2 tablespoons whole wheat flour
1½ cups chicken stock
   salt, pepper to taste
2 cups milk
4 to 5 cups fresh Swiss chard,* leaves and ribs (approximately ½ lb.)

Preheat oven to 400°F.

Cut out the tops of the tomatoes, then scoop out the easy-to-remove pulp. Saute onion in oil. Mix ½ cup of pulp with onion, bread crumbs and seasonings. Fill tomato shells approximately one-third full with crumb mixture. Break an egg into each tomato and cover with grated cheese. Place each tomato in a greased ramekin and bake in preheated oven for 12 to 15 minutes or until eggs are just set and tomatoes are soft but not collapsing. Be careful not to overcook the eggs. Serve immediately.

Yield: 4 servings

Baked Tomatoes and Eggs

4 large tomatoes
1 small onion, minced
1 tablespoon oil
½ cup dry whole grain bread crumbs
1 teaspoon basil
½ teaspoon fennel
   salt, pepper to taste
4 eggs (at room temperature)
½ cup grated cheddar cheese

Combine ingredients in electric blender and process until liquid.

Yield: approximately 3 cups

Tomato Dressing

2 medium-size tomatoes
½ green pepper
1 stalk celery
1 cup mayonnaise
1 teaspoon dry mustard

Green Tomato and Apple Mince Pie

1½ recipe Whole Wheat Flaky
     Pastry (see Index) or
     Oat and Rice Flaky
     Pastry (see Index)
  3 cups chopped green tomatoes
     (1 lb. before
     preparation)
  3 cups tart apples, peeled and
     chopped (1 lb. before
     preparation)
  ¼ cup raisins
  ¼ cup currants
  ½ cup honey
  ¼ cup vinegar
  ¼ cup water
  ½ teaspoon salt
  ½ teaspoon cloves
  1 teaspoon cinnamon
  ¾ teaspoon nutmeg
  ¼ cup brandy (optional)

Using either of the suggested recipes, make a 9-inch pie shell but do not bake it. Reserve remaining pastry for lattice top.

Combine all ingredients, except brandy. Simmer over low heat for 20 minutes. Add brandy at the end if using it. *Preheat oven to 400°F.*

Pour green tomato and apple mixture into unbaked 9-inch pie shell.

Basic Method for Making Lattice Top

Roll out remaining pastry into an oblong. Cut into strips ½ inch wide. Lay strips across the filling, parallel to each other approximately an inch apart. Turn pie slightly and instead of laying the top layer of strips perpendicular (or at right angles) to the bottom layer of strips, lay them diagonally, or on a slant. This gives the impression that the strips are woven, without actually doing so. Lay a strip of pastry all around the rim of the pan, covering the ends of the strips. Pinch this to make an attractive edge all around the pie.

Bake in preheated oven for 30 minutes. Serve warm.

Yield: 1 9-inch pie

Combine sliced green tomatoes and onions. Sprinkle with salt. Let mixture stand for 12 hours. Pour fresh water over mixture and drain. Heat vinegar to boiling point, and add green and red peppers, garlic, honey, dry mustard and ginger. Then add tomato-onion mixture. Tie the whole spices in a square of cheesecloth and drop into the mixture. Simmer for approximately 1 hour, or until tomatoes are transparent, stirring frequently. Remove spice bag. Pour into hot jars, leaving ¼-inch headspace. Adjust caps. Process quarts 15 minutes in boiling-water bath.

Yield: approximately 3 quarts

Green Tomato Pickle

4 *quarts sliced green tomatoes*
6 *large onions, sliced*
½ *cup salt*
6 *cups vinegar*
6 *green peppers, sliced*
3 *sweet red peppers, diced*
6 *cloves garlic, minced*
2¼ *cups honey*
1 *tablespoon dry mustard*
1 *tablespoon ginger*
1 *tablespoon whole cloves*
1 *stick cinnamon*
½ *tablespoon celery seed*

Preheat oven to 400°F.

Make pie shell according to preferred recipe. Bake shell in preheated oven for 8 minutes.

Meanwhile, saute onion in butter until soft, but not brown. Put 1½ cups cheese in pie shell, topped with sauteed onion. Sprinkle tomato slices with flour and basil and saute them for 2 minutes—1 minute on each side. Arrange them on top of onion and cheese. Combine eggs and half-and-half and pour over tomatoes. Salt and pepper to taste. Sprinkle remaining ½ cup cheese over top of quiche.

Bake for 10 minutes in preheated oven, then turn heat to 350°F. and bake 15 to 20 minutes longer or until set.

Yield: 4 to 6 servings

Tomato Quiche

1 *9-inch unbaked pie shell*
1 *large onion, sliced*
4 *tablespoons butter*
2 *cups grated cheese*
   (4 ounces—half Swiss
   and half cheddar)
2 *large tomatoes, skinned,*
   sliced ½ inch thick
   and drained
2 *tablespoons whole wheat*
   flour
2 *teaspoons basil*
3 *eggs, beaten*
½ *cup half-and-half*
salt, pepper to taste

Tomato Sauce

4 *green onions, thinly sliced*
1 *clove garlic, minced*
1 *tablespoon oil*
2 *tablespoons tomato paste*
1 *cup tomato juice*
1 *cup meat or vegetable stock*
½ *teaspoon fennel*
½ *teaspoon oregano*
¼ *teaspoon salt*
2 *tablespoons cornstarch*
4 *tablespoons cold water*

Saute green onions and garlic in oil for a minute or two. Add tomato paste and blend in. Stir in tomato juice and stock. Season with herbs and salt. Dissolve cornstarch in cold water and stir into boiling liquid, stirring constantly. Cook until thickened.

Yield: approximately 2½ cups

Glazed Turnips

12 *ounces small white turnips,*
peeled if necessary
(approximately
1½ cups)
½ *teaspoon salt*
water (about 1 inch in
bottom of saucepan)
2 *tablespoons apple juice*
1 *tablespoon butter*

Boil turnips in salted water until they are tender and water has boiled off. Add apple juice and continue boiling (uncovered) until juice has been absorbed. Add butter and shake pot constantly, turning the turnips until all are coated and shiny golden brown.

Yield: 4 servings

Grated Turnip and Potato Salad

2 *medium-size potatoes*
water to cover
3 *cups grated turnips*
1½ *teaspoons caraway seeds*
3 *tablespoons vinegar*
3 *tablespoons yogurt*
salt, pepper to taste

Cook potatoes in water to cover until tender. Drain and reserve liquid for soup. Peel and grate potatoes and combine with remaining ingredients. Toss together lightly. Chill and serve.

Yield: 6 servings

Slice beef very thin, across the grain. Peel turnips, if necessary, slice thin, and cut slices into ½-inch strips. Slice onions thin. Mix cornstarch and water.

Heat oil in *wok* or heavy skillet which has a lid. Stir-fry beef, uncovered, until nearly tender. Add turnips and continue stirring for 2 minutes, then add onions and stir for 1 minute longer. Add salt and pepper, cover and simmer for 5 minutes. Stir in cornstarch mixture, cook a few minutes and serve.

Yield: 4 servings

Stir-Fried Turnips with Beef

1 *lb. lean chuck*
6 *medium-size turnips (approximately 12 ounces)*
2 *green onions, including tops*
2 *tablespoons cornstarch*
2 *tablespoons water*
2 *tablespoons oil*
½ *teaspoon salt*
⅛ *teaspoon pepper*

Peel turnips if necessary and cut into ½-inch cubes. Cook in salted water until tender. Drain, reserving liquid. Using the same saucepan, cook peas in turnip liquid until tender. Drain, reserving liquid. Butter a casserole and add turnips and peas. *Preheat oven to 350°F.*

In a small pan, heat butter or oil, add flour and stir until smooth. Stir in 1 cup reserved vegetable stock or water. Cook until thick, then pour over vegetables in casserole. Mix grated cheese and crumbs and sprinkle evenly over mixture in casserole. Bake in preheated oven for 45 minutes.

Yield: 4 to 6 servings

Turnips and Peas au Gratin

6 *medium-size turnips (approximately 12 ounces)*
½ *teaspoon salt*
water to cover
2 *cups fresh peas or 1 10-ounce package frozen*
2 *tablespoons butter or oil*
1 *tablespoon whole wheat flour*
1 *cup vegetable stock or water*
1 *cup grated cheddar cheese*
½ *cup whole wheat bread crumbs*

Avocado Watercress Salad with Tamari Dressing

2 *cloves garlic, minced*
4 *tablespoons oil*
4 *teaspoons unhulled sesame seeds*
4 *tablespoons tamari soy sauce*
3 *tablespoons lemon juice*
¼ *bunch watercress (or enough for 4 plates)*
1 *ripe avocado*

Saute minced garlic in oil over low heat for approximately 2 minutes, stirring constantly. Add sesame seeds and continue to saute for 1 minute longer, taking care that they don't burn. Remove from heat and add soy sauce and lemon juice.

Wash watercress and make a bed of it on four individual salad plates. Peel, remove pit and slice avocado. Arrange on watercress and top with dressing.

Yield: 4 servings

Stir-Fried Beef and Watercress

2 *tablespoons tamari soy sauce*
2 *tablespoons sherry*
1 *teaspoon honey*
1 *lb. lean, ground beef*
2 *bunches watercress*
4 *green onions, including tops*
1 *tablespoon cornstarch*
2 *tablespoons water*
2 *tablespoons oil*
1½ *tablespoons oil*
½ *teaspoon salt*
½ *cup beef stock*

In large bowl, combine soy sauce, sherry and honey. Blend well. Stir soy sauce mixture into ground beef with a fork. Marinate for 30 minutes, stirring occasionally.

Cut off thick stems of the watercress and save them to use at a later date. Wash watercress sprigs well. Drain thoroughly and pat dry gently with paper towels. Slice green onions, including tops. In a small bowl, mix cornstarch and water.

In a *wok* or large, heavy frying pan, heat 2 tablespoons oil. Add ground beef mixture and stir-fry until the redness is nearly gone. Use a large fork to break up lumps as the beef is cooking. Remove beef from pan with a slotted spoon and discard remaining fat. Wipe the pan dry. In the same pan, heat 1½ tablespoons oil. Stir-fry watercress until just wilted. Add salt and mix well. Return beef to pan, add green onions and stir-fry just to heat. Pour in stock and heat to boiling. Stir cornstarch mixture thoroughly and add to beef. Continue to stir until sauce thickens. Serve immediately.

Yield: 4 servings

Add ingredients to electric blender in order given. Process until dressing is smooth, then refrigerate until ready to use.

Yield: 1½ cups

Watercress Dressing

1 *cup mayonnaise (homemade)*
½ *cup yogurt*
1 *medium-size onion, chopped*
1 *tablespoon cider vinegar*
1 *tablespoon lemon juice*
1 *clove garlic*
1 *cup watercress leaves*
½ *teaspoon salt*
⅛ *teaspoon pepper*

Using a large, heavy-bottom saucepan or skillet, saute onion, green pepper and then zucchini in butter for a few minutes, stirring to coat vegetables with butter. Add water, cover pan and simmer for 5 minutes. Add tomato and corn and cook another 5 minutes or until vegetables are done. Season to taste and serve.

Yield: 4 to 6 servings

Zucchini, Corn and Tomato Saute

1 *small onion, chopped*
1 *green pepper, seeded and cut into strips*
3 *medium-size zucchini, sliced ¼ inch thick*
2 *tablespoons butter*
½ *cup water*
1 *large tomato, peeled and cubed*
freshly cut corn from 3 or 4 ears
salt, pepper to taste

Preheat oven to 350°F.

Place zucchini in buttered casserole. Sprinkle with salt, pepper, dill and cayenne. Pour yogurt over zucchini and sprinkle with cheese. Cover casserole and bake in preheated oven for 30 minutes. Uncover and bake until zucchini is tender and lightly browned.

Yield: 4 to 6 servings

Zucchini in Yogurt Sauce

3 *medium-size zucchini, cut into ¼-inch slices*
salt, pepper to taste
1 *tablespoon dill*
cayenne to taste
¾ *cup yogurt*
¼ *cup Parmesan cheese*

Zucchini Dollar Cakes

½ lb. zucchini (approximately
   1½ cups)
3 egg yolks
½ cup cottage cheese
1 clove garlic, minced
3 tablespoons whole wheat or
   rye flour
½ teaspoon salt
⅛ teaspoon pepper
⅛ teaspoon marjoram
3 egg whites
butter

Grate zucchini, using small holes in grater. Add to egg yolks, along with rest of ingredients except egg whites and butter. Mix well. Beat egg whites stiff and fold gently into zucchini mixture. Melt butter in a skillet and drop batter by tablespoons into it. Turn each cake when the surface is a bit dry and looks "set." Saute until they are golden brown on both sides. Serve immediately.

Yield: 4 to 6 servings

Zucchini Frittata

1 small onion, minced
2 cups sliced zucchini
2 tablespoons butter
1 tablespoon oil
6 eggs, beaten
salt, freshly ground black
   pepper to taste
1 teaspoon fennel
1 tablespoon chopped parsley
2 tablespoons grated Swiss
   cheese

Using a 10-inch skillet, saute onion and zucchini in butter and oil until tender and evenly browned. Combine eggs, seasonings, fennel and parsley and pour into skillet over sauteed onion and zucchini. Cook over medium heat, without stirring, until bottom of mixture is set but top is still soft. Sprinkle cheese on top and place under broiler to melt cheese and brown top. Cut into portions and serve.

Yield: 3 servings

Zucchini, Pepper and Tomato Relish

2 small zucchini, grated
2 green peppers, diced
2 tomatoes, diced
2 green onions, thinly sliced
½ cup oil
3 tablespoons wine vinegar
½ teaspoon tarragon
½ teaspoon marjoram

Combine vegetables. Combine oil, vinegar and seasonings and pour over vegetables, tossing lightly. Serve on a bed of salad greens.

Yield: 4 servings

Fruits, the

Infinite Variety Treat

One of the greatest things about fruit is its infinite variety. Consider the wide swing between a blueberry and a watermelon, or between dates and a grapefruit. Even the fussiest eaters can find a few fruits that please them.

Fruits add carbohydrates, vitamins and minerals to our diet. Some also have a trace of fat and some protein. Their caloric value is somewhat higher than that of vegetables, because they usually contain more sugar. Fruits also contain a high percentage of cellulose which furnishes some of the bulk we need for digestion.

Even within the same variety, the vitamin content of fruits can vary. Pink grapefruit, for instance, has a higher vitamin A content than the white.

The difference in vitamin C content of melon varieties is quite remarkable. Cantaloupes are richest. The concentration of the vitamin is in the soft flesh toward the center. Honeydew melons have less vitamin C and watermelons almost none.

Berries are good vitamin sources, especially the strawberry. If you use strawberries wash them before you hull them, otherwise they lose much of their vitamin C during the washing process. In many European countries strawberries eaten for dessert are not hulled at all. They are carefully washed and dried so as not to bruise them, brought to the table on a bed of green leaves in a pretty bowl, and people just eat them out of hand.

Avocado for Weight Control

The avocado contains more fat (mostly unsaturated) than any other fruit except the olive, and that fat is the type which helps to control cholesterol and stabilize weight. The avocado we find in food stores usually comes from Florida (smooth skinned, often dotted with yellow) or California (called "alligator pear" because of its rough skin). It's best to buy avocado when it is firm and then leave it at room temperature to ripen from five to seven days. It is ready to eat when uniformly soft but not spongy.

215

Don't try to solve the riddle of whether a tomato is a fruit or a vegetable. Use it as both. A dish of tomato slices, with a few drops of lemon juice and some honey, is as refreshing as a dish of strawberries.

Fruit juices are great thirst quenchers, but they can't compete with the nutritional value of the whole fruit. When you have a choice, take the whole prune, or the entire orange, not the juice, to get optimal benefits.

Some Fruits Go Well with Meats

Apples, pears, prunes, cherries, and grapes are some of the fruits which go well in meat dishes. White grapes added to chicken gravy, prunes and apples with pork or beef are delicious combinations. *Himmel und Erde*, an appetizing mixture of potatoes and apples, with some onions thrown in if you like, is a good accompaniment for any pork dish, from sausage to chops. Prunes combine beautifully with lentils and other legumes. Many kinds of fruit (white grapes and lemons, for example) enhance the taste of stewed or baked fish.

Himmel und Erde
(mashed potatoes with apples)

8 *medium-size potatoes, cubed (approximately 4 cups)*	2 *tablespoons butter*
	salt to taste
4 *medium-size tart apples, cubed (approximately 3 cups)*	¼ *cup dry whole grain bread crumbs*
	2 *tablespoons melted butter*

Cook potatoes and apples separately until tender. Mash potatoes and add butter to them. Salt to taste. Add cooked apples tossing together lightly. Combine crumbs and butter and sprinkle over potato-apple mixture at serving time.

Yield: 6 servings

And there are all those delicious fruit soups that have been introduced to this country by our ancestors who came from Europe, particularly the Scandinavian countries. They are easy to prepare and provide a refreshing change.

Strawberry Soup

3 *pints (approximately) fresh* *strawberries or* 1½ *packages frozen* *strawberries (30 ounces)*	2½ *tablespoons cornstarch* ½ *cup orange juice, fresh* *or frozen*
3 *tablespoons honey*	2 *tablespoons honey* ½ *cup sour cream or yogurt*

Wash and slice enough fresh strawberries to make 3¾ cups. Add honey and stir well to coat the berries evenly. Set aside for an hour or so. If using frozen strawberries, slice them, drizzle honey over them, stir well and thaw completely.

Drain berries. You should have approximately 1½ cups strawberry juice and 2¼ cups berries. Put juice into electric blender and add half of the berries, processing to make a very liquid puree. Heat puree to the boiling point.

Dissolve cornstarch in orange juice and stir into boiling strawberry puree. Cook a minute or two, until mixture is clear and thickened. Cool slightly, add honey, and remaining strawberries. Chill completely and serve with a dollop of sour cream or yogurt on top of each bowl. Or, if desired, add sour cream or yogurt to the soup, stirring a little of the soup into the sour cream or yogurt first, to thin it and then stirring it into the rest of the soup. Chill completely before serving.

Yield: 4 to 6 servings

If you stew fruit, try to avoid using an aluminum or cast-iron container because the tannins and other organic compounds which are part of the fruit and add to their color, might change. The taste might also be affected.

Some fruits turn dark when peeled or cut. This can be avoided by sprinkling lemon juice on the fruit as soon as it is cut.

Most fruits keep best in the refrigerator because the cold slows the enzyme activity, thus retarding spoilage. Exceptions are the banana and avocado, which should be allowed to ripen in a cool, not cold place. However, once ripe, a banana will hold for several days in the refrigerator. The skin will turn brown, but the flesh will remain firm.

Dried fruits rival any candy for taste and sweetness. They also provide more carbohydrates and minerals than you get from the fresh fruit. Through the loss of water during the drying process, the vitamin content diminishes some, but the fruit flavor increases. When buying dried fruit try to avoid the kind that has been sulfured to preserve the color. It's just another additive you don't need.

Like most vegetables, fruit is better for you when it's fresh and uncooked. If you do cook fruit for any reason, be careful not to sweeten it unnecessarily. Rhubarb, for instance, gets much sweeter when baked than when boiled. Just drizzle a little honey on top and bake it in a low oven (about 200°F.) for half an hour to an hour.

When you peel citrus fruits for fruit salad or other purposes, leave as much of the white membrane on the fruit as possible. It is a good source of the bioflavonoids, an important companion to vitamin C.

Make fruit a habit and experiment with those you've never tried before, like guava, kiwi fruit, persimmon or pomegranate. Depending on where you live and the season, some of them might be expensive, but think of what you pay for a dish of ice cream or a slice of pie for dessert in a restaurant. Here is a treat that's a new experience and it's so much better for you!

Try unusual fruit combinations for a welcome surprise. Also, combine fruits and vegetables for marvelous salads or desserts.

Apfelkuchen Souffle

2½ *cups sliced tart apples*
 2 *tablespoons butter*
¼ *cup yogurt*
 4 *egg yolks*
 2 *tablespoons whole wheat flour*
½ *teaspoon lemon rind*
 2 *tablespoons lemon juice*
¼ *cup honey*
¼ *cup sliced almonds*
 4 *egg whites*
⅛ *teaspoon salt*
¼ *teaspoon cinnamon*
 2 *tablespoons wheat germ*
¼ *cup sliced almonds*
whipped cream

Saute apples in butter just until tender.

Combine yogurt and egg yolks. Add whole wheat flour, then lemon rind and juice and honey. Add this mixture to the apples and cook over low heat until thickened, stirring constantly. Add almonds. *Preheat oven to 325°F.*

Beat egg whites and salt together until stiff. Fold into apple mixture. Turn souffle into buttered cake pan or shallow casserole dish. Sprinkle top with cinnamon, wheat germ and almonds. Bake in preheated oven for 35 to 40 minutes or until egg white is set. Serve warm or cold, with whipped cream.

Yield: 6 to 8 servings

In a saucepan, bring apricots to a boil in water to cover and simmer until soft. Add apples, cover pan and simmer until apples are soft. Add lime or lemon slices, garlic and spices. Continue to cook for a minute or two. Add cashew nuts and cool. Serve at room temperature.

Yield: approximately 2 cups

Apple and Apricot Chutney

½ *cup dried apricots*
   water to cover
 2 *tart apples, chopped*
 1 *lime or ½ lemon, seeded*
      and thinly sliced,
      including rind
 1 *clove garlic, minced*
½ *teaspoon ginger*
 4 *whole cloves*
½ *teaspoon coriander*
   chili powder to taste
½ *cup cashew nuts*

If using cracker or bread crumbs, you may want to add wheat germ, sesame seeds or ground almonds. There should be 4 cups of crumbs including any additions. In heavy skillet, saute crumbs lightly in butter and oil, stirring constantly. Add honey and cinnamon to crumbs, stirring to blend, then remove from heat. If using cookie or cake crumbs, use less butter, oil and honey.

In a glass serving bowl, make a thin layer (½-inch) of crumbs, then a little thicker layer of applesauce, then another thin layer of crumbs and so on, alternating until both have been used up. End with a layer of crumbs on top.

Whip heavy cream and spread over entire surface. Decorate with small spoonfuls of currant jelly or raspberry jam. Chill for several hours before serving.

Yield: 6 to 8 servings

Danish Apple Cake

 4 *cups whole grain dried*
      crumbs (cookie, cake,
      cracker or bread)
   wheat germ, unhulled
      sesame seeds or ground
      almonds (optional)
 2 *to 4 tablespoons butter*
 1 *to 2 tablespoons oil*
 3 *to 4 tablespoons honey*
1½ *teaspoons cinnamon*
 4 *cups applesauce, seasoned*
      to taste
½ *cup heavy cream*
 2 *to 3 tablespoons currant*
      jelly or raspberry jam

Apple Strudel Slices

Pastry

2 cups whole wheat flour
½ teaspoon salt
⅔ cup butter
4 tablespoons ice water
¼ cup melted butter

Filling

3 cups chopped tart
　　cooking apples
½ cup raisins
½ cup chopped walnuts
2 to 3 tablespoons honey
　　(depending on tartness
　　of apples)
cinnamon to taste

Syrup

1 cup honey
2 cups water
½ teaspoon cinnamon
¼ cup butter

Make Pastry

Combine flour and salt. Grate in butter and work lightly with your fingertips until it is evenly distributed, as in pie crust. Add ice water while tossing dough lightly with a fork. Knead briefly to incorporate water. Roll out dough ¼ inch thick into an oblong shape. Brush the dough with melted butter.

Make Filling

Spread chopped apples, raisins and nuts evenly over dough, leaving an inch wide margin along all four sides. Drizzle honey and sprinkle cinnamon over the fruit.

Assemble

Carefully roll up pastry, starting with the long side, as you would a jelly roll. Cut slices 1¼ inches wide and lay slices flat in a buttered, shallow ovenproof dish. *Preheat oven to 375°F.*

Make Syrup

Combine honey, water and cinnamon. Boil for 10 minutes. Add butter and stir to melt. Pour syrup over strudel slices and bake in preheated oven for 30 minutes or until pastry is brown and apples are tender.

Yield:　6 to 8 servings

Applesauce

(unsweetened)

3 medium-size apples
　　(approximately 1 lb.)
⅓ to ⅔ cup unsweetened apple
　　juice (depending on
　　juiciness of apples)
½ teaspoon cinnamon

Wash and peel apples and remove core. Place in saucepan. Add juice to the apples. Cover pan tightly and simmer for 5 to 10 minutes or until apples are tender. Add cinnamon. Cool and serve.

Yield:　approximately 2 cups

Combine yogurt, lemon juice and honey, mixing well to blend. Shred apples right into yogurt mixture, stirring after each addition, to keep apples from discoloring. Stir in nuts and serve immediately.

Yield: 4 servings

Raw Apple and Black Walnut Cream

1 *cup yogurt*
1 *tablespoon lemon juice*
1½ *tablespoons honey*
4 *medium-size tart eating apples, peeled and cored*
1 *cup chopped black walnuts*

Prepare pie shell according to preferred recipe.

Place apricots and prunes in saucepan with just enough water to cover them. Bring to a boil, cover, lower heat and simmer for approximately 10 minutes. Set aside to cool slightly. *Preheat oven to 375°F.* Combine apple slices, honey, cinnamon and lemon juice. Mix thoroughly.

Arrange fruit in pie shell, alternating apricot, prune and apple until shell is filled. Pour over the top any juice remaining from apricot-prune mixture and apple mixture. Bake in preheated oven for approximately 45 minutes or until apples are tender.

Yield: 1 9-inch pie

Apricot Prune Apple Tart

1 *9-inch unbaked pie shell*
1 *cup dried apricots*
1 *cup dried prunes, pitted and halved*
water to cover
1 *cup apple slices (approximately ¼ inch thick)*
2 *tablespoons honey*
½ *teaspoon cinnamon*
1 *teaspoon lemon juice*

Combine all ingredients in a small saucepan and cook slowly for approximately 20 minutes. Cool, then puree in electric blender. Serve hot or cold.

Can be used as an alternate to cognac in Crepes Suzette recipe or as a topping for ice cream or puddings.

Yield: approximately 1 cup

Apricot Sauce

½ *cup dried apricots*
2 *slices lemon, including rind*
1 *cup hot water*
¼ *cup honey*

Apricot Soup

4 *cups pitted fresh apricots or*
1 1¼-lb. package
frozen unsweetened
apricots
2 *cups water*
6 *tablespoons honey*
¼ *cup cornstarch*
¼ *cup water*
½ *teaspoon almond extract*
(optional)

Combine apricots and water in a saucepan and bring to a boil. Turn heat down and simmer for 5 minutes or until apricots are tender but still firm. Lift out about 1 cup apricots and set aside. Puree remaining apricots and water in electric blender. Return puree to saucepan and heat. Add honey. Dissolve cornstarch in water and stir into puree when it is boiling. Continue to cook, stirring, for approximately 1 minute, until soup is thickened and clear. Remove from heat, add almond extract, if desired, and cool. Cut reserved apricots into quarters and add to soup. Chill completely before serving.

Yield: 4 servings

Avocado Banana Dressing

2 *ripe avocados*
1 *ripe banana*
1 *tablespoon lemon juice*
¼ *cup wheat germ*
¼ *cup chopped sunflower seeds*

Peel and pit the avocados. Mash with a fork until smooth. Add banana and mash with the avocado. Add lemon juice, wheat germ and sunflower seeds. Mix until well combined.

Serve as a spread or a dressing for fruit or vegetable salad.

Yield: 1½ cups

Avocado Grapefruit Soup*

¾ *cup grapefruit juice,*
fresh or frozen
1 *avocado*
¼ *teaspoon salt*
¾ *cup yogurt or sour cream*
(half yogurt and half
sour cream may be
substituted)
½ *cup grapefruit segments*
(optional)

Put grapefruit juice into electric blender. Peel and pit avocado. Dice ½ cup of pulp and set aside. Put remaining avocado into blender with juice, add salt and process until smooth. Add yogurt or sour cream and blend briefly.

Add reserved diced avocado and grapefruit segments, if desired, and chill thoroughly before serving.

Yield: 4 to 6 servings

*This soup is best made and served on the same day because avocado, as it is in contact with the air, tends to turn an unappetizing gray color.

Arrange a bed of salad greens topped with slices of avocado, then oranges and finally onions on six individual salad plates.

Combine remaining ingredients and just before serving, pour dressing over salads.

Yield: 6 servings

Avocado, Orange and Onion Salad with Molasses Dressing

salad greens for 6 plates
1 *avocado, peeled and sliced*
3 *medium-size oranges, peeled, seeded and sliced*
1 *medium-size onion, peeled and very thinly sliced*
⅓ *cup oil*
¼ *cup lime juice*
4 *teaspoons molasses*
¼ *teaspoon white pepper*
½ *teaspoon dry mustard*
½ *teaspoon salt*
4 *teaspoons unhulled sesame seeds*

Peel and pit avocados, carefully dicing ¾ cup to add later. Sprinkle lemon juice over the ¾ cup to keep it from discoloring.

Heat chicken stock to boiling and then cool slightly. Chop remaining avocado coarsely and put into electric blender along with chicken stock. Process to a smooth puree. Add onion juice, salt and white pepper if desired.

Combine yogurt, mayonnaise and, if using it, heavy cream, stirring carefully to make a smooth paste. Add to avocado puree, along with reserved ¾ cup diced avocado, and refrigerate for several hours. Serve very cold, garnished with finely diced fresh tomato and chopped parsley.

Yield: approximately 8½ cups

Creamy Avocado Soup

2 *medium-size avocados, fully ripe*
1 *tablespoon lemon juice*
5 *cups chicken stock*
juice from ½ small onion, grated
¼ *teaspoon salt*
white pepper to taste
1 *cup yogurt*
1 *tablespoon mayonnaise*
1 *cup heavy cream (1 more cup yogurt may be substituted)*
1 *tomato, seeded and finely diced*
chopped parsley

NOTE: This soup should be used within 2 days after it is made, as it tends to darken slightly during storage in the refrigerator.

Avocado Spread

1 *ripe avocado, mashed*
½ *clove garlic, minced*
½ *teaspoon chili powder*
½ *teaspoon prepared mustard*
½ *teaspoon lemon juice*
2 *tablespoons chopped onion*
½ *teaspoon salt*

Combine all ingredients, mix well and serve as a spread or dip.

Yield: approximately 1 cup

Jellied Avocado and Cheese Ring

1½ *envelopes unflavored*
    gelatin
½ *cup cold water*
2 *teaspoons lemon juice*
2 *teaspoons vinegar*
4 *teaspoons oil*
1 *tablespoon honey*
6 *tablespoons cottage cheese*
1 *cup yogurt*
2 *tablespoons mayonnaise*
1 *avocado*
1½ *sweet red peppers or 2*
    canned pimientos,
    diced
4 *tablespoons diced sweet*
    pickle
4 *tablespoons chopped pecans*
1 *teaspoon grated onion*
1 *orange, peeled and*
    segmented
1 *grapefruit, peeled and*
    segmented

In small saucepan, soften gelatin in cold water. Dissolve by slowly heating while stirring constantly. Set aside.

Put lemon juice, vinegar, oil and honey into electric blender. Add cottage cheese and process until smooth. Add yogurt and mayonnaise. Blend to combine. Add dissolved gelatin and blend to mix. Pour into mixing bowl.

Cut avocado in half, but do not peel. Reserve half for garnish. Peel and dice the other half. Add this with red pepper, pickle, pecans and onion to gelatin mixture. Mix well and pour into oiled 1-quart ring mold. Chill in refrigerator until firm.

Unmold salad just before serving and fill center of ring and surround it with segments of orange and grapefruit and slices of avocado on a bed of salad greens.

Yield: 4 to 6 servings

Peel, remove pits and mash avocados. Add next five ingredients, combining well.

Make tomato flowers: Cut stem center out; cut across tomato 3 ways, to make 6 sections, but leave them attached at bottom. Pull sections apart and fill with curried avocado. Serve on a bed of salad greens.

Yield: 6 servings

Tomatoes Filled with Curried Avocado

3 *ripe avocados*
1 *tablespoon grated onion*
2 *tablespoons lemon juice*
¾ *teaspoon salt*
½ *teaspoon curry powder*
⅛ *teaspoon chili powder*
6 *tomatoes*

Preheat oven to 375°F.

Combine whole wheat flour, non-fat dry milk and salt. Combine beaten egg yolks, oil, honey and water. Stir wet ingredients into dry, to make a smooth batter. Beat egg whites until stiff. Fold them into batter.

Put oil into iron skillet or shallow baking dish and coat bottom and sides evenly. Pour half of batter into it. Slice bananas over batter, drizzle honey over them and sprinkle with nutmeg or cinnamon. Pour the remaining half of batter on top.

Bake in preheated oven for 15 minutes. Then turn oven to 325°F. and continue to bake for 20 minutes more. Serve immediately with whipped cream, if desired.

Yield: 6 to 8 servings

Baked Banana Pancake

1 *cup whole wheat flour*
½ *cup non-fat dry milk*
½ *teaspoon salt*
3 *egg yolks, beaten*
1 *tablespoon oil*
2 *teaspoons honey*
1½ *cups water*
3 *egg whites*
1 *tablespoon oil*
3 *bananas*
2 *tablespoons honey*
nutmeg or cinnamon to taste
whipped cream (optional)

Process cashews and water in electric blender. Add other ingredients and blend until bananas are liquefied. Chill and serve.

Yield: 3 cups

Banana Cashew Shake

½ *cup raw cashew nuts*
1½ *cups water*
3 *ripe bananas*
⅛ *teaspoon lemon juice*

Banana Cookies

¾ *cup sunflower seeds*
¼ *cup oats*
1 *banana*
1 *egg*
1 *tablespoon oil*
2 *tablespoons honey*

Preheat oven to 350°F.

Grind sunflower seeds and oats to a meal in electric blender. Mash banana with a fork. Mix together all ingredients and drop by rounded teaspoons onto an oiled baking sheet. Bake in preheated oven 15 to 20 minutes, until lightly browned on the bottom. Cool on a wire rack.

Yield: approximately 20 cookies

Caribbean Banana Soup

½ *cup brown rice*
6 *ripe bananas*
    (approximately 1½
    cups), coarsely mashed
4 *cups beef stock*
½ *cup minced onion*
¼ *cup diced green pepper*
2 *cloves garlic, minced*
2 *tablespoons oil*
¼ *cup freshly grated or dried*
    unsweetened coconut
¼ *cup ground peanuts*
salt, cayenne pepper to taste

Cook brown rice according to preferred method. (See "Cooking with Cereal Grains.")

Combine bananas and beef stock in saucepan and simmer for 10 minutes, stirring occasionally.

Saute onion, green pepper and garlic in oil for a few minutes. Add coconut and saute until it is golden brown, stirring constantly. Add sauteed mixture to banana soup, then the ground peanuts and cooked rice. Season with salt and cayenne pepper to taste. Simmer, covered, for approximately 15 minutes. Serve hot.

Yield: 6 to 8 servings

Blackberry and Cantaloupe Salad with Cottage Cheese

salad greens for 6 plates
3 *cups blackberries, washed*
1 *small cantaloupe, peeled,*
    seeded and sliced
3 *peaches, peeled and halved*
2 *cups cottage cheese*
Lime Honey Dressing
    (see Index)

Make a bed of crisp salad greens on six individual salad plates. Arrange blackberries, slices of cantaloupe, and peach halves on salad greens. Top with cottage cheese and serve Lime Honey Dressing with it.

Yield: 6 servings

Reserve 1 cup blackberries. Combine remaining berries with water, lemon and honey. Simmer for 5 minutes, mashing berries to extract all the juice. Strain, pressing the pulp to remove juice. There should be approximately 3 cups of juice.

Reheat juice, dissolve cornstarch in water and stir into boiling juices. Turn down heat and cook until thickened. Cool. Add reserved berries and spices. Chill completely and serve with a dollop of sour cream or yogurt.

Yield: 4 cups

Blackberry Soup

1 *quart blackberries or*
  1 1¼-lb. frozen
  unsweetened
  blackberries
2 *cups water*
4 *slices lemon*
6 *tablespoons honey*
2½ *tablespoons cornstarch*
¼ *cup water*
¼ *teaspoon cinnamon*
⅛ *teaspoon cloves*
  sour cream or yogurt

If fresh mint leaves are not available, make an infusion by pouring 1 cup boiling water over peppermint tea and allowing to steep 5 minutes. Strain and use instead of water.

Combine pineapple juice, mint infusion or water and strawberries in electric blender and process until pureed. Add cantaloupe, honey and fresh mint, if using it, and process until smooth. Chill.

If you want to serve in a punch bowl, freeze some of the punch in a small container which will fit into the punch bowl. Use this instead of ice when serving to avoid diluting punch.

Yield: approximately 4 cups

Minted Strawberry Cantaloupe Punch

16 *fresh mint leaves or*
   2 tablespoons dried
   peppermint tea
1 *cup water*
1 *cup pineapple juice*
1 *cup sliced fresh strawberries*
  or ⅓ package
  frozen unsweetened
  strawberries
½ *cantaloupe, peeled and*
  cut into chunks, or
  ½ package frozen
  unsweetened cantaloupe
  balls
2 *tablespoons honey*

Peach and Cantaloupe Soup

2½ cups orange juice, fresh
        or frozen
4 cups sliced fresh peaches or
        frozen unsweetened
        peaches
2 cups cubed cantaloupe
1 20-ounce can pineapple,
        drained (reserve juice)
4 tablespoons cornstarch
3 to 4 tablespoons honey
mint sprigs

Put ½ cup orange juice, 1 cup sliced peaches, ½ cup cantaloupe cubes and ½ cup pineapple into electric blender and puree. Repeat, using same amounts of fruit juice and fruits.

In a saucepan, dissolve cornstarch in 1½ cups cold orange juice. Heat to boiling and cook for 1 minute, stirring constantly. Stir in honey. Combine with fruit puree, adding the remaining 2 cups sliced peaches, 1 cup cubed cantaloupe and 1 cup diced pineapple with reserved pineapple juice. Chill completely before serving. Decorate with mint sprigs.

Yield: approximately 10 cups

Cherry Custard Cake

1 cup whole grain dry
        bread crumbs
1 cup ground hazelnuts
        (filberts)*
½ teaspoon cinnamon
2 tablespoons melted butter
2 tablespoons oil
2 tablespoons honey
3 pints fresh bing cherries or 2
        cups frozen unsweetened
        bing cherries
⅓ cup water (omit if using
        frozen cherries)
2 to 4 tablespoons honey
        (depending on sweetness
        of cherries)
3 eggs
4 tablespoons honey
¾ cup yogurt

Combine bread crumbs, ground nuts and cinnamon in a medium-size bowl. Combine melted butter, oil, honey and pour into crumb mixture, working it with your fingers until all ingredients are well blended. Press on the bottom and around the sides of a 9-inch layer cake pan. Chill for several hours.

Meanwhile, wash and remove stems from 3 pints fresh sweet cherries. Add water and honey to taste and bring to a boil. Turn down heat and simmer for 5 to 10 minutes, until tender. Drain and reserve juice for another use. When cherries are cool, remove pits. There should be approximately 2 cups pitted cherries. If using frozen cherries, add honey to taste, thaw completely and drain well.

Preheat oven to 325°F. Beat eggs. Add honey and yogurt, beating until smooth. Combine with cherries and pour into cake pan.

Bake in preheated oven for 40 minutes until custard is set and top is lightly browned. Serve warm.

Yield: 6 to 8 servings

*Ground almonds, walnuts, Brazil nuts or pecans may also be used.

Put all ingredients into electric blender and process until cherries are liquefied. Chill for at least 1 hour. Freeze by preferred method.

Yield: approximately 3 cups

Cherry Ice Cream
(with egg)

1 *cup pitted fresh black sweet cherries or frozen unsweetened black cherries*
1 *egg*
¾ *cup heavy cream*
¾ *cup yogurt, milk or light cream*
4 *to 6 tablespoons honey (to taste)*

Using either of the suggested recipes, make a 9-inch pie shell but do not bake it. Reserve remaining pastry for lattice top.

Coarsely chop cranberries in blender. Combine cranberries and remaining ingredients, mixing well, and turn into unbaked pie shell. *Preheat oven to 400°F.*

Make lattice top. (See recipe for Green Tomato and Apple Mince Pie.) Bake in preheated oven for 15 minutes, then at 325°F. for approximately 30 minutes or until apples are tender. Serve warm or cold.

Yield: 1 9-inch pie

Cranberry Apple Tart

1½ *recipe Whole Wheat Flaky Pastry (see Index) or Oat and Rice Flaky Pastry (see Index)*
2½ *cups fresh or frozen cranberries*
1½ *cups coarsely chopped apples*
¼ *cup orange juice*
2 *tablespoons water*
½ *cup honey*
¼ *teaspoon salt*
½ *teaspoon ginger*
3 *tablespoons quick-cooking tapioca*
2 *tablespoons cornstarch*

Cranberry-Applesauce

2 *cups fresh or frozen cranberries*

2 *cups sliced tart apples*

½ *cup water*

¼ *cup orange juice*

¼ *cup honey*

grated rind of 1 *orange*

Combine cranberries, apples, water and orange juice. Bring to a boil, turn heat down and simmer for 5 to 10 minutes until cranberries have popped and apples are tender. Add honey and orange rind. Puree in electric blender. Serve warm or cold.

Yield: approximately 3 cups

Cherry Soup

4 *cups pitted fresh black sweet cherries or frozen unsweetened black cherries*

1⅓ *cups orange juice*

2½ *tablespoons cornstarch*

3 *tablespoons lemon juice*

6 *tablespoons honey*

⅛ *teaspoon cinnamon*

⅛ *teaspoon allspice*

yogurt

Set aside 1 cup cherries. Put remaining cherries and orange juice in electric blender and process until cherries are liquefied. Heat cherry mixture to boiling. There should be approximately 4 cups. Dissolve cornstarch in lemon juice and add to soup, stirring until it is thickened. Remove from heat, add honey and spices. Cut reserved cherries in quarters and add to soup. Chill completely and serve with a dollop of yogurt.

Yield: 4 to 6 servings

Cranberry Anadama Bread

1 *cup fresh or frozen cranberries*

⅓ *cup honey*

⅓ *cup orange juice*

1 *tablespoon grated orange rind*

3 *tablespoons dry yeast*

⅓ *cup lukewarm water*

⅓ *cup orange juice*

½ *cup cornmeal*

⅓ *cup molasses*

2 *tablespoons oil*

1½ *teaspoons salt*

4½ *cups whole wheat flour*

In electric blender, combine cranberries, honey, ⅓ cup orange juice and orange rind. Process very briefly—only until cranberries are coarsely chopped.

Sprinkle yeast over lukewarm water and allow to soften for 10 minutes.

In a small saucepan, combine ⅓ cup orange juice with cornmeal. Gradually bring to a boil, stirring constantly, then lower heat and cook for 2 minutes or until thick. Remove from heat and stir in molasses, oil and salt. Add cranberry mixture and allow to cool.

Next, add the yeast mixture and then gradually add about 4 cups flour, beating until the dough leaves the sides of the bowl. Turn the dough out onto a lightly floured surface and knead in approximately ½ cup flour. Continue to knead for 10 minutes.

Put the dough in a large oiled bowl, cover with a towel and let rise in a warm place for 1½ hours, or until it has doubled in bulk. Punch down the dough and knead for another 5 minutes. Divide the dough in half, shape into 2 loaves and put each loaf in a buttered 8x4x3-inch loaf pan. Cover with towel and let loaves rise for 1 hour, or until double in bulk.

Preheat oven to 350°F. Bake the loaves for approximately 45 minutes. Cool on a rack before serving.

Yield: 2 loaves

Make Dough

In a small bowl, combine water and honey. Sprinkle yeast over surface and set aside for 10 minutes until mixture becomes frothy.

In a large bowl, mix butter and honey until smooth; then beat in the egg. Combine yeast and butter-egg mixtures, then add vanilla, cream and salt. Add flour a little at a time, adding enough to make a dough which can be rolled. Knead the dough on a floured board until it is smooth and elastic. Place in an oiled bowl, cover with a towel and let rise in a warm place for 1½ hours, or until it is double in bulk.

Make Filling

In a heavy saucepan, combine cranberries, orange juice and honey. Cook, covered, over low heat for approximately 10 minutes. Let the mixture cool, then puree in electric blender. Return to saucepan. Combine cornstarch and water and add slowly to cranberry puree. Bring to a boil and cook until thickened. Cool.

Assemble

Preheat oven to 450°F.

Roll out dough on a floured board, making a 12-inch circle. Lift onto a buttered baking sheet, make a slightly raised border around the edge of the circle and crimp the edges. Spread the cranberry filling on the dough and bake for 10 minutes. Serve warm with pouring cream or whipped cream.

Yield: 6 to 8 servings

Cranberry Galette

Dough

¼ cup lukewarm water
1 tablespoon honey
1 tablespoon dry yeast
2 tablespoons butter
1 tablespoon honey
1 egg
1 teaspoon vanilla
¼ cup light cream
⅛ teaspoon salt
1¼ to 1½ cups whole wheat flour

Filling

2 cups fresh or frozen cranberries
1 cup orange juice
½ cup honey
2 tablespoons cornstarch
2 tablespoons cold water

heavy cream

Fig Sauce for Meat Loaf or Pork Roast

2½ *teaspoons cornstarch*
1 *tablespoon lemon juice*
1½ *cups unsweetened pineapple juice*
¼ *teaspoon salt*
1 *cup diced dried figs*
honey to taste

In a saucepan, combine cornstarch and lemon juice. Gradually stir in pineapple juice and salt. Bring mixture to a boil, stirring constantly. Turn down heat and simmer for 5 minutes. Stir in diced figs. Simmer approximately a minute longer. Remove from heat, add honey to taste, pour into sauceboat and serve with meat loaf or pork roast.

Yield: 2 cups

Gooseberry Meringue Pie

1 *9-inch unbaked pie shell*
1 *pint fresh gooseberries*
¼ *cup water*
6 *tablespoons honey*
2 *tablespoons cornstarch*
½ *teaspoon cinnamon*
½ *teaspoon nutmeg*
2 *tablespoons cold water*
1 *teaspoon lemon rind*
3 *tablespoons honey*
3 *egg whites*

Make pie shell according to preferred recipe.

Wash gooseberries and combine with water and honey in saucepan. Simmer until tender. Combine cornstarch, spices and cold water and stir into cooking gooseberries. Continue to simmer until thickened. Add lemon rind. Cool.

Preheat oven to 300°F. Measure honey and put it into preheating oven to thin it. Beat egg whites until stiff. Add warm honey gradually, while continuing to beat.

Spoon gooseberries into pie shell and top with meringue. Bake in preheated oven for 15 minutes or until meringue is golden. Cool. Serve slightly warm.

Yield: 1 9-inch pie

Grape Juice

Cover grapes with boiling water. Heat slowly to a simmer and continue to simmer until fruit is very soft. Keep below the boiling point. Strain through dampened jelly bag or a strainer which has been lined with several thicknesses of dampened cheesecloth. Leave to drain or hang up bag, until it has stopped dripping. Measure juice. There should be approximately 3¾ cups white grape juice and 8 cups blue grape juice. Refrigerate for at least 24 hours and up to 48 hours. Strain once more. Heat to a simmer, add honey, stirring until it is dissolved.

Pour hot juice into hot clean jars. Wipe rims clean, adjust caps and process pints and quarts in hot water bath, held at 180° to 190°F. for 20 minutes.

White Grape Juice

8 *cups grapes, washed and stemmed*

boiling water to cover

4 *to 6 tablespoons honey to taste*

Yield: approximately 4 cups

Blue Grape Juice

8 *cups grapes, washed and stemmed*

boiling water to cover

8 *to 10 tablespoons honey to taste*

Yield: approximately 8 cups

Basic Oil and Vinegar Dressing

Combine all ingredients in a glass quart jar and store in a cool place. Shake well before using and be careful that the garlic stays in the jar, and doesn't get poured into the salad by mistake.

Yield: 2 cups

1½ *cups oil*

¼ *cup apple cider vinegar*

2 *tablespoons water*

2 *tablespoons lemon juice*

2 *cloves garlic, peeled*

½ *teaspoon salt*

¼ *teaspoon celery salt*

1 *tablespoon crushed basil leaves*

Lemon Dressing

Combine all ingredients in a glass jar and store in a cool place. Shake well before using.

Yield: 1½ cups

1 *cup oil*

½ *cup lemon juice*

½ *small onion, minced*

1 *teaspoon salt*

½ *teaspoon coriander*

Lemon Orange Gelatin

1 *envelope unflavored gelatin*
½ *cup cold water*
½ *cup boiling water*
¼ *cup honey*
  pinch of salt
  grated rind of 1 *lemon*
½ *cup lemon juice*
½ *cup orange juice*
3 *medium-size oranges,*
    peeled and separated
    into segments

Soften gelatin in cold water, then combine with boiling water, stirring until gelatin is dissolved. Add honey, salt, lemon rind and juices. Chill in refrigerator until partially set. Fold in oranges and continue to chill until completely jelled.

Yield: 4 servings

Zucchini Lemon Pie

1 *8-inch baked pie shell*
10 *ounces zucchini*
    (approximately 2
    small zucchini)
1 *cup water*
1 *tablespoon butter*
6 *tablespoons honey*
4 *tablespoons cornstarch* ·
  pinch of salt
  grated rind of 1 *lemon*
¼ *cup lemon juice*
2 *egg yolks*
2 *egg whites*
1 *tablespoon honey, warmed*
    to a thin consistency

Make pie shell according to preferred recipe.

Peel zucchini, cut into slices, put into electric blender with water and puree. There should be 2 cups zucchini mixture. Heat this in a large saucepan along with butter and honey.

Combine cornstarch, salt and lemon rind and juice, mix well and stir into hot zucchini mixture. Cook stirring constantly, until thickened.

Beat egg yolks and add a little of the hot mixture to them, stirring, then stir this back into zucchini mixture, and cook for approximately 1 more minute. Remove from heat and pour into baked pie shell. *Preheat oven to 400°F.*

Make meringue by beating egg whites until stiff and adding the warmed honey, gradually, during the beating process. Pile meringue on top of filling, covering it completely. Leave a rough surface on the meringue so it will brown more attractively.

Bake in preheated oven for approximately 5 minutes until meringue is golden brown. Cool and serve.

Yield: 1 8-inch pie

In a small saucepan, sprinkle gelatin over cold water. Heat to dissolve gelatin, stirring constantly. Remove from heat; stir in honey. Add lemon rind, juice and remaining water and chill for at least 1 hour. Beat egg whites stiff; fold into lemon mixture. Freeze by preferred method.

Yield: 1 quart

Lemon Sherbet
(milkless)

1 *envelope unflavored gelatin*
¼ *cup cold water*
½ *cup honey*
  grated rind of 1 lemon
10 *tablespoons lemon juice*
1½ *cups water*
2 *egg whites*

Combine all ingredients in a jar. Close tightly and shake well before serving.

Yield: 1⅔ cups

Lime Honey Dressing

1 *cup oil*
  grated rind of 1 lime
⅓ *cup lime juice*
1 *teaspoon grated onion*
⅓ *cup honey*
¼ *teaspoon salt*
¼ *teaspoon dry mustard*
1 *teaspoon paprika*
1 *teaspoon celery seeds*

Make pie shell according to preferred recipe. In a saucepan mix cornstarch, salt and honey and add boiling water slowly, stirring constantly, to avoid lumps. Add yogurt, milk or cream, blending in thoroughly. Bring mixture to a boil, then turn heat down and simmer, stirring, for a minute or so. Add lime juice, blending in well. Transfer mixture to the top of a double boiler, and cook over hot water, covered, for 25 to 30 minutes or until the taste of raw cornstarch is no longer evident. Add beaten egg yolks, stirring constantly, then lime rind and butter. Cool mixture at room temperature for approximately 10 minutes.

Whip cream and fold half of it into lime mixture. Beat egg whites until stiff and fold them gently into lime mixture. Pour into baked pie shell and chill in refrigerator until set. Spread remaining whipped cream over the top of the chilled pie before serving.

Yield: 1 9-inch pie

Key Lime Pie

1 *9-inch baked pie shell*
6 *tablespoons cornstarch*
⅛ *teaspoon salt*
¾ *cup honey*
1 *cup boiling water*
½ *cup yogurt, milk or*
   light cream
⅓ *cup lime juice*
2 *egg yolks, beaten*
  grated rind of 1 lime
½ *tablespoon butter*
1 *cup heavy cream*
2 *egg whites*

Papaya Shrub

1 *papaya*
1½ *cups water*
½ *teaspoon lemon juice*
fresh mint sprigs

Peel papaya, remove seeds and cut into pieces. Put in electric blender, add water and lemon juice and process until smooth. Chill and serve in parfait glasses, topped with sprig of fresh mint.

Yield: approximately 3 cups or 4 servings

Peach Almond Torte

3 *cups sliced peaches*
4 *tablespoons honey*
1 *tablespoon lemon juice*
½ *cup soy grits*
½ *cup water*
2 *eggs, beaten*
2 *egg yolks, beaten*
1⅔ *cups almonds, (ground to a meal in electric blender)*
¼ *cup melted butter*
6 *tablespoons honey*
grated rind of 1 lemon
2 *egg whites*
whipped cream

Combine peaches, honey and lemon juice in electric blender and puree. Cook over low heat until thick. Cool.

Soak soy grits in water for 10 minutes. Drain on paper towel. Combine eggs, egg yolks, almonds and soy grits. Combine melted butter, honey, lemon rind and stir into egg mixture. Meanwhile, *preheat oven to 350°F.* Beat egg whites until stiff and fold them into batter.

Spread cooled peach puree over bottom of buttered 9-inch cake pan. Pour batter over it, spreading it evenly. Bake in preheated oven for 1 hour. Turn out cake immediately, onto a cake plate. Cool. Serve with whipped cream.

Yield: 8 to 10 servings

Peach Fritters

2 *eggs*
2 *egg yolks*
4 *tablespoons whole wheat or rye flour*
2 *teaspoons honey*
¼ *teaspoon cinnamon*
2 *peaches, pitted, peeled and chopped coarsely*
2 *egg whites*
butter
cinnamon

Beat eggs and egg yolks, stir in flour, honey, cinnamon and peaches. Beat egg whites until stiff but not dry and fold into batter.

Melt butter in a medium-hot skillet and drop batter by tablespoon into it. Cook to a golden brown on both sides. Serve warm with butter and cinnamon.

Yield: 4 servings

Preheat oven to 400°F.

Make pie shell according to preferred recipe.
Combine all ingredients except eggs and orange juice.
Beat eggs, stir in orange juice and add to pear mixture.
Turn into pie shell. Bake in preheated oven for 30 minutes
or until pears are tender and custard is set. Cool on rack.
Serve warm or cold.

Yield: 1 9-inch pie

Pear and Orange Custard Tart

1 *9-inch unbaked pie shell*
5 *cups Seckel or other winter pears, peeled, cored and sliced*
2 *tablespoons honey*
2 *tablespoons lemon juice*
2 *tablespoons quick-cooking tapioca*
2 *tablespoons cornstarch*
¼ *teaspoon cinnamon*
1 *teaspoon orange rind*
2 *eggs*
6 *teaspoons orange juice*

Preheat oven to 350°F.

Place pears and apple juice in a casserole and sprinkle
with lemon juice and spices. Drizzle with honey.
Combine nuts and seeds and spread evenly over the
pears. Bake in preheated oven for 30 to 40 minutes or until
pears are tender.

Yield: 4 servings

Winter Pear Crunch

4 *cups peeled, sliced winter pears*
¾ *cup unsweetened apple juice*
2 *tablespoons lemon juice*
¼ *teaspoon cinnamon*
¼ *teaspoon ginger*
2 *tablespoons honey*
½ *cup almonds and/or walnuts (ground in electric blender)*
¼ *cup sunflower seeds (ground in electric blender)*
¼ *cup pumpkin seeds (ground in electric blender)*

In electric blender combine all ingredients and process
to a thick, shrub consistency.

Yield: 4 cups

Pineapple-Carrot Shrub

1¾ *cups unsweetened canned pineapple with juice*
1 *cup water*
2 *large carrots, washed, scraped and cut into 1-inch pieces*
¼ *-inch slice of lemon with rind*

Pineapple Pudding

2 *20-ounce cans unsweetened crushed pineapple (approximately 5 cups)*
¼ *cup melted butter*
⅓ *cup honey*
1 *teaspoon cinnamon*
1 *cup wheat germ*
½ *cup pumpkin seeds (finely ground in electric blender)*
1 *cup coconut*
2 *tablespoons butter (optional)*

Preheat oven to 350°F.

Drain 1 cup juice from pineapple and reserve for another use. Combine all remaining ingredients except pineapple and 2 tablespoons butter. Put half the pineapple in a baking dish, then make a layer using half the combined mixture; repeat layers of pineapple and the dry mixture. Dot with more butter, if desired, and bake in preheated oven for 15 minutes. Serve warm or cold.

Yield: 8 servings

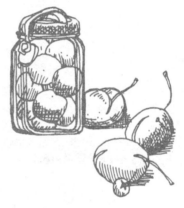

Plum Custard Tart

1 *9-inch unbaked pie shell*
1 *tablespoon cornstarch*
1 *tablespoon tapioca*
½ *teaspoon cinnamon*
2 *lbs. blue prune plums, halved and pitted*
4 *tablespoons honey*
1 *teaspoon cornstarch*
2 *eggs, beaten*
3 *tablespoons honey*
½ *cup milk or light cream, warmed*

Preheat oven to 400°F.

Make pie shell according to preferred recipe.

Combine cornstarch, tapioca and cinnamon and sprinkle over bottom of pie shell. Lay plum halves in pie shell, skin side up, overlapping each other. Drizzle honey over the top. Bake in preheated oven for 30 minutes or until filling is bubbling and pastry is golden brown.

Dissolve cornstarch in beaten eggs. Add honey and then warm milk or light cream. Pour custard over top of pie, distributing it evenly. Turn oven down to 350°F. and continue to bake pie until custard is set and an inserted silver knife comes out clean (15 to 20 minutes). Cool. Serve warm.

Yield: 1 9-inch pie

Combine all ingredients. Simmer for 10 minutes. Lift out fruit and put into glass dessert bowl. Simmer juice for another 20 minutes to concentrate it. Remove cinnamon stick. Pour juice over fruit. Chill. Serve cold accompanied by a dish of sour cream or yogurt.

Yield: 4 servings

Plum, Peach and Nectarine Compote

8 *large red plums, washed, pitted and halved*
2 *peaches, washed, pitted, peeled and halved*
2 *nectarines, washed, pitted, peeled and halved*
½ *cup water*
¼ *cup lemon juice*
¼ *cup dry red wine*
¼ *cup honey*
1 *stick cinnamon*

Wash firm, slightly underripe red plums. Prick them all over with a sterilized needle.

Combine wine, honey and spices and bring to a boil. Turn heat down and simmer for 5 minutes. Add plums and bring slowly to a simmer using medium-low heat. Remove from heat. Allow plums to remain covered with syrup at room temperature for 12 hours or more. Bring slowly to a simmer once again. Allow to remain at room temperature for another 12 hours approximately, and bring them to a simmer slowly, again. Continue to simmer plums this time, until they are tender, but still firm. Cool and serve or store in refrigerator for future use.

Yield: 4 to 6 servings

Spiced Plums in Wine

2 *lbs. red plums*
2 *cups dry red wine*
½ *cup honey*
3 *whole cloves*
3 *whole allspice*
1 *stick cinnamon broken in 4 pieces*

Put all ingredients except ice cubes into blender and process until fruit is liquefied. Add ice cubes and blend a few seconds longer. Serve immediately.

Yield: 4 cups

Sunshine Zap

2 *cups unsweetened orange juice*
1½ *medium-size bananas (approximately 1 cup)*
1 *cup unsweetened pineapple juice*
3 *ice cubes (optional)*

Yellow Plum Ice Cream

18 *large ripe yellow plums,*
      washed
 1 *envelope unflavored gelatin*
 4 *tablespoons water*
½ *cup honey*
 4 *teaspoons lemon juice*
 3 *cups light or heavy cream or*
      a mixture of both
 2 *egg whites*

Mash and cook plums in their own juice over low heat for approximately 10 minutes. Remove pits and put plums through a food mill or strainer. There should be approximately 2 cups puree. Soften gelatin in water. Heat just long enough to dissolve gelatin and combine with honey and lemon juice. Stir into puree. Add light and/or heavy cream and pour into freezer trays. Freeze for several hours.

Before serving, let soften at room temperature for approximately 15 minutes. Add unbeaten egg whites and beat with electric mixer until fluffy and of ice cream consistency. Serve at once.

NOTE: This ice cream can be refrozen several times. But be sure to beat it again each time before serving.

Yield: 8 to 10 servings

Quince Paste
(old-fashioned quince candy)

 5 *quinces*
   water to cover
½ *cup honey*

Wash, core, peel and chop quinces. Cover with water. Bring to a boil and simmer until quinces have turned a deep pink orange color (45 minutes to an hour). Drain off juice. Reserve for jelly. Puree pulp, add honey and cook in a heavy-bottom saucepan over low heat, stirring frequently, until it is as thick as possible.

Line a cookie sheet or flat pan or platter with cheesecloth, spread the puree on it ½ inch thick and cover with more cheesecloth. Leave in a cool, airy place for 1 to 2 weeks to dry, turning it every few days to enable it to dry on both sides. When the paste peels off of the cheesecloth easily, lay it between two sheets of wax paper or plastic wrap. Roll out as thin as possible with a rolling pin. Roll up paste in the plastic into a tube and store in cool dry place.

To serve, allow people to tear off the size piece they desire.

Yield: approximately 1¾ cups paste

Using either of the suggested recipes, make a 9-inch pie shell but do not bake it. Reserve remaining pastry for lattice top.

Combine quinces, honey and lemon juice in a bowl. Toss to mix evenly. Pile in unbaked pie shell. Sprinkle with cinnamon and cut butter into small pieces and distribute them over surface of pie. *Preheat oven to 350°F.*

Make lattice top. (See recipe for Green Tomato and Apple Mince Pie.) Bake in preheated oven for 30 minutes or until quince is tender.

Yield: 1 9-inch pie

Quince Tart

1½ recipe Whole Wheat Flaky
    Pastry (see Index) or
    Oat and Rice Flaky
    Pastry (see Index)
  6 cups sliced quinces
  ½ cup honey
  2 tablespoons lemon juice
    cinnamon to taste
  2 tablespoons butter

Preheat oven to 400°F.

Make pie shell according to preferred recipe.

If using frozen rhubarb, slice into ½-inch pieces, then thaw completely and drain, reserving juice to use instead of orange juice.

Combine tapioca, spices and salt. Combine orange juice or rhubarb juice and orange rind, honey and molasses. Add dry and wet ingredients to rhubarb, tossing well to combine. Put into unbaked pie shell. Top with slivers of butter. Bake in preheated oven for 10 minutes.

Meanwhile, prepare custard by combining egg yolks, heavy cream or yogurt and honey. After pie has baked for 10 minutes, remove it from the oven and pour custard over the top, gently stirring to distribute it evenly. Turn oven down to 350°F. and return pie to oven for 20 to 30 minutes longer or until the custard has set and the rhubarb is tender. Cool slightly before serving.

Yield: 1 9-inch pie

Rhubarb Custard Pie

  1 9-inch unbaked pie shell
  4 cups fresh rhubarb (cut into
    ½-inch slices) or
  1 1¼-lb. package
    frozen rhubarb
  2 tablespoons quick-cooking
    tapioca
  ¼ teaspoon ginger
    pinch of cloves
  ¼ teaspoon salt
  ¼ cup orange juice or
    rhubarb juice
  ½ teaspoon orange rind
  6 tablespoons honey
  4 tablespoons molasses
  2 tablespoons butter
  2 egg yolks
  2 tablespoons heavy cream or
    yogurt
  1 to 2 tablespoons honey (use
    larger amount
    if using yogurt)

Hot Rhubarb Soup

2 *lbs. fresh or frozen rhubarb
   (approximately 8 cups
   sliced rhubarb)*
4 *cups cold water*
4 *tablespoons cornstarch*
¼ *cup cold water*
½ *to ¾ cup honey*
¼ *teaspoon cinnamon*
½ *cup heavy cream*
1 *egg yolk*

Wash, trim and cut rhubarb into 2-inch lengths. Bring to a boil in cold water. Turn down heat and simmer for 5 minutes or until tender. Drain. There should be approximately 4 cups. Return liquid to pot and bring to a boil.

Dissolve cornstarch in cold water, stir into boiling rhubarb liquid and cook a minute or two until thickened. Remove from heat. Add ½ cup honey, cinnamon and then the drained rhubarb.

Whip the cream and stir the egg yolk into it, combining them. Stir some of the hot rhubarb into the cream mixture and then gradually add this to the hot soup, stirring gently to combine. Taste for sweetness. Add more honey if desired. Serve immediately.

Yield: 4 to 6 servings

Rhubarb Fool

1 *lb. fresh rhubarb*
3 *tablespoons honey*
4 *teaspoons cornstarch*
1 *recipe Thick Custard
   (see Index)*
whipped cream

Wash, trim and slice rhubarb into ½-inch pieces. Add honey and steam in top of double boiler until it is tender (20 to 30 minutes). Do not stir it or it will become mushy. Drain well. You should have approximately 1 cup juice.

Cool juice to lukewarm, dissolve cornstarch in it and bring to a boil, simmering it just until it is clear and begins to thicken. Combine with rhubarb and chill.

Combine chilled Thick Custard with chilled rhubarb. Serve topped with dollop of whipped cream.

Yield: 4 servings

Strawberry Cream Roll

(a festive strawberry shortcake)

1 *recipe Jelly Roll (see Index)*
5 *pints fresh strawberries or
   2 1¼-lb. bags
   frozen, unsweetened
   strawberries*
6 *to 8 tablespoons honey*
1 *cup heavy cream*

Make jelly roll, omitting jelly. Cool completely.

Wash and slice fresh strawberries. Drizzle honey over them. If using frozen strawberries, slice them, drizzle honey over them and allow them to thaw completely. Drain them well. Taste for desired sweetness, adding the full amount of honey if needed.

Whip the cream, fold in 2 cups drained strawberries. Spread cooled cake with strawberry cream. Reroll cake, slice and serve topped with remaining strawberries.

Yield: 6 to 8 servings

Preheat oven to 400°F.

Make pie shell according to preferred recipe.

Combine next six ingredients in electric blender and process until smooth. Pour into unbaked pie shell and bake in preheated oven for 10 minutes. Lower oven temperature to 325°F. and continue to bake for 35 to 40 minutes or until inserted table knife comes out clean. Remove from oven and cool for 45 minutes.

While pie is cooling, prepare strawberry glaze. Wash and halve or slice strawberries, separating the very ripe ones from the firmer ones. There should be approximately 1 cup soft berries and 1½ cups firm ones. Add honey to the soft berries, mash them slightly and bring them to a boil over medium heat. Dissolve cornstarch in cold water and stir into boiling berries, cooking about a minute stirring constantly.

Remove from heat and drain off clear juice. Pour cooked berries over top of pie, then arrange uncooked berries, cut side down, over entire surface of pie. Carefully pour clear juice glaze over all the strawberries coating each one, completely covering the filling of the pie. Refrigerate for several hours.

Yield: 6 to 8 servings

Strawberry Custard Pie

1   *9-inch unbaked pie shell*
3   *eggs*
¼   *cup melted butter*
¼   *cup honey*
1½ *cups yogurt*
    pinch of salt
1½ *teaspoons vanilla*
1½ *pints fresh strawberries*
¼   *cup honey*
1   *tablespoon cornstarch*
1   *tablespoon cold water*

Wash strawberries and remove stems.

Make a bed of lettuce on each individual salad plate. Then make a layer of chopped nuts, next a layer of whole strawberries and finally a layer of chopped celery.

Combine remaining ingredients and pour over salads. Chill and serve.

Yield: 4 to 6 servings

Strawberry Salad

1   *pint fresh strawberries*
1   *head Boston or*
        garden lettuce, washed
        with leaves separated
½   *cup pecans or walnuts,*
        coarsely chopped
1   *cup finely chopped celery*
¼   *cup olive oil*
2   *tablespoons lemon juice*
½   *teaspoon honey*
½   *teaspoon salt*
½   *teaspoon pepper*
    pinch of paprika

English Plum Pudding*

½ *cup figs*
1½ *cups currants*
2 *cups raisins*
2 *cups sultanas (light-colored raisins)*
¾ *cup chopped dried apricots*
1 *cup chopped pitted dates*
¾ *cup chopped dried pineapple*
¼ *cup chopped honey-dipped papaya*
1 *cup slivered almonds (blanched if desired)*
2 *apples, peeled, cored and grated*
1 *carrot, grated*
4 *tablespoons grated orange rind*
2 *teaspoons grated lemon rind*
1 *cup apple juice, cider or brandy*
2 *cups whole wheat flour*
4 *cups soft whole grain bread crumbs*
⅓ *cup honey*
1 *teaspoon allspice*
1 *teaspoon nutmeg*
1 *teaspoon cinnamon*
1 *teaspoon salt*
½ *lb. suet or hard butter, coarsely grated*
6 *eggs*
⅓ *cup orange juice*
¼ *cup lemon juice*

In a large bowl, combine first fourteen ingredients. Mix thoroughly and set aside. In another bowl, combine flour, bread crumbs, honey, spices, salt, suet or butter and mix well with your hands.

Beat eggs until light and lemon colored. Stir in orange juice and lemon juice. Combine with fruit mixture. Add flour mixture to fruit mixture and beat with wooden spoon and knead with your hands until all ingredients are well combined. Cover the bowl with a damp towel and refrigerate overnight, at least 12 hours.

The mixture can then be placed in four 1-quart or two 2-quart buttered bowls (stainless steel, Pyrex or ceramic) and filled to within 2 inches of the top. Cover each bowl with oiled or buttered cloth and tie securely under the rim of the bowl. Then place aluminum foil over the cloth and pinch it tightly around the rim, to keep all steam or water out.

Place each bowl in a large pot and pour enough boiling water around it to come three-quarters of the way up the side of the bowl. Cover the pot tightly with a lid. Keep heat at lowest possible point and steam the puddings for 6 to 8 hours. It's vital to tend the puddings very carefully so that the hot water doesn't boil away. Keep adding boiling water from time to time. When finished, remove puddings from pots and cool to room temperature. Remove foil and cloth and put on fresh foil and store for 3 to 4 weeks in refrigerator before serving.

To prepare for serving, place the puddings, again covered with cloth and aluminum foil, in a covered pot with boiling water, but steam only 2 to 4 hours. To remove puddings from bowls, loosen carefully with rubber spatula around the outside and invert on serving plate. If desired, the puddings may be set aflame by warming brandy over low heat, igniting it with a match and pouring it as it flames over the pudding.

Yield: 4 puddings, each approximately 8 servings or 2 puddings, each approximately 16 servings

*If any of the dried fruit isn't available, increase amounts of other fruit accordingly.

Prepare two loaf tins, 9x5x3-inch size, by lining them with buttered parchment paper or brown wrapping paper. Let the paper extend above the long sides of the pan about 2 inches.

Combine 1¾ cups whole wheat flour with the spices and salt. Cut all fruit (except raisins and sultanas) into small pieces. Sprinkle and separate all fruit with ½ cup flour. Chop walnuts coarsely and add to fruit. *Preheat oven to 275°F.*

Cream butter until soft. Beat in honey and molasses. Add egg yolks and vanilla and beat until fluffy. Add flour mixture and apply juice alternately to butter mixture, beating after each addition. Carefully fold in floured fruits and nuts. Beat egg whites until stiff, but not dry, and fold them carefully into batter. Turn batter into prepared pans. Lay whole blanched almonds on top of each loaf in desired design.

Bake in preheated oven on middle rack for approximately 3 hours. Cool in the pan for 30 minutes at least. Remove from pan, remove paper and cool completely on cake rack.

Wrap in several thicknesses of cheesecloth which have been drenched with apple juice, cider or brandy. Then wrap in waxed paper and aluminum foil and store in a refrigerator or a cool, dry place. Check the moisture of the cake every week or so and drench the cheesecloth with fresh liquid if needed.

Yield: 2 loaves

*If any of the dried fruit isn't available, increase amounts of other fruit accordingly.

Holiday Fruitcake*

1¾ *cups whole wheat flour*
1 *teaspoon cinnamon*
½ *teaspoon allspice*
½ *teaspoon nutmeg*
¼ *teaspoon ground cloves*
⅛ *teaspoon ground cardamom*
½ *teaspoon salt*
½ *cup honey-dipped papaya*
1 *cup pitted dates*
1 *cup dried pineapple*
1 *cup dried apricots*
1½ *cups raisins*
1 *cup sultanas (light-colored raisins)*
½ *cup whole wheat flour*
1½ *cups walnuts*
1 *cup butter*
½ *cup honey*
¼ *cup molasses*
6 *egg yolks*
1 *tablespoon vanilla*
½ *cup apple juice, cider or brandy—plus extra for storing cakes*
6 *egg whites*
whole blanched almonds

Dried Fruit Shake

½ cup mixed dried fruit or
    4 dates, pitted;
    4 prunes, pitted;
    2 halves dried peaches
2 cups milk
1 to 2 teaspoons honey
    to taste
1 to 3 teaspoons molasses
    to taste

Bring dried fruit to a boil in water to cover. Simmer until soft. Drain and reserve liquid for another use.

Process all ingredients in electric blender until smooth.

Yield: approximately 3 cups

Watermelon and Onion Salad

salad greens for 6 plates
1½ to 2 lbs. watermelon,
    cut in balls or cubes
    (rind removed)
6 green onions, with tops
Lime Honey Dressing
    (see Index)

Make a bed of crisp salad greens on six individual salad plates.

Prepare watermelon and divide into six portions, piling it on salad greens. Slice 1 green onion, thinly, on top of each portion of watermelon, using as much of green top as possible.

Spoon Lime Honey Dressing generously over each salad. Chill and serve as appetizer or accompaniment to a meal.

Yield: 6 servings

Discover
Seeds and Nuts

❊❊ Seeds

Of course seeds are super foods. They are the nucleus of plant life—the storehouse of nourishment that sustains growth. And they bring these values to the people who eat them. But best of all they taste good and add a welcome new dimension to many ordinary dishes.

You will find edible seeds of all varieties for sale in natural food stores.

Seeds are not complete protein but they can add a great deal to your total protein intake when they are eaten along with other protein foods.

Most seeds are super foods, but here are some real standouts:

Pumpkin seeds, for instance, readily available from natural food stores and by mail, are very special. They offer plenty of zinc, iron, protein and B vitamins. Enjoy them raw or roast them lightly if you prefer that flavor.

Most seeds, though rich in phosphorus, are "poor" in calcium but *sesame seeds* are a notable exception. They contain twice as much calcium as phosphorus—if the sesame seeds you get are unhulled. These can be purchased in any natural food store at a fraction of the cost of the hulled variety on sale at the spice shelves of supermarkets.

Sesame oil, pressed from the sesame seeds, is valuable because it contains most of the same properties as the seeds.

Tahini is sesame seed butter. Its availability is confined almost exclusively to health food stores and mail-order health product suppliers. Tahini has a mild but unique flavor and it can be used in the same way you would use peanut butter.

For a very special way to experience the unique appeal of sesame seeds, try this salad dressing created by the chef at Yes!, a natural foods restaurant in the fashionable Georgetown section of our nation's capital.

Lemon-Sesame Dressing

½ cup lemon juice
2 tablespoons tamari
   soy sauce
2 tablespoons water
¼ cup plus 2 tablespoons oil
¼ cup tahini

¼ teaspoon garlic powder
pinch of salt
¼ teaspoon celery seeds
¼ green pepper, chopped
¼ cup sliced onions

Combine all ingredients in electric blender and process until smooth.

Yield: 2 cups

In old Czarist Russia, as a hedge against starvation, every soldier in the field received what was known as "iron rations," consisting of a bag of *sunflower seeds* weighing one kilogram. The large wave of Russian immigrants that came to New York City at the turn of the century, brought the tradition of sunflower seeds with them. For them, paper bag lunches weren't complete without "polly" seeds (as sunflower seeds were called), and they were, far and away, the snack of choice!

Abundantly endowed with a highly digestible, polyunsaturated oil, this tiny seed also contains 12 different minerals, 17 vitamins, a good supply of protein, plus its own enzymes and pectin. They are available in most supermarkets as well as health food stores.

Nuts

Squirrels pack nuts away to stock up on high-energy food for winter, and we should do the same. Nuts are one of the most widely available natural foods. They're carefully packed in strong shells by nature, so they need no preservatives to stay fresh as long as the shell is intact.

Nuts are amazingly rich in food energy, pound for pound far exceeding the caloric power of bread, meat and fruits. And a variety of nuts can add new flavor dimensions to the diet. They offer plenty of unsaturated oils, protein, minerals and some vitamins.

Cashews contain almost as much high-quality protein as soybeans.

Peanut Butter Began as a Prescription

Although most people think of it as a nut, the peanut is neither a seed nor a nut, but a legume. Without a doubt the most popular form of peanuts is peanut butter, which was invented around 1890 by a nutrition-conscious physician as a high-protein "prescription" for his patients. The worth of his idea is clear: peanuts are higher in amino acids, polyunsaturated fatty acids, calcium, phosphorus and niacin than beefsteak. Besides the endless variations of the peanut butter sandwich, peanut butter is used in stews, sauces and that delicious concoction, peanut soup. Peanut flour is a good protein source that can be used in baking bread or cookies.

Most people use nuts in cake and icing ingredients, or as fried and salted snacks. To get even more out of nuts start thinking about them the way the vegetarians do—as a basic food that is eaten raw or even cooked as an ingredient of various dishes. Eat nuts out of hand, but eat them raw and unsalted to get the most nutritional benefit. And keep in mind that nuts—especially when they are served as part of a mixture—can take the place of meat or other main-dish foods.

Why a mixture? Because the protein in nuts is not complete, that is, individual nuts don't contain eight essential amino acids in proper balance the way meat, fish and eggs do. No plant source of protein has them all. Soybeans come close, but still aren't perfect. When eaten in the right combination, plant foods can supply protein that's every bit as useful as animal protein, but you have to plan the mixture with some care. Some native cultures do it instinctively, though, the way Latin Americans traditionally eat beans and rice together—a perfectly complementary combination of amino acids.

There's nothing really complicated about swinging your diet partly away from meat to include a variety of nuts. It's simple, mainly because nuts taste so good and can be easily worked into meal planning in a multitude of ways.

Sesame Cookies

Toast sesame seeds in a dry, medium-hot skillet, stirring constantly, until seeds begin to darken and give off a roasted fragrance. Remove seeds from hot pan. *Preheat oven to 350°F.*

Combine all ingredients and drop batter by teaspoon onto oiled cookie sheet, leaving enough room for cookies to spread 2 inches across.

Bake in preheated oven for 8 minutes. Remove from cookie sheet immediately. Cool on rack before serving.

Yield: approximately 3 dozen cookies

½ *cup unhulled sesame seeds*
½ *cup melted butter*
6 *tablespoons honey*
1 *egg, beaten*
1 *cup oat flour (oatmeal may be ground to flour in electric blender)*
½ *cup brown rice flour*
½ *teaspoon vanilla*

Sunflower Mayonnaise

Using an electric blender, process egg yolks until thick. Add vinegar and blend a few minutes longer. Gradually add oil, then lemon juice, salt and curry powder. Process until smooth and thick.

Yield: approximately 1 cup

2 *egg yolks*
1½ *tablespoons apple cider vinegar*
1 *cup sunflower seed oil*
2 *tablespoons lemon juice*
½ *teaspoon salt*
¼ *teaspoon curry powder*

Sunflower Oil Dressing

2 *tablespoons lemon juice*
½ *cup sunflower seed oil*
½ *cup yogurt*
½ *teaspoon seasoning salt*

Combine all ingredients in a bowl and blend until smooth.

Yield: 1 cup

Sunflower Seed Cookies

2 *egg whites*
¼ *cup honey*
1 *teaspoon vanilla*
1 *cup sunflower seeds
    (ground to a meal
    in electric blender)*

Preheat oven to 275°F.

Beat egg whites until stiff, then gradually beat in honey and vanilla. Carefully fold in sunflower seed meal. Drop batter by teaspoon onto a well-buttered cookie sheet and bake in preheated oven for 30 minutes.

Loosen cookies from baking sheet as soon as possible after removing them from oven. They will be a bit soft to the touch but will harden as they cool. Store in airtight container.

Yield: 2 dozen cookies

Sunflower Seed Spread or Dip

1 *cup sunflower seed meal
    (sunflower seeds
    can be ground
    in electric blender)*
2 *tablespoons sunflower
    seed oil*
¼ *cup peanut butter*
¼ *teaspoon seasoning salt*

Combine ingredients in a bowl and mix until smooth. Use as sandwich spread, filling for stuffed celery or as a dip for raw vegetables.

Yield: 1½ cups

Preheat oven to 375°F.

In a bowl combine flour, sunflower seed meal and salt. In another bowl, beat egg yolks, then add oil, molasses or honey, milk and raisins. Combine wet and dry mixtures. Fold in beaten egg whites. Bake in oiled muffin tins in preheated oven for 25 minutes.

Yield: 12 muffins

Sunflower Seed Muffins

¾ *cup whole wheat flour*
¾ *cup sunflower seed meal*
    (sunflower seeds
    can be ground
    in electric blender)
¼ *teaspoon salt*
2 *egg yolks*
1 *tablespoon oil*
2 *tablespoons molasses*
    or honey
¾ *cup milk*
¾ *cup raisins*
2 *egg whites, well beaten*

Cook millet according to preferred method. (See "Cooking with Cereal Grains.") There should be approximately 1 cup cooked millet. Use ¾ cup for this recipe and reserve remainder for another use.

Preheat oven to 350°F. Combine soy grits and tomato juice and set aside to soften for 5 minutes. Combine grated carrots, cooked millet, onion, green pepper, oil, eggs, soy flour and peanut flour. Stir in soy grit mixture, season with herbs and salt and pepper to taste. Turn into oiled loaf pan and bake in preheated oven for 1 hour. Serve hot or cold.

Yield: 4 servings

Carrot Peanut Loaf

¼ *cup millet*
1 *tablespoon soy grits*
¼ *cup tomato juice*
1½ *cups grated carrots*
½ *small onion, minced*
½ *cup minced green pepper*
1 *tablespoon oil*
2 *eggs, beaten*
2 *tablespoons soy flour*
¾ *cup peanut flour*
    (if unavailable, peanuts
    may be ground fine
    in electric blender)
¼ *teaspoon dill*
1 *teaspoon oregano*
salt, pepper to taste

Crunchy Peanut Bread

1 *cup lukewarm water*
2 *tablespoons plus*
    2 teaspoons honey
2 *teaspoons dry yeast*
1 *cup peanuts (finely ground*
    in electric blender)
¼ *cup non-fat dry milk*
1 *teaspoon salt*
3 *cups whole wheat flour*
1 *egg, beaten*

Combine lukewarm water and honey. Sprinkle yeast over surface and set aside for 5 minutes to activate. Combine ground peanuts, non-fat dry milk, salt and whole wheat flour. Combine yeast mixture with egg and stir into dry mixture, mixing well.

Turn into oiled loaf pan (3¾x7½x2-inch). Smooth surface with wet spatula. Set the pan in a cold oven, turn oven temperature to 325°F. and bake for 1¼ hours. Cool for 5 minutes, remove loaf from pan and cool completely on rack before serving.

Yield: 1 small loaf

Dutch Peanut Croquettes

1½ *cups whole wheat bread*
    crumbs (made in electric
    blender from dry bread)
½ *cup wheat germ*
1 *cup peanuts (finely ground*
    in electric blender)
½ *cup grated cheddar or*
    Swiss cheese
½ *teaspoon salt*
1 *cup milk*
¼ *cup wheat germ*

Preheat oven to 350°F.

Combine all ingredients except ¼ cup wheat germ. Shape into logs approximately 1 inch in diameter and 3 inches long. Roll in wheat germ and bake on an oiled baking sheet in preheated oven for 20 minutes or until browned.

These can be eaten warm, cold or at room temperature, plain or dipped into catsup, mustard or mayonnaise. What you don't eat, store in the refrigerator for future nibbling.

Yield: 14 croquettes

In heavy skillet, saute onions, garlic, peanuts and spices together in oil until onions are tender. Add potatoes, saute for 2 minutes or so, then add mushrooms and tomatoes and finally the cabbage. Stir vegetables to coat them with spice mixture, add tomato juice or water, then cover skillet and steam for 5 or 10 minutes until cabbage is tender but still green and firm. Serve immediately accompanied by yogurt, over brown rice.

Yield: 4 to 6 servings

Peanut and Cabbage Curry

4 *medium-size onions,*
     chopped
4 *small cloves garlic, minced*
1 *cup peanuts*
2 *tablespoons basil*
2 *teaspoons ground cumin*
1 *teaspoon Garam Masala*
     (see Index)
1 *tablespoon ground*
     coriander
6 *tablespoons oil*
2 *medium-size potatoes, diced*
4 *cups sliced fresh mushrooms*
4 *medium-size tomatoes,*
     chopped
4 *cups shredded cabbage*
1 *cup tomato juice or water*
yogurt

Combine cornmeal, non-fat dry milk, salt and water. Cook, stirring constantly, until thick (approximately 5 minutes). Cool slightly, then stir in ground peanuts. *Preheat oven to 350°F.*

Place dough between two sheets of waxed paper and roll ¼ inch thick. Cut into 1½-inch rounds and bake on an oiled baking sheet for 20 minutes in preheated oven.

Yield: 24 snaps

Peanut Cornmeal Snaps

⅓ *cup cornmeal*
¼ *cup non-fat dry milk*
½ *teaspoon salt*
¾ *cup water*
2 *cups peanuts (finely ground*
     in electric blender)

Raised Peanut Cookies

⅓ *cup honey*
½ *cup apple juice*
1 *tablespoon dry yeast*
2½ *cups oatmeal (ground
        briefly in electric blender
        to resemble coarse oat
        flour)*
½ *cup soy flour*
½ *teaspoon salt*
1 *cup raw peanut flour
        (peanuts may be
        finely ground in
        electric blender)*
2 *eggs*
⅓ *cup oil*
1 *teaspoon vanilla*
1 *cup raisins*

Combine honey with apple juice and heat to luke-warm. Sprinkle yeast over surface and leave to soften. Combine oatmeal, soy flour, salt and peanut flour. Beat eggs and add oil and vanilla to them. Combine yeast mixture and egg mixture and add to dry ingredients. Stir in raisins. Cover bowl and leave batter in a warm place for 25 minutes. *Preheat oven to 375°F.*

Drop batter by teaspoon onto greased cookie sheets. Bake in preheated oven for 12 minutes or until cookies are brown around the edge and on the bottom. Cool cookies on a rack.

Yield: 4 dozen cookies

Gado Gado

*(Indonesian main course or
salad course)*

2 *large potatoes, scrubbed
        and diced*
1 *cup sliced carrots*
1 *cup cut green beans*
1 *cup shredded cabbage*
½ *cucumber, sliced*
1 *cup bean sprouts*
½ *large green pepper, slivered*
4 *hard-cooked eggs, sliced*

Place diced potatoes in a vegetable steamer set over boiling water, cover and steam 10 minutes. Add carrots and green beans, cover, and continue to steam for 5 minutes. Add shredded cabage and steam for 3 minutes. Arrange steamed and raw vegetables and sliced eggs on a serving platter and serve with *Gado Gado* Sauce (see below).

*Yield: 4 servings as a main course;
             8 servings as a salad course*

Combine all ingredients in saucepan and heat gently until smooth and thickened (approximately 20 minutes).

Yield: 2 cups

6 *tablespoons peanut butter*
1 *clove garlic, minced*
1 *teaspoon crushed red pepper
     or to taste*
   grated rind of 1 *lemon*
1½ *teaspoons molasses*
½ *teaspoon salt*
1½ *cups water or chicken, beef
     or vegetable stock*

Molasses and Peanut Butter Log Confection

In medium-size bowl combine peanut butter and molasses. Mix together thoroughly. Stir in soy flour, mixing until well combined. Gradually add ⅓ cup non-fat dry milk, blending thoroughly with a wooden spoon. Sprinkle a little of the remaining non-fat dry milk on a bread board. Knead mixture in this until all of the non-fat dry milk has been incorporated. Roll into log shape, 2 inches thick. Roll in chopped nuts and transfer to a cookie sheet. Place in refrigerator to chill for at least 1 hour before serving. Cut log in ¼-inch slices and serve.

Yield: approximately 1 pound

1 *cup peanut butter*
⅔ *cup molasses*
¼ *cup soy flour*
⅔ *cup non-fat dry milk*
¾ *cup chopped peanuts or
     chopped walnuts*

Peanut Butter Soup

Saute onion and celery in oil until tender. Stir peanut butter into sauteed mixture. Add chicken stock, tomato juice and seasonings. Bring to a boil and simmer for 10 minutes or so. Just before serving, stir in yogurt and salt to taste. Heat but do not boil. Serve hot.

Yield: approximately 4½ cups

1 *medium-size onion,
     chopped*
1 *cup chopped celery*
2 *tablespoons oil*
¼ *cup peanut butter*
2½ *cups chicken stock*
1 *cup tomato juice*
⅛ *teaspoon white pepper*
½ *teaspoon ground coriander*
1 *cup yogurt*
   salt to taste

Crumb Crust

6 *tablespoons butter*
1 *cup dry whole grain*
    bread crumbs
1 *cup almonds (finely ground*
    in electric blender)
1 *cup unsweetened coconut*
    (small shreds)
2 *tablespoons honey*

Melt butter in large skillet. Combine crumbs, almonds and coconut and stir into butter. Continue to cook on low heat, stirring constantly, for 1 or 2 minutes. Remove from heat. Add honey, blend in thoroughly, and press mixture lightly into two oiled 9-inch pie plates. The crust may be baked at 325°F. for 8 minutes, or it may be left unbaked, in which case it must be refrigerated for several hours before serving.

Yield: 2 9-inch pie shells

Walnut Cheese Spread

7 *ounces Gouda cheese,*
    finely grated
1 *cup finely chopped walnuts*
1 *tablespoon butter*
1 *teaspoon finely chopped*
    garlic
1 *tablespoon chopped fresh*
    coriander or parsley
salt to taste

Combine cheese, nuts, butter and seasonings in a bowl, and beat until as smooth as possible. This spread can be refrigerated until needed. Serve at room temperature.

Yield: 4 to 6 servings

Walnut-Onion Dip or Spread

1 *cup walnuts*
¼ *cup chopped onion*
¼ *cup chopped parsley*
1 *teaspoon salt*
⅛ *teaspoon black pepper*
¼ *cup wine vinegar*
1 *teaspoon prepared mustard*
1 *teaspoon chopped chives*

Combine all ingredients in electric blender and process until smooth.

Serve as a dip with fresh vegetable sticks or as a spread on herbed crackers or whole grain bread.

Yield: 1½ cups

Preheat oven to 350°F.

Walnut Torte

Grind walnuts, ½ cup at a time, in electric blender. Beat egg whites until stiff, then set aside. Beat egg yolks, then beat in honey and vanilla, and finally, mix in ground nuts. Fold in beaten egg whites carefully, then turn batter into greased 9x9-inch pan or a 9-inch layer cake pan.

Bake for 10 minutes in preheated oven. Then turn oven down to 325°F. and continue to bake for approximately 25 minutes longer or until cake tests done when an inserted toothpick comes out clean. Cool for 10 minutes, then remove from pan if desired. Serve warm or cold with a fruit sauce.

Yield: 6 servings

2 *cups walnuts*
4 *egg whites*
4 *egg yolks*
6 *tablespoons honey*
1 *teaspoon vanilla*

Preheat oven to 375°F.

Whole Wheat and Walnut Pastry

Combine nuts, flour, wheat germ, salt and oil. Add cold water gradually, tossing mixture gently to distribute evenly. Press into a 9-inch pie pan. Bake in preheated oven for approximately 15 minutes or until nicely browned.

Yield: 1 9-inch pie shell

¼ *cup ground walnuts*
1 *cup whole wheat*
   pastry flour
¼ *cup wheat germ*
¼ *teaspoon salt*
¼ *cup oil*
2 *tablespoons cold water*

Making Their Mark

At last, beans and peas and other legumes are resuming their rightful place on our nation's dinner plate among our most nutritious and versatile foods. They are both inexpensive and rich in protein, a particularly desirable combination.

As food prices go higher and as people become more concerned about nutrition, they are getting away from the overemphasis on meat and are busy exploring the "legume market."

A heavy emphasis on meat makes for a rather dull diet. After all, there are only five different kinds of meat plus poultry. And when you look at the menu of an average restaurant, you'll find that it rarely lists all five of them, and most certainly not all types of meat from the animals.

Looking at other protein-rich foods for variety, legumes top the list. There are at least 24 different kinds of beans, peas and lentils.

It is a fallacy to suggest that legumes are starchy, just because they are very filling and satisfying and some of them have a mealy texture. Their ratio of protein to carbohydrates is very high. The average legume is made of 20 to 24 percent protein, and that little wonder, the soybean, has an even higher protein content. In addition to the valuable protein, all legumes have an appreciable amount of the B vitamins, calcium, phosphorus, magnesium and iron. They're good food for weight-watchers and penny-watchers and they need no refrigeration for long storage.

Here is a selection of popular types from among the different kinds of beans, peas and lentils we know about.

❈ Beans

Black beans (or black turtle soup beans)—They are used in thick soups and in Oriental, Mediterranean and South American dishes.

Black-eyed peas (also called black-eyed beans or "cow peas")—These beans are small, oval shaped and creamish white with a black spot on one side. They are used primarily as a main dish vegetable. Black-eyed peas are beans. There is no difference in the product, but different names are used in some regions of the country.

261

Garbanzo beans—Known as chick-peas, these beans are nut flavored and very good when pickled in vinegar and oil for salads. Cooked, mashed with garlic, lemon juice and seasonings, they make a delicious dip especially when scooped up with pita (Arab bread) or any other flat bread. They can also be used as a main dish in the "unpickled" form.

Chick-Pea and Lentil Curry

1⅓ cups chick-peas
1 cup lentils
2 medium-size onions, chopped
¼ cup oil
3 to 4 teaspoons grated fresh gingerroot or 1 to 2 teaspoons ginger

¼ to ½ teaspoon cayenne pepper
¼ teaspoon ground cloves
½ teaspoon cinnamon
3 teaspoons cumin
1 teaspoon turmeric
salt to taste
3 tablespoons lemon juice
chopped parsley

Cook chick-peas and lentils according to preferred methods. (See "Basic Methods for Cooking Beans and Other Legumes.") Drain and reserve liquid.

Saute onions in oil with spices for approximately 5 minutes, then stir in chick-peas and lentils. Season with salt to taste and lemon juice. Add some of the final cooking water from chick-peas if it is needed. Garnish with parsley before serving.

Yield: 8 to 10 servings

Kidney beans—These beans are large and have a red color and kidney shape.

Pinto beans—Although of the same species as the kidney beans, these beige-colored, speckled beans have a more delicate flavor.

Kidney and pinto beans are both popular for chili con carne and add zest to salads and many Mexican dishes.

Lima beans—Not widely known as dried beans, lima beans make an excellent main dish vegetable and can be used in casseroles. They are broad and flat. Lima beans come in different sizes, but the size does not affect the quality.

Navy beans—This is a broad term which includes Great Northern, Marrow and pea beans.

Pea beans—Small, oval, and white, pea beans are a favorite for home-baked beans, soups and casseroles. They hold their shape even when cooked tender.

Frijoles Refritos

(Refried Beans)

2 *cups black, pinto or kidney beans*	2 *cloves garlic, minced (optional)*
¼ *to* ½ *cup oil*	¾ *cup tomato puree (optional)*
2 *onions, chopped*	*salt to taste*
	cayenne to taste

Cook beans according to preferred method. (See "Basic Methods for Cooking Beans and Other Legumes.") Drain beans and reserve liquid.

Using as little oil as possible, saute onions and garlic (if using it), then add some beans, mashing them well and stirring them around as they cook. They may be seasoned with tomato puree, salt and cayenne, if desired. If too dry, add a little of the bean liquid, when mashing them. Cook them until they are dry and crispy, but be careful that they do not burn.

Yield: 6 to 8 servings

✿ Peas

Dried peas are an interesting and versatile food group that adds variety to meals. They may be green or yellow and may be bought either split or whole.

Dried *green peas* have a more distinct flavor than dried yellow peas and enjoy their greatest popularity in the United States, England and north European countries. They are gaining in popularity in Japan.

Dried *yellow peas* are preferred in eastern Canada, the Caribbean and South America.

Timetable for Cooking Legumes

	Traditional Method	Pressure Cooker
	(soaked beans)	*(using 15 lbs. pressure)* *(unsoaked beans)*
Black Beans	1½– 2 hours	30– 35 minutes
Black-eyed Peas	1½– 2 hours	20– 25 minutes
Chick-peas (garbanzo beans)	3– 4 hours	45 minutes
Great Northern Beans (white)	1½– 2 hours	25 minutes
Kidney Beans	1½– 2 hours	25– 30 minutes
Lentils	1 hour	10– 15 minutes
Lima Beans (large)	1½– 2 hours	25 minutes
Lima Beans (small)	1 hour	20 minutes
Marrow Beans (white)	2– 3 hours	30– 35 minutes
Pea Beans (white, navy)	1½– 2 hours	25 minutes
Pinto Beans	1½– 2 hours	25– 30 minutes
Soybeans	2– 3 hours	25 minutes
Split Peas	45 minutes– 1 hour	10– 15 minutes

Basic Methods for Cooking Beans and Other Legumes

There are several methods of cooking legumes including one for the traditionalists who believe in long, slow cooking and another for those who want to find a short cut. Then for those who don't eat legumes because of the discomfort or flatulence they can cause, we offer a method which helps to overcome this drawback by removing as many of the offending carbohydrates as possible before the legumes are eaten.

The amount of water used for cooking legumes is generally three to four times the volume of the legumes. During the cooking process, 1 cup of legumes will expand to approximately 2½ to 3 cups. The amount of water needed, the length of time needed for cooking and the amount of expansion are all variable, depending on the quality of legume, mineral content of the water and type and size of cooking utensil.

Pressure cooking legumes requires a little less water than the three to four times the volume of the legumes recommended above, because less water escapes as steam in this method. However, the longer cooking legumes will absorb almost three times their volume of water by the time they are soft. It is not necessary to soak any legumes which are to be cooked under pressure. Be sure to fill your pressure cooker only three-quarters full.

Legumes cooked in an unsealed pot must be stirred from time to time and more water may need to be added partway through the cooking process. Some legumes tend to foam up and overflow the pot. Soybeans especially do this. For this reason, do not cover soybeans tightly with a lid and add 1 to 2 tablespoons vinegar or oil to the water when cooking them. This inhibits the foaming. It is especially important to add the vinegar or oil to soybeans when cooking them in the pressure cooker, to prevent clogging the air vents in the cover. Salt should be added only during the last half hour of cooking legumes because it retards their softening.

Choose Cooking Method Best for You

Traditional Method: Soak legumes overnight. (If soaking soybeans overnight in warm weather, refrigerate them.) Bring legumes to a boil in soaking water, turn down the heat, and simmer legumes, covered, for required time.

Variation of Above: To rid legumes of carbohydrates that can cause intestinal gas, discard soaking water, bring legumes to a boil in fresh water, simmer covered, for 30 minutes. Drain and discard water. Bring to a boil again in fresh water, then simmer until legumes are soft. There will be a slight loss in minerals, protein and some water-soluble vitamins which may be compensated for by adding nutritional yeast to the finished product.

Short-Cut Methods: 1. No soaking. Bring water to a boil, drop legumes into pot slowly so that boiling does not stop. When the legumes are all in the pot, lower the heat and simmer them, covered, until they are soft. This method will save from ½ to 1 hour of cooking time.

2. No soaking. Cook legumes in pressure cooker. This method cuts down cooking time. To rid legumes of gas-inducing carbohydrates while using pressure cooking method, discard cooking water after half the required cooking time has elapsed, then resume cooking, using fresh water, for the remainder of the time.

3. Soak legumes overnight and sprout them for 2 days. Cook by traditional method above. This method increases nutrients and cuts down on cooking time. This method also rids legumes of carbohydrates, and the gas they cause.

Dried *split peas* have been "skinned" and split mechanically and are mainly used for split pea soup, though they combine well with many foods. The splitting treatment cuts down on cooking time.

Split Peas with Barley

(This recipe can be cooked in a crockery pot. See marker 🍲 *for method below.)*

2 tablespoons oil	3½ cups stock
¼ cup chopped onion	2 tablespoons chopped parsley
¼ cup chopped green pepper	3 tablespoons chopped fresh
¾ cup split peas	dill or 1 teaspoon dried
¼ cup soy grits	½ teaspoon salt
¾ cup pearled barley	chopped fresh parsley

🍲 (If using crockery pot, omit the following steps and continue with method below.)

Heat oil in a heavy saucepan and saute onion and green pepper for approximately 5 minutes. Add split peas, soy grits and barley, stirring constantly, until they are coated with oil (approximately 3 minutes). Add stock, parsley, dill and salt.

Cover pot and simmer for approximately 1¼ hours or until barley is tender. Serve hot, garnished with chopped parsley.

Yield: 6 servings

🍲 Soak split peas for at least 4 hours in water to cover. Drain. Omit oil. Combine soaked split peas with remaining ingredients. Cook on low for 8 to 10 hours.

Green and yellow whole peas and split peas, although they vary in taste a little, are used interchangeably in many recipes according to individual preference.

Dried *whole peas* can be served "just plain boiled," with butter and also go well with egg dishes or as a side dish with fish, poultry and game. They can also be used pureed in dips or in patties, croquettes and stuffed peppers.

Pea soup may be made from either whole or split peas. Cooked with other vegetables, with or without meat, pea soup is one of the best one-dish meals. It warms body and soul on a cold winter day.

❀❀ *Lentils*

One of the most delicious and easiest to prepare of the legumes is the lentil, an old-world favorite. Most of us think of lentils as an ingredient in soup. But that's just the beginning.

In India, for example, there are numerous varieties of lentils and lentil dishes. *Dal,* a sauce made from lentil or pea puree seasoned with spices, onion or garlic, is eaten with rice or bread. At least one kind of *dal* is part of every East Indian meal.

In Europe lentils often serve as the base for one-dish meals. When cooked with meat or soup bones, carrot, leek, onion and sometimes potatoes, a pot of lentils is good to have around on moving or spring cleaning day. Lentils are also used as a vegetable, cooked together with dried prunes or pears or apples, and sometimes lentils are served with dumplings. They sprout easily, too.

Lentils need no coddling and cook to puffed tenderness in about 30 minutes.

Lentil, Rice and Prune Pilaf

1 *cup brown rice*	1 *tablespoon honey*
2 *cups water*	3 *tablespoons lemon juice*
½ *teaspoon salt*	1 *stick cinnamon*
1 *cup lentils*	3 *cloves*
4 *cups water*	½ *teaspoon salt*
½ *teaspoon salt*	3 *tablespoons butter*
2 *cups prunes*	¼ *teaspoon dried mint*
2 *cups water*	⅛ *teaspoon tarragon*

Cook rice in salted water for approximately 35 minutes, or until tender and all water is absorbed.

While the rice is cooking, cook lentils in another saucepan in salted water for approximately 25 minutes, or until they are just tender but firm. Drain and combine with rice.

In a saucepan, combine prunes, water, honey, lemon juice, cinnamon stick and cloves. Cook for 20 minutes. Drain the prunes, reserving the juice. Remove seeds and cut into quarters. Add to rice and lentil mixture and stir in salt, butter, mint and tarragon. Strain the reserved prune juice and add enough to moisten the dish. Simmer for 3 to 5 minutes and serve.

Yield: 6 servings

Hopping John

(black-eyed peas, rice and pig's feet)

(This recipe can be cooked in a crockery pot. See marker 🍲 *for method below.)*

    2 *cups black-eyed peas*
    5 *or 6 cups water*
    2 *teaspoons salt*
    ¾ *cup chopped onion*
    ¼ *cup chopped celery*
    1 *pair pig's feet*
       (approximately
       1½ to 2 lbs.)
    1 *cup brown rice*
    ¼ *teaspoon black pepper*

🍲 (If using crockery pot, omit the following steps and continue with method below.)

Soak black-eyed peas in 6 cups water overnight. Next morning add salt, onion, celery and pig's feet to peas and soaking water and cook, covered, until peas are almost tender but still whole (approximately 45 minutes). Add rice, additional salt, if needed, and black pepper. Simmer for approximately 1 hour, or until rice is tender. Remove meat from pig's feet and discard bones and fat. Mix meat into peas and rice. Serve hot.

Yield: 6 to 8 servings

🍲 Put unsoaked black-eyed peas in bottom of crockery pot. Place pig's feet on top of peas. Add onion, celery, rice, salt and pepper. Bring 5 cups, not 6, of water to a boil and pour over mixture in crockery pot, poking a bit with a spoon to distribute water evenly. Cover and cook on low for 6 to 8 hours, until peas are tender and meat is done. Remove meat from pig's feet and discard bones and fat. Mix meat into peas and rice and serve.

NOTE: It is traditional to serve Hopping John on New Year's Day throughout the Carolinas. Eaten then, this dish is believed to bring good luck and plenty of everything the rest of the year.

Cook black beans according to preferred method. (See "Basic Methods for Cooking Beans and Other Legumes.") Drain and reserve liquid for soup.

In saucepan or skillet saute onion, celery, carrot and green pepper for approximately 5 minutes in oil. Add rice and continue to saute for 5 minutes more. Add chicken stock and seasonings. Bring to a boil, cover, lower heat and simmer for approximately 1½ hours or until rice is tender. *Preheat oven to 325°F.*

Add ¼ cup cheese, chopped parsley and cooked black beans. Mix thoroughly. Stir in beaten eggs and spoon into oiled casserole. Top with remaining ¼ cup cheese and bake in preheated oven for 30 minutes or until firm and nicely browned.

Yield: 6 to 8 servings

NOTE: This mixture can also be used to stuff tomatoes or green peppers.

Black Bean and Rice Bake

1 *cup black beans*
¼ *cup chopped onion*
¼ *cup chopped celery*
¼ *cup grated carrot*
¼ *cup chopped green pepper*
3 *tablespoons oil*
1 *cup brown rice*
2 *cups chicken or vegetable stock*
½ *teaspoon salt*
¼ *teaspoon black pepper*
½ *teaspoon basil*
½ *teaspoon thyme*
½ *cup grated Parmesan or Swiss cheese*
3 *tablespoons chopped parsley*
6 *eggs, beaten*

Soak the beans overnight in enough cold water to cover. Drain and add fresh water to cover, then simmer until they are almost tender (approximately 2 hours). Cook all the chopped vegetables in oil until they are almost tender. Add to the beans, with chicken stock, then simmer until beans are tender. Remove from heat and allow to cool slightly. When cool, puree in electric blender. Return to the pot, add salt and lemon juice. Heat and serve with snipped chives.

Yield: 6 to 8 servings

Black Bean Soup

1 *cup black beans*
1 *onion, chopped*
1 *green pepper, chopped*
1 *stalk celery, chopped*
1 *carrot, chopped*
2 *cloves garlic, chopped*
3 *tablespoons oil*
2 *cups chicken stock*
salt to taste
lemon juice to taste
snipped chives

Soul Food Crackers

1 *cup black-eyed peas*
3 *cups hot water*
1 *cup oatmeal (ground lightly in electric blender)*
½ *cup whole wheat flour*
¼ *teaspoon salt*
½ *cup water*
5 *tablespoons oil*
1 *tablespoon honey*

Make black-eyed pea flour: Sort and wash black-eyed peas, then soak them in 3 cups hot water for 4 hours. *Preheat oven to 350°F.* Drain peas and spread them out in a single layer on an ungreased baking sheet. Roast in preheated oven for 35 minutes, stirring occasionally. Remove peas and turn off oven. When peas are cool, grind to a powder in electric blender. There will be ½ to ¾ cup black-eyed pea flour. Use ½ cup flour for this recipe. Reserve remaining black-eyed pea flour for another use.

Combine ½ cup black-eyed pea flour with ground oatmeal, whole wheat flour and salt. Combine wet ingredients and stir into dry mixture, making a cohesive ball. *Preheat oven to 350°F.* Oil baking sheet, pat out dough on sheet and roll to a thickness of ⅛ inch, using a rolling pin.

Score with a knife in desired shapes and bake in preheated oven for 15 minutes. Cool 5 minutes before removing crackers from baking sheet. Finish cooling on a rack before storing.

Yield: 4 dozen 2-inch-square crackers

Chick-Pea and Cabbage Soup

1½ *cups chick-peas*
2 *cloves garlic, minced*
1 *slice whole grain bread, diced in ¾-inch pieces*
2 *tablespoons oil*
2 *tablespoons chopped parsley*
1 *large potato, peeled and diced*
1 *large tomato, chopped*
1 *bay leaf*
½ *head of cabbage or 4 cups shredded*
6 *cups bean liquid and water*
salt to taste
½ *lb. spinach, chopped*

Cook chick-peas according to preferred method. (See "Basic Methods for Cooking Beans and Other Legumes.") Drain and reserve liquid.

Saute garlic and bread in oil until garlic begins to deepen in color. Remove pan from heat and stir in parsley. Combine mixture with potato, cooked chick-peas, tomato, bay leaf, cabbage, bean liquid and water, and salt to taste in large pot and cook until potato is done (approximately 15 to 20 minutes). The bread will soften and thicken the soup. Approximately 5 minutes before serving, add spinach and continue cooking until it is done, but still keeps its bright green color. Serve hot.

Yield: 6 to 8 servings

Cook chick-peas according to preferred method. (See "Basic Methods for Cooking Beans and Other Legumes.")

Combine cooked chick-peas, bean liquid and water, garlic, lemon juice, salt and tahini in electric blender and process to a smooth puree. Thin to desired consistency with more bean liquid or water. Serve as a dip or sandwich filling.

Yield: approximately 3 cups

Hummus

¾ *cup chick-peas*
½ *to 1 cup bean liquid and*
  water
2 *cloves garlic*
6 *to 8 tablespoons lemon juice*
1 *teaspoon salt*
½ *cup tahini*
  (sesame seed butter)

Cook garbanzo beans according to preferred method. (See "Basic Methods for Cooking Beans and Other Legumes.") Drain if desired.

Preheat oven to 350°F. In a large skillet, saute onion, garlic, celery and green pepper in oil until tender. Add tomatoes with their juice, breaking up the tomatoes into smaller pieces. Combine sauteed vegetables with cooked garbanzo beans in a casserole, season with herbs, spices and salt to taste. Bake in preheated oven for 45 minutes to 1 hour.

Yield: 4 to 6 servings

Mexican Garbanzo Beans

1 *cup garbanzo beans*
1 *medium-size onion,*
  chopped
2 *cloves garlic, minced*
1 *stalk celery, chopped*
1 *green pepper, chopped*
3 *tablespoons oil*
1 *16-ounce can tomatoes*
1 *teaspoon oregano*
1 *teaspoon basil*
½ *teaspoon cumin*
⅛ *teaspoon chili powder*
salt to taste

Cook kidney beans according to preferred method. (See "Basic Methods for Cooking Beans and Other Legumes.") Drain and reserve liquid for soup.

Process next seven ingredients in electric blender until pureed. Add kidney beans gradually, working them in with a spatula until they are evenly pureed. Add mayonnaise and continue to blend until it is mixed in evenly.

Serve immediately or refrigerate in closed container. It will keep well for a week.

Yield: approximately 5½ cups

Kidney Bean Dip

1 *cup kidney beans*
3 *tablespoons tarragon*
  vinegar
2 *tablespoons oil*
½ *cup kidney bean liquid*
1 *small onion, peeled*
4½ *tablespoons soy flour*
1 *tablespoon dill seed*
¾ *teaspoon salt*
1½ *cups mayonnaise*

Kidney Bean Curry

2½ *cups dried kidney beans*
 4 *to 6 cups water*
 ½ *teaspoon turmeric*
 2 *teaspoons salt*
 ¼ *cup butter*
 2 *bay leaves*
 ½ *teaspoon ginger*
 ½ *teaspoon ground cumin*
 ½ *teaspoon ground coriander*
 ¼ *teaspoon white pepper*
 ¼ *teaspoon ground cardamom*
 3 *large tomatoes, peeled
      and chopped*
 ½ *cup yogurt*

Soak kidney beans in water to cover overnight. Add turmeric and salt and cook slowly for 1 to 2 hours, until beans are tender but firm. Drain, reserving liquid.

Heat butter in large skillet. Add bay leaves, spices and tomatoes. Cook for approximately 5 minutes. Remove bay leaves. Add drained kidney beans and ½ cup reserved bean liquid. Simmer for 15 minutes and, just before serving, stir in yogurt.

Yield: 6 to 8 servings

Dried Lima Bean Casserole

⅔ *cup dried lima beans*
water to cover
 1 *large green pepper, diced*
 2 *stalks celery, diced*
 1 *large onion, chopped*
 2 *cloves garlic, finely chopped*
 2 *tablespoons oil*
1½ *teaspoons salt*
1½ *cups bean liquid or
      chicken stock*
1½ *tablespoons unhulled
      sesame seeds*
 ½ *cup raisins*
1½ *cups shredded cheddar
      cheese*

Cook beans in water to cover until tender (see "Timetable for Cooking Legumes"). Drain and reserve liquid.

Preheat oven to 375°F. Saute vegetables in oil until tender. Combine with cooked lima beans, salt, liquid or stock, sesame seeds and raisins. Mix well and add half of the cheese. Bake in oiled casserole 25 minutes in preheated oven. Sprinkle with remaining cheese, bake 15 minutes at 400°F., and serve.

Yield: 4 to 6 servings

Combine lentils and water in a saucepan, partially cover pan with a lid and bring to a boil. Watch carefully to prevent lentils from boiling over. Turn heat down and simmer for 45 minutes to 1 hour or until lentils are tender.

Meanwhile, saute garlic and onion in oil, adding the spices and then the tomato juice. Cook until onions are soft and mixture is well blended.

Add onion and spice mixture to lentils and salt to taste. Puree *dal* in electric blender and serve with brown rice.

Yield: approximately 3½ cups

Indian Lentil *Dal*

1 *cup lentils*
3 *cups water*
1 *clove garlic, minced*
1 *medium-size onion, sliced*
1 *tablespoon oil*
1 *teaspoon Garam Masala (optional; see Index)*
½ *teaspoon turmeric*
½ *teaspoon ginger*
¼ *teaspoon chili powder*
¼ *cup tomato juice*
salt to taste

Cook kidney beans according to preferred method. (See "Basic Methods for Cooking Beans and Other Legumes.") Drain and reserve liquid for soup.

Break salmon into bite-size chunks. Add cooked beans and remaining ingredients and toss lightly. Chill before serving. Serve on a bed of salad greens.

Yield: 4 servings

Salmon Kidney Bean Salad

½ *cup kidney beans*
1 *7¾-ounce can salmon, drained*
¼ *teaspoon dill*
¼ *teaspoon salt*
1 *tablespoon chopped onion*
2 *tablespoons chopped parsley*
1 *tablespoon lemon juice*

Cook lentils in water or stock for approximately 25 minutes or until tender. Add salt and set aside. *Preheat oven to 350°F.*

Heat oil in a large skillet. Saute onion, mushrooms and bulgur for approximately 5 minutes. Combine the lentil mixture, including the liquid, with the bulgur mixture, and place in a buttered casserole. Cover and bake in preheated oven for 20 minutes.

Serve with yogurt and chopped green onions or chives.

Yield: 6 servings

Bulgur and Lentil Pilaf

¾ *cup lentils*
3 *cups water or stock*
1 *teaspoon salt*
3 *tablespoons oil*
1 *medium-size onion, chopped*
¼ *lb. mushrooms, sliced (approximately 1½ cups)*
¾ *cup bulgur*
yogurt
chopped green onions or chives

Lentil and Potato Pie

1½ *cups lentils*
1 *bay leaf*
3 *cups water or stock*
2 *medium-size potatoes*
¼ *cup milk*
1 *to 2 tablespoons butter*
   salt to taste
1 *large onion*
1 *16-ounce can tomatoes,*
      drained
2 *tablespoons oil*

Cook lentils and bay leaf in water or stock for 45 minutes or until they are soft. Remove bay leaf. Mash lentils thoroughly and set aside.

Boil potatoes in their jackets, then skin and mash, adding approximately ¼ cup milk and 1 tablespoon butter. Salt to taste. Chop onion and tomatoes and cook in oil until soft. *Preheat oven to 375°F.*

Butter an ovenproof dish, place the lentils in it, cover with the onion-tomato mixture, and top with mashed potatoes. Dot with extra bits of butter and bake in preheated oven approximately 30 minutes, or until casserole is hot and bubbling.

Yield: 6 servings

Cheese and Bean Crepes

1 *cup pinto beans*
1 *clove garlic, minced*
¼ *cup oil*
1 *teaspoon chili powder*
1 *teaspoon cumin*
⅓ *cup bean liquid or stock*
      (optional)
1 *cup shredded cheddar cheese*
   salt to taste
1½ *recipe Rice and Soy Crepes*
      (see Index)
   Parmesan cheese (optional)
1 *recipe Tomato Sauce*
      (see Index)

Cook pinto beans according to preferred method. (See "Basic Methods for Cooking Beans and Other Legumes.") Drain and reserve liquid.

Saute garlic in oil, add beans, mashing them in the pan with a potato masher. Add spices. Continue to saute beans for a few minutes, adding bean liquid or stock if necessary. Stir constantly. Add cheese and continue to heat only until cheese has melted. Salt to taste. Remove from heat and fill crepes, using 2 tablespoons filling for each crepe. Fold or roll crepes, top with Parmesan cheese if desired, and serve with Tomato Sauce.

Yield: 18 8-inch crepes

Cook navy beans according to preferred method. (See "Basic Methods for Cooking Beans and Other Legumes.") Drain and reserve liquid.

Meanwhile, cook green beans in water to cover until tender. Drain and reserve liquid for soup.

Combine all ingredients and mix well. Allow to marinate for several hours or overnight.

Yield: 6 to 8 servings

Navy Bean Salad

1 *cup navy beans*
1 *lb. green beans*
water to cover
1 *cup chopped onion*
1 *cup chopped green pepper*
1 *clove garlic, minced*
⅓ *cup vinegar*
⅔ *cup oil*
⅓ *cup bean liquid*
1 *teaspoon prepared mustard*
1 *teaspoon tamari soy sauce*

The Soybean

The queen of the legumes is the soybean. And its status is growing. From a relatively unknown commodity—considered cattle feed, an oil-producing crop or "that exotic vegetable the Asians eat"—it has finally come into its own in this country as an important food.

The soybean is the vegetable that most nearly provides the complete protein necessary for good health. It is rich in calcium and B vitamins, and lower in carbohydrates than any other bean. We Americans have begun to experiment with soybeans and are sprouting them as well as eating the green beans as a fresh vegetable.

Many varieties are suited to the family garden. The Fiskeby V Vegetable Bean, containing from 39 to 40 percent protein, is a flavorful soybean that crops in a short 45 days. This variety is available from Thompson & Morgan, P.O. Box 24, Somerdale, New Jersey 08083.

Methods of preparation for these garden soybeans vary from steaming the beans and serving them with butter or in salads to stir-frying them in a little oil alone or with other vegetables. A fresh succotash made with green soybeans and corn contains ample complete protein for a meal from that dish alone, making a meat dish unnecessary. Or you can create other low-cost, complete-protein combinations by serving soybeans in a casserole or soup with homemade whole wheat bread on the side.

Green Soybean and Corn Succotash

12 *cobs of corn*
2 *quarts green soybeans (still in the pod)*
butter (optional)

Cut corn off cobs. Pour boiling water over soybean pods (enough to cover them) and allow to stand 5 minutes, then drain and cool. Remove pods from soybeans. Put water to the depth of 1 inch in a medium-size saucepan and bring it to a boil. Add corn and soybeans, cover pan, cook 10 minutes over medium heat or until soybeans are tender. Drain and serve topped with a bit of butter, if desired.

Yield: 6 to 8 servings

For convenience in shelling, boil the soybeans for five minutes, then slip the beans out of the pods whether for immediate consumption, or for freezing or canning.

If you can't grow your own vegetables, you might find fresh green soybeans at a farmer's market. Otherwise, you can rely on getting the dried varieties at any supermarket.

Cooked soybeans can be used to make soup, chili con carne, barbecued baked beans, stuffed peppers or soyburgers—to name just a few of the many possibilities.

Soy Flour for Added Values

If you have a mill or grinder and are accustomed to making your own flour from whole rye, corn or other grain, restrain yourself when it comes to making soy flour. If you try to grind the uncooked bean, you will find that there's too much of the natural oil of the bean in the flour. Then if you use it immediately, you might find the taste a bit strong; if you keep it over a prolonged period of time, it might spoil. Good soybean flour is made from beans that have been cooked and then dried before they are ground. You will find this kind in health food stores or in the natural foods section that some supermarkets have. If you belong to a food co-op, you might buy it in large quantity.

You can boost the nutritive value of many recipes by adding small amounts of soy flour to them. Try adding a few tablespoons to cakes, cookies, pancakes and muffins.

In cooking with soy flour, keep its unique characteristics in mind. Don't expect soy flour to act like wheat flour. Soy flour has almost no starch—which means of course, that it can't be used as thickening. It also has no gluten, so don't replace more than two tablespoons per cup of flour in recipes which call for yeast. Soy flour in bread will help to keep it fresh and moist, but if you add too much, the bread will be heavy. Baking temperatures should be lowered by 25 degrees if the recipe contains soy flour, as it browns more quickly than other flours. Much more soy flour can be added to recipes where the gluten isn't so important. Delicious pancakes can be made using over one-half soy flour in the batter.

Soy Pancakes

6 *tablespoons buckwheat flour*	2 *egg whites*
6 *tablespoons cornmeal*	2 *egg yolks*
½ *cup soy flour*	1¾ *cups buttermilk*
¼ *teaspoon salt*	

Combine dry ingredients. Beat egg whites stiff but not dry, then beat egg yolks and buttermilk together and stir into dry ingredients. Gently fold in beaten egg whites. Spoon batter into medium-hot oiled skillet. When pancakes are brown, turn them to brown on the other side. Serve immediately.

Yield: approximately 30 3-inch pancakes

Soy grits or granules are crushed raw soybeans. They can be used in meat loaf, stews, even in cake recipes which call for ground nuts. They are inexpensive and rather bland in flavor so that they can be added to almost any dish and can even be used in making granola.

Soy Cheeseburgers

1 *cup soy grits*
1 *cup tomato juice*
4 *eggs, beaten*
¼ *cup water*
6 *tablespoons minced onion*

6 *tablespoons minced green pepper*
4 *teaspoons tamari soy sauce*
2 *teaspoons basil*
1 *cup grated cheese*

Combine soy grits and tomato juice. Add remaining ingredients, except for cheese, mixing thoroughly. Spoon into medium-hot, oiled skillet. Flatten burgers with the spoon and turn them when they are brown underneath. Top browned side with grated cheese. Cover skillet just long enough to melt cheese. Serve immediately.

Yield: 6 servings

Soy milk is extracted from dried beans. It can be made at home (see Index) or bought in powdered form called soy powder. Like soy flour (only somewhat finer), this is an important ingredient in cooking and baking for people who have allergies to milk and wheat. Soy flour and soy powder can be used interchangeably.

The versatile soybean also provides one of the finest oils, high in polyunsaturates. It can be used for salad dressing, baking and cooking, either by itself or mixed with safflower, peanut or other oils.

If you sprout soybeans, be sure to use only beans of the current season's crop. The sprouts may be eaten raw, they may be cooked by themselves or with other vegetables.

Tofu (Soybean Curd)

Tofu, as soybean curd is called throughout East Asia, is a custardlike food made from soybean milk. The process involves cooking the milk, then adding a solidifier, preferably magnesium chloride or calcium chloride taken from seawater. This causes the curd to separate from the whey. After the whey is drained off, the curd is pressed to form a firm block.

Tofu is prepared fresh each morning at 38,000 shops in Japan. It can be found in Oriental groceries and natural food stores all over the United States. It may be ordered by mail from companies specializing in Oriental foods and it is available in fresh, dried or canned form. However, tofu can also be made right in your own kitchen. A tofu kit, complete with pressing box, solidifier and instructions, is available from The Learning Tree, Box 620, Occidental, California 95465.

This low-cost protein food, which has been the backbone of the East Asian diet for more than 2,000 years, is at present the single most important soybean food for more than one billion people, according to William Shurtleff and Akiko Aoyagi, authors of *The Book of Tofu* (1975, Autumn Press, Inc., P.O. Box 469, Soquel, California 95073). This is an authentic, informative book containing 500 intriguing recipes for tofu, soybean milk and *okara* (the soybean pulp from which the milk is pressed).

Tofu is used extensively in Japanese and Chinese cooking. The most popular way to serve it in Japan is simply chilled and topped with soy sauce and finely slivered green onions or fresh ginger. Of course tofu is an ingredient in soups, it can also be deep fried, made into tofu-burgers, pureed to make dips, stir-fried with vegetables, even slivered to make french fries.

Soy Sauce *(Shoyu)*

The finest soy sauce, a basic ingredient in Oriental cooking, is made from whole soybeans, natural salt and well water that have been fermented for 12 to 18 months. All natural soy sauce, some of which is called tamari, is imported from Japan. There is a high-quality product called *shoyu* which is now produced in the United States. This less costly soy sauce is usually prepared from defatted soybean meal and brewed for 4 to 6 months. Some of the domestic soy sauce which is sold under various Chinese brand names is not fermented or brewed but made from hydrolyzed vegetable protein (HVP) by the reaction of defatted soybeans with hydrochloric acid. It is flavored with corn syrup and caramel. It may contain sodium benzoate or alcohol preservatives.

Herbed Soybean Salad

1 *cup soybeans*
2 *cups cubed zucchini*
½ *cup chopped parsley*
⅛ *teaspoon dill*
⅛ *teaspoon basil*
1 *clove garlic, minced*
1 *teaspoon salt*
1 *teaspoon prepared mustard*
2 *tablespoons vinegar*
¼ *cup oil*

Cook soybeans according to preferred method. (See "Basic Methods for Cooking Beans and Other Legumes.") Meanwhile, cook zucchini in a little water until tender, but not soft.

Combine cooked soybeans, zucchini and herbs. Mix garlic, salt, mustard, vinegar and oil. Pour dressing over soybean mixture and toss until well combined. Chill several hours or overnight, stirring occasionally.

Yield: 6 to 8 servings

Fresh Vegetable and Fruit Stew with Soybeans

1½ *cups soybeans*
 2 *medium-size onions, sliced*
 1 *teaspoon minced garlic*
 4 *to 6 tablespoons oil*
 4 *cups soybean liquid and
      water*
 3 *tablespoons tomato puree*
 4 *medium-size potatoes,
      peeled and diced*
 ¼ *medium-size head cabbage,
      cored and cut in chunks*
 ¼ *medium-size head cauli-
      flower, separated
      into flowerets*
 2 *cups winter squash, peeled,
      seeded and diced*
 2 *cups green beans, tipped
      and cut in 2-inch lengths*
 1 *tablespoon dried basil or
      2 sprigs fresh basil,
      snipped*
 2 *sprigs parsley, snipped*
    salt to taste
 2 *cups fresh blueberries*
 6 *to 8 fresh plums, halved
      and pitted*
 2 *apples, peeled, cored and
      sliced*
1½ *cups fresh cherries, halved
      and pitted*

Cook soybeans according to preferred method. (See "Basic Methods for Cooking Beans and Other Legumes.") Drain and reserve liquid.

Place soybeans in casserole. Saute onions and garlic in a little oil. Add soybean liquid, water and tomato puree. Pour this over soybeans. *Preheat oven to 350°F.* Arrange vegetables in layers on top of soybeans. Add herbs, season to taste, cover casserole and bake in preheated oven for 30 minutes.

Remove casserole from oven and top with fruit arranged in four rows, starting with a row of blueberries on one side, then plum halves, skin-side up, the apple slices and then cherry halves, skin-side up. Cover casserole and bake for 10 to 15 minutes more or until fruit is tender. Serve immediately from the casserole.

Yield: 6 to 8 servings

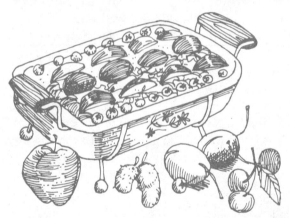

Soybean-Cabbage Casserole

1¼ *cups soybeans*
 6 *cups coarsely grated cabbage*
 1 *cup chopped walnuts*
1½ *teaspoons salt*
 1 *cup raisins*
 5 *egg yolks*
 5 *egg whites, stiffly beaten*

Cook soybeans according to preferred method. (See "Basic Methods for Cooking Beans and Other Legumes.") Drain and reserve liquid for soup.

Preheat oven to 400°F. Combine all ingredients except egg whites. Mix well. Fold in beaten egg whites. Pour into an ungreased large casserole and bake for 40 minutes in preheated oven.

Yield: 10 servings

Preheat oven to 350°F.

Soybean Coffee

1 *lb. soybeans*

Pick over and wash soybeans. Place them on a cookie sheet and roast them in preheated oven for 20 to 25 minutes, shaking the pan every 10 minutes. The soybeans have roasted long enough when the bean inside the skin is a deep chocolate color. Don't leave them until they are black. Remove soybeans from the oven and from the hot pan immediately and allow them to cool completely. Grind them, 1 cup at a time, in an electric blender.

Use 1 tablespoon of this "coffee" to every coffee cup of water, bringing the water to a boil in a small saucepan, then adding the soybean "coffee," covering the pan, removing it from the heat, and steeping the beverage for 5 minutes. Strain "coffee" through a fine strainer.

Yield: enough powder for approximately 30 cups

Cook soybeans according to preferred method. (See "Basic Methods for Cooking Beans and Other Legumes.")

Meanwhile, make pie shell according to preferred recipe.

Drain and reserve liquid from beans. Put soybeans through meat grinder or puree in electric blender, using a little of reserved liquid if necessary. Use 1½ cups ground or pureed soybeans for this recipe. *Preheat oven to 450°F.*

Combine all ingredients and mix thoroughly. Pour into unbaked pie shell and bake in preheated oven for 15 minutes. Lower heat to 350°F. and bake approximately 35 minutes, or until lightly browned.

Soybean Custard Pie

¾ *cup soybeans*
1 *9-inch unbaked pie shell*
¾ *cup honey*
¼ *teaspoon salt*
1 *teaspoon cinnamon*
½ *teaspoon ginger*
½ *teaspoon nutmeg*
2 *eggs, slightly beaten*
1 *cup milk*

Yield: 1 9-inch pie

Soy Milk

1⅓ *cups soybeans*
8 *cups water*
1⅓ *teaspoons baking soda*
8 *cups water*
5½ *cups water*
2½ *to 3 teaspoons honey
   (optional)*
salt to taste

Soak soybeans in 8 cups water for 16 hours. If weather is hot, refrigerate soaking soybeans.

Drain soybeans and discard soaking water. In large saucepan dissolve baking soda in 8 cups fresh water, add drained soybeans and bring to a boil. Simmer for 5 minutes, stirring constantly to prevent them from boiling over. Drain, wash soybeans in fresh water, pouring off the floating hulls and drain again.

Put one-quarter of the drained soybeans (approximately ¾ cup) in electric blender, add ½ cup water or just enough to cover them, and process for approximately 2 minutes to make a thick, smooth puree. Then add ¾ cup water, process just long enough to thin the puree and pour into the top of a double boiler. Puree remaining soybeans in the same way, using ½ cup water to ¾ cup soybeans and then adding ¾ cup water to thin the puree. All together 5 cups of water should be used along with all the drained soybeans (approximately 3 cups).

Pour all pureed soybeans into top of double boiler, add ½ cup more water, stirring it into puree. Cover with a lid and cook over rapidly boiling water for 30 minutes, stirring the puree occasionally so that it will cook evenly.

Meanwhile line a colander with about four layers of cheesecloth and set it over a bowl. When the 30 minutes are up, pour the soybean puree into the colander. Let it drip for 30 minutes, gently lifting the cheesecloth on one side and then the other to help the milk drain off the pulp, but don't squeeze or press the pulp or it will go through the cheesecloth into the milk. If you want to, you can gather up the edges of the cheesecloth and make a sort of "bag," wrapping a piece of string around the neck and tying it to a cupboard knob, suspended over a bowl.

If desired, season the soy milk, adding 1 teaspoon honey and a few grains of salt for every cup of milk.

Use soy pulp (*okara*) in making bread, meat or vegetarian loaves or to thicken cream soup or gravy. *Okara* should be frozen for future use as it will not keep very long in the refrigerator. Soy milk too is quite perishable but if sweetened with honey, will keep up to a week in the refrigerator.

*Yield: 2½ to 3 cups soy milk;
3 to 4 cups soy pulp* (okara)

Preheat oven to 350°F.

Combine all ingredients. Pack into a buttered 9x5x3-inch loaf pan and bake in preheated oven for approximately 40 minutes, or until firm and nicely browned.

Yield: 6 to 8 servings

Using a meat grinder with a fine blade, put through cooked liver, hard-cooked egg and onion. Combine remaining ingredients and add to liver mixture. Mix well and store in refrigerator. Use as spread for sandwiches or as a dip for crackers or raw vegetables.

Yield: approximately 3 cups

Carrot Soy Loaf

2 *cups chopped onions*
4 *tablespoons chopped parsley*
2 *tablespoons chopped celery*
2 *cups grated carrots*
2 *cups soy pulp (from preparation of Soy Milk—see above) or 1 cup soy grits and 1 cup water simmered together for 8 minutes*
1 *cup tomato sauce*
2 *eggs, beaten*
1 *cup wheat germ*
1 *teaspoon crushed thyme*
1 *teaspoon sweet basil*
1 *teaspoon salt*

Liver Pate

4 *medium-size pieces fried or broiled beef or pork liver, or a mixture of both (approximately 2⅔ cups when ground)*
1 *hard-cooked egg, peeled*
½ *small onion, peeled*
½ *cup mayonnaise*
1 *cup soy pulp (from preparation of Soy Milk—see above) or ½ cup soy grits and ½ cup water simmered together for 8 minutes*
1 *tablespoon lemon juice*
1 *tablespoon tamari soy sauce*
2 *teaspoons dry basil leaves*
1 *teaspoon powdered sage*
½ *teaspoon poultry seasoning*
pinch of celery salt
pinch of white pepper

Mock Pumpkin Pie

1   *8-inch unbaked pie shell*
2   *eggs, beaten*
¼   *cup honey*
1   *tablespoon molasses*
1   *teaspoon vanilla*
¾   *teaspoon cinnamon*
½   *teaspoon ginger*
¼   *teaspoon salt*
1¼   *cups soy pulp (from
        preparation of Soy
        Milk—see above) or 10
        tablespoons soy grits
        and 10 tablespoons
        water simmered together
        for 8 minutes*
1   *cup yogurt*

Make pie shell according to preferred recipe.

Preheat oven to 400°F. Combine all ingredients and mix well. Pour into pie shell. Bake in preheated oven for 10 minutes, then turn oven to 350°F. and bake 30 minutes more or until pie is set.

Yield: 1 8-inch pie

Scroggin

(backpacker's food)

3   *cups soybeans*
3   *cups wheat berries*
2⅔   *cups hulled oats*
1½   *cups water*
2   *cups raisins*
4   *cups sunflower seeds*
1   *cup walnuts or almonds*
2   *cups dry cottage cheese
        (optional)*
4   *cups fresh or frozen blue-
        berries (or any berries
        in season)*
2   *cups unsweetened coconut
        (optional)*

Cook soybeans by preferred method. (See "Basic Methods for Cooking Beans and Other Legumes.") Drain and reserve liquid for soup.

Combine wheat berries and hulled oats in pressure cooker with 1½ cups water. Cook for 7 minutes, then remove cooker from heat and allow pressure to drop of its own accord. Drain and reserve liquid for soup.

Combine cooked soybeans, wheat berries and oats and mix in all other ingredients. Pack into freezer containers and freeze. Remove to refrigerator 24 hours before using to allow scroggin to thaw. If you are planning to take scroggin along on a hike in hot weather, leave it in its frozen state. When you are ready to eat it, it will be thawed but cold and refreshing.

Yield: 14 pints or 7 quarts

Soy-Potato Dumplings

Cook potatoes in water to cover, drain and reserve liquid for soup. Mash and use ½ cup for this recipe.

Combine all ingredients and mix thoroughly. Chill for approximately 1 hour. Drop by tablespoon into a pot of boiling water or spoon carefully onto simmering stew. Cover the pot tightly and steam for 10 minutes.

Yield: 14 small dumplings

2 *medium-size potatoes*
water to cover
½ *cup soy flour*
1 *teaspoon salt*
3 *eggs, beaten*
3 *tablespoons water*
1 *tablespoon oil*

Soy Salad Dressing

Stir soy flour or powder into oil. Add other ingredients slowly, stirring continuously.

Yield: approximately 1½ cups

¾ *cup soy flour or powder*
1 *cup oil*
½ *teaspoon salt*
¼ *cup lemon juice*

Sprouts—

Making Seeds and Beans Even Better

Sprouting is a time-honored technique for expanding the impressive nutritional treasure seeds and legumes have been endowed with by nature. It is merely a matter of providing the setting where seeds can do what comes naturally—put forth slender green shoots—and reaping the additional harvest of vitamins the shoots contain. And you have a whole new flavorsome food to work with, in the bargain. Sprouts are a natural for salads, make a fine ingredient in soups, serve well as a hot vegetable, part of a casserole or as a simple snack.

To begin with, the seed contains the best food value plants have to offer. For example, protein is higher in the seed than in any other part of the plant, and vitamins, minerals, unsaturated oils and valuable carbohydrates are also contained generously in seeds.

Seeds store well. Whole seeds don't have to be preserved or frozen to prevent spoilage. And if they're sprouted, seeds can quickly be converted into a low-cost ingredient for almost any dish.

Compared with most other worthwhile foods, seeds and beans are cheap. They expand tremendously during sprouting and each serving (approximately half a cup) costs less than a penny. While many people interested in low-cost food are gratefully taking advantage of the economy of sprouts, the average victim of food-cost inflation hasn't yet discovered this bonanza.

Look at the whole range of seeds that is available as a source for sprouts and plan to include more of them in your diet. Beans and other legumes, such as peas and lentils, are worth special attention. By sprouting, you can eat and enjoy the seeds of numerous plants you probably never considered using as food.

The Chinese Started It All

Most Americans tend to think of sprouts as "Chinese food" which, indeed, they are. Thousands of years ago, the Chinese faced the same kind of population pressures and the food and energy shortages that plague us today. Seed sprouting, usually mung beans, was one solution to their problems.

No heat energy is needed to sprout seeds for eating. The seed does not have to be ground into flour, nor does it have to be cooked. Only a little moisture is needed. The basic process of regular sprouting is simple. Merely wash the seeds in water and soak them overnight. Then keep them moist for several days until the sprout portion is long enough to suit your taste. Experts say sunflower seed sprouts and wheat sprouts are most delicious when the sprout is the same length as the seed. Mung bean sprouts are best at 1½ to 3 inches. Let the green leaves develop fully on alfalfa sprouts by putting them in the light so the chlorophyll can develop. Pea and soybean sprouts are good short or long.

The biggest plus is that sprouting triggers a process of vitamin expansion that is truly remarkable. The vitamin C content of soybeans, for example, is said to increase as much as 553 percent during sprouting. The same kind of vitamin C explosion happens in other plants too.

B vitamins also zoom in sprouting seeds. Riboflavin quadruples, as does pyridoxine which is B₆. Pantothenic acid increases dramatically. Vitamins A, E and K go up in varying amounts when seeds sprout.

The vitamin-boosting power of the sprouting process is so impressive that it's truly a wonder sprouting is not used much more widely to make grains, beans and other seeds into convenience foods of outstanding nutritional value.

Start with Mung Beans

Mung beans are the best choice for beginners in sprouting. They sprout quickly with almost total germination, grow rapidly and taste delicious. After a few batches of mung beans, a sprouter will want to graduate to alfalfa seeds, lentils, rye and wheat. Each has a unique flavor and special nutritional characteristics. A common favorite is alfalfa sprouts, which are delicate and have a uniquely pleasant flavor. Alfalfa is a tremendously nutritious food but it can only be eaten by people in the form of sprouts.

Seeds that are intended for planting in farm or garden may have been treated with pesticides, so get sprouting seeds in health food stores, from food mail-order houses or from supermarkets.

Always start by presoaking seeds overnight, or for 8 to 12 hours. Then get your seeds into a container that will keep them moist and preferably away from light for several days. It is necessary to rinse the seeds with water several times a day, and then drain them. Don't keep the seeds sitting in water—just make sure they're damp.

How do you do that?

One of the most popular and simplest techniques is the "wide-mouthed-jar" method. All you need is a canning jar or similar glass jar with a wide mouth, to make it easy to flush with water and drain. The seeds are put inside and soaked, and the top of the jar is covered with cheesecloth held in place with a rubber band. You can also buy special wire screens for the tops of sprouting jars, made from galvanized wire mesh or even stainless steel mesh. They work well.

Keep the jar in a dark place, such as a closet or cupboard. Pour in water a few times a day, swish it around a little, then drain the water off and leave it inverted so no excess water remains. Harvesttime differs from seed to seed, and according to personal taste. Lentils and mung beans take from three to four days, wheat two days, and alfalfa six to seven days. Alfalfa sprouts should be exposed to the light when leaves form, to allow photosynthesis to create added nutritional value as the leaves turn green.

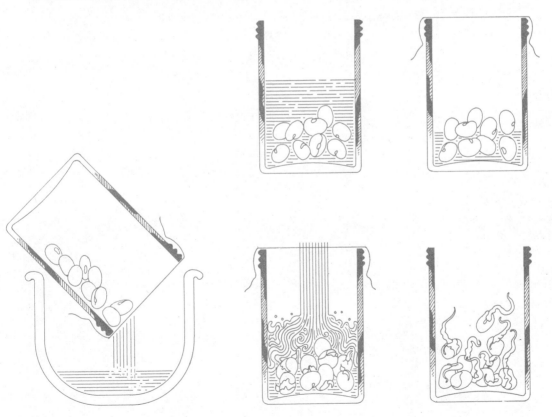

Alternative Sprouting Methods

There are other ways to sprout seeds for eating. Some people wrap them in cloth towels, or cover seeds with damp paper towels. The Japanese sprout seeds in a series of wooden trays with holes in the bottom. They can be stacked five-high, so that water poured over the top tray drains down through all of them. An advantage of this method is that one of the stacked trays can be "charged" with seeds each day, so that a fresh batch of sprouts will be ready at regular intervals. For a big family or a restaurant, that could be an important advantage.

All these sprouting devices are fun to use. But you might prefer the casual, direct approach used by Helen K. Nearing of Harborside, Maine, who wrote in *Farmstead Magazine* (Spring 1975):

"We take a small china bowl, any size, and put a handful of mung beans in it and then more than cover it with water, putting a saucer on top. We leave this by the kitchen sink overnight. Next day we pour the water off by tilting the bowl and draining with saucer held on. (This water can be added to soup or cereal or you can drink it straight for the vitamins it contains.) Pour more water onto the seeds and pour right off again, draining with saucer held on. Rinse in this way two or three times a day until sprouts are the length you want."

Alfalfa Sprout Gazpacho

1 *cup alfalfa sprouts*
4 *cups tomato juice*
½ *cucumber, chopped*
1 *stalk celery, chopped*
1 *green onion, chopped*
1 *1-inch slice green pepper, chopped*
2 *medium-size tomatoes, skinned and chopped*

Combine all ingredients in electric blender and process until completely liquefied. Chill 1 hour. Serve as a beverage or a soup.

Yield: 6 cups

Put wheat sprouts through a meat grinder, using the fine blade. Combine all ingredients and let stand at room temperature for 20 minutes. *Preheat oven to 325°F.* Form into two oval loaves and place on oiled baking sheet. Bake in preheated oven for 1 hour. Cool on rack.

Yield: 2 small loaves

Sprouted Wheat Bread

(unleavened)

> 2 *cups sprouted wheat*
> *(sprouted for 24*
> *to 36 hours)*
> ½ *cup oil*
> 1¼ *cups milk*
> 2 *cups whole wheat flour*
> 2 *cups wheat germ*

Combine all ingredients, mixing by hand until you have a soft, moist, well-blended mixture. Form into patties. Broil or saute them according to preferred method of cooking.

Yield: 4 servings

Beef and Sprout Patties

> 1 *lb. ground beef*
> 1 *cup chopped mung bean*
> *sprouts*
> 1 *clove garlic, minced*
> ¼ *medium-size onion, minced*
> ¼ *cup tomato juice*
> 2 *tablespoons tamari*
> *soy sauce*
> 1 *tablespoon basil*

Chop sprouts and peanuts together, or put through meat grinder using blade with large holes. Cut in peanut butter, then add milk. Mix thoroughly. In another bowl, combine seeds, flour and salt. Mix together the sprout and seed mixtures to form a stiff dough. *Preheat oven to 275°F.*

Divide dough in half and spread each half on an oiled cookie sheet. Cover with wax paper and roll out to ¼ inch thick. Cut into 1½-inch squares and bake in preheated oven for 1 hour or until browned. Remove from pan and cool on rack. Store in airtight container.

Yield: 80 squares

Garbanzo (Chick-Pea) Sprout Snack

> 2 *cups garbanzo (chick-pea)*
> *sprouts*
> 1½ *cups peanuts*
> ¾ *cup peanut butter*
> 1 *cup milk*
> 1½ *cups unhulled sesame seeds*
> 1½ *cups sunflower seeds*
> 1½ *cups whole wheat flour*
> ½ *teaspoon salt*

Sprouted Wheat Tabouli

2 *cups sprouted wheat*
1 *cucumber, peeled and diced*
1 *green pepper, seeded and
    diced*
1 *green onion, sliced*
¼ *cup diced celery with leaves*
2 *tablespoons chopped parsley*
salt to taste
½ *cup oil*
½ *cup cider vinegar*

Combine all ingredients. Toss to mix. Cover and refrigerate at least overnight before serving. Mixture will keep several days in the refrigerator. Serve on salad greens.

Yield: 6 to 8 servings

Sprouted Wheat Sticks

3 *to 4 cups sprouted wheat*
2 *tablespoons crushed
    caraway seeds*
1 *egg, lightly beaten*
cornmeal

Preheat oven to 400°F.

Put sprouted wheat through fine blade of meat grinder. Mix with seeds and egg. Form into cigar shapes, roll in cornmeal and place on an oiled baking sheet. Let dry 5 minutes.

Bake 10 minutes in preheated oven, lower heat to 325°F. and continue baking until done, about 5 minutes longer.

Yield: 1 dozen sticks

Sprouts and Avocado Crepes

2 *ripe medium-size avocados,
    peeled and pitted*
1 *clove garlic, minced*
3 *tablespoons lemon juice*
¼ *cup sesame seed butter*
1 *teaspoon tamari soy sauce*
salt, pepper to taste
1 *cup mung bean sprouts*
1¼ *recipe Rice and Soy Crepes
    (see Index)*

Mash avocados and combine with all ingredients, except sprouts, to make filling. Put 2 tablespoons filling and 1 tablespoon sprouts on each crepe. Roll or fold crepe and serve.

Yield: approximately 16 8-inch crepes

Separate broccoli bunch into stalks. Trim stalks and cut stem off below the flower. Reserve the flowers. Slice stalks ¼ inch thick. Heat oil to medium-hot in large skillet or *wok*. Stir-fry onions for a minute or two, then add cabbage, broccoli stalks, turnips and ginger. Stir-fry for approximately 5 minutes. Finally, add broccoli flowers, bean sprouts, tamari soy sauce, water and salt to taste. Stir-fry for a few more minutes until vegetables are tender but still firm. Pan may be covered briefly toward the end of the cooking process to hasten tenderizing. Serve immediately.

Yield: 4 servings

Stir-Fried Bean Sprouts

½ *large bunch broccoli*
¼ *cup oil*
4 *green onions, thinly sliced*
4 *cups coarsely chopped Chinese cabbage (celery cabbage)*
2 *cups sliced turnips*
2 *tablespoons minced fresh ginger*
2 *cups mung bean sprouts*
¼ *cup tamari soy sauce*
¼ *cup water*
salt to taste

Place all ingredients, except sesame seeds, through fine blade of meat grinder. Mix well and shape into balls the size of marbles. Roll in sesame seeds and refrigerate before serving.

Yield: 30 balls

Wheat Sprout Candy

1 *cup wheat sprouts*
1 *cup walnuts*
1 *cup coconut*
1 *cup raisins*
unhulled sesame seeds

Carob, Better

Than Chocolate

It's true. When the pod of the carob tree is ground up it can be used in candy, drinks, cake and icing as a very acceptable substitute for chocolate. But down through the ages, carob has been known, not as a substitute for chocolate, but as a delicious food in its own right. The Israelites called it *Boecksur* or "God's Bread." Mohammed's conquering armies enjoyed it and relied on it as survival food under the name of *Kharub*. The Romans called it *Carobi*. More familiar are the terms "Honey Locust" and Saint-John's-bread, which are still widely used.

Carob flour carries trace amounts of no less than 15 minerals. And while carob can hardly be described as a mineral supplement, it does make a definite contribution to our total nutrition. The contribution is especially significant because it displaces chocolate, a food with definite nutritional disadvantages.

Carob is low in calories, low in fat, high in natural sugars, contains vitamins A and B complex which help to digest it, along with its miniature reservoir of minerals.

This sweet confection, which is just about the same price as cocoa, can satisfy the craving many people have for chocolate, without kicking up allergies in those who are sensitive to chocolate and without encouraging tooth cavities as chocolate does. And it is certainly better than chocolate for diabetics. Carob is naturally sweet and the natural sugar in it does not require insulin to metabolize it.

Chocolate, on the other hand, is naturally bitter. (Nibble some baking chocolate and you'll see.) The sweet chocolate bars and other chocolate candies that delight kids contain more than 40 percent added white sugar. One hundred grams (about 3½ ounces) of chocolate candy contain 528 calories.

An Answer for Allergies

Dr. Joseph A. Fries, the Director of the Allergy Service at the Methodist Hospital of Brooklyn, said that in tests of 300 allergic children, 70 percent had reactions after eating chocolate; some had difficulty with breathing and digestion and they also suffered rashes. When the chocolate was taken out of their diet, their breathing returned to normal and their rashes cleared up noticeably, Dr. Fries said. He searched for a food with chocolatelike flavor that would satisfy his young patients, but would not possess the allergenic properties in chocolate that made them sick.

He reported the result of his search in the *Annals of Allergy* (September 1966): "Recently there have appeared on the market confections made from carob bean (Saint-John's-bread), the fruit of the carob tree. These mimic to a remarkable degree the appearance, the texture and most important the taste of chocolate. Carob is a legume of low-allergenic potential."

By now, carob has been rediscovered by many people as a useful addition to the kitchen shelf. With carob as the central ingredient, you can make chocolatelike syrups, hot and cold milk drinks, fudge, cake, brownies, puddings, ice cream and even frosting.

Carob Carrot Candy

½ cup sunflower seeds
  (finely ground
  in electric blender)
½ cup walnuts (finely ground
  in electric blender)
½ cup chopped walnuts
1¼ cups finely grated carrots
½ cup non-fat dry milk
¼ cup carob, sifted

Combine all ingredients in order given. Mix well, then shape into a roll approximately 9 inches by 2 inches. Roll in wax paper or plastic wrap and put into freezer for several hours. When hardened, slice into ¼-inch pieces.

Yield: 35 to 40 slices

Carob Honey Cake

1 cup whole wheat
  pastry flour
½ cup carob, sifted
2 teaspoons cinnamon
6 egg yolks
⅓ cup softened butter
½ cup honey
⅓ cup water
2 teaspoons vanilla
6 egg whites, stiffly beaten

Preheat oven to 350°F.

Combine flour, carob and cinnamon. Mix well. Beat egg yolks with butter and honey. Add water and vanilla. Combine dry and wet mixtures and mix thoroughly, then fold in beaten egg whites.

Turn into a buttered 9-inch spring-form pan and bake for approximately 40 minutes in preheated oven. Frost with Carob Nut Frosting (see Index), if desired.

Yield: 1 9-inch cake

Carob Cottage Cheese Pie

Preheat oven to 300°F.

Combine sesame seeds and coconut and place in a shallow baking pan in a preheated oven. Bake until lightly browned (8 to 10 minutes) stirring or shaking occasionally.

Meanwhile, oil a 9-inch pie pan. When sesame seeds and coconut are brown, sprinkle the mixture on the bottom and sides of the pan, reserving 2 tablespoons for decoration later. Raise oven temperature to 375°F.

Combine honey, vanilla and cottage cheese and puree in electric blender until very smooth. Beat eggs until thick. Add to cheese mixture and mix well. Pour into prepared pie pan and bake in a preheated 375°F. oven for approximately 35 minutes or until firm. Remove from oven and allow to cool for 30 minutes.

Meanwhile, combine yogurt, honey, almond extract, carob, cinnamon and non-fat dry milk. Mix until very smooth. Spread the topping carefully over the cooled pie and make a 1-inch border of the remaining coconut-sesame mix. Bake in 375°F. oven for 5 minutes. Refrigerate for 2 or 3 hours before serving.

Yield: 8 servings

3 *tablespoons unhulled sesame seeds*
½ *cup shredded coconut*
1 *tablespoon oil*
¼ *cup honey*
2 *teaspoons vanilla*
1½ *cups cottage cheese*
3 *eggs*
1 *cup yogurt*
2 *tablespoons honey*
¼ *teaspoon almond extract*
¼ *cup carob, sifted*
½ *teaspoon cinnamon*
3 *tablespoons non-fat dry milk*

Carob Nut Brownies

Preheat oven to 350°F.

Combine eggs, honey, molasses, butter and almond extract. Mix flour, carob and salt, then combine the wet and dry mixtures. Mix thoroughly, add nuts and turn into an oiled 8x8-inch baking pan. Bake in preheated oven for 25 minutes. Remove from oven and cut while warm. Cool on rack.

Yield: 16 brownies

2 *eggs, beaten*
½ *cup honey*
1 *tablespoon molasses*
¼ *cup melted butter*
¼ *teaspoon almond extract*
1 *cup whole wheat pastry flour*
1 *cup carob, sifted*
½ *teaspoon salt*
⅔ *cup chopped walnuts*

Carob Nut Frosting

3 *tablespoons honey*
3 *tablespoons softened butter*
⅔ *cup non-fat dry milk*
⅓ *cup carob, sifted*
4 *tablespoons cottage cheese
    (pureed in electric
    blender until smooth)*
½ *cup chopped nuts*

In electric mixer, beat honey and butter together, then stir in non-fat dry milk and carob. Add pureed cottage cheese, mixing until smooth. Spread over cake and top with chopped nuts.

*Yield: frosting to cover 1
          9-inch loaf cake or
          2 8-inch layers*

Carob Peanut Butter Pudding

¼ *cup honey*
1 *tablespoon butter or oil*
½ *cup peanut butter*
½ *cup carob, sifted*
1½ *cups milk*
3 *eggs, beaten*
¼ *teaspoon almond extract*

Combine honey, butter or oil, peanut butter and carob in the top of a double boiler. Heat and stir constantly until mixture is smooth. Add milk and stir constantly until mixture is hot.

Gradually add ½ cup hot mixture to beaten eggs, then stir this back into the hot mixture. Cook, stirring constantly, until pudding is thick. This will take approximately 5 to 8 minutes. Add almond extract and pour into serving dish. Chill for several hours.

Yield: 6 servings

Carob Potato Bonbons

4 *medium-size potatoes*
3 *tablespoons carob, sifted*
¼ *teaspoon salt*
2 *tablespoons honey*
1 *teaspoon vanilla*
2 *tablespoons non-fat
    dry milk*
3 *cups coconut
    (approximately)*

Cook potatoes in water to cover, drain and reserve liquid for soup. Mash potatoes and chill. Use 2 cups for this recipe.

Combine mashed potatoes, carob and salt. Mix thoroughly, then add honey, vanilla and non-fat dry milk. Mix in 1 cup coconut, shape into balls about the size of a walnut and roll balls in remaining coconut. Refrigerate approximately 8 hours or overnight before using.

Yield: 40 bonbons

Combine water, non-fat dry milk, carob, butter and lecithin granules in electric blender and process until smooth. Pour carob mixture over peanuts and raisins, mixing until they are evenly coated. Drop mixture by teaspoon onto lightly buttered baking sheet, forming it into clumps.

Starting in a cold oven, bake clusters on a rack in the middle of the oven at 300°F. for 10 minutes, or until the tops begin to look dry. Remove from oven and cool before taking clusters from the sheet. Harden in refrigerator before serving.

Yield: 30 large clusters

Carob Raisin Clusters

⅓ *cup warm water*
⅓ *cup non-fat dry milk*
½ *cup carob, sifted*
2 *tablespoons butter*
2 *rounded tablespoons lecithin granules*
1 *cup peanuts*
1 *cup raisins*

In a small saucepan, combine carob, honey, salt and cornstarch. Add water and bring to a boil, stirring constantly. Boil slowly for 5 minutes, remove from heat, cool and add vanilla. Serve hot or cold as a sauce with ice cream or cake or add 2 teaspoons to 1 cup milk for a carob drink.

Yield: 1 cup

Carob Syrup

⅓ *cup carob*
⅓ *cup honey*
⅛ *teaspoon salt*
1 *teaspoon cornstarch*
⅔ *cup hot water*
½ *teaspoon vanilla*

Heat honey and peanut butter. Quickly add carob and then all the seeds, coconut and fruit. Pour into greased 8x8-inch pan and refrigerate to harden. Cut into squares and keep refrigerated if possible.

Yield: approximately 25 squares

Super Fudge

1 *cup honey*
1 *cup peanut butter*
1 *cup carob*
1 *cup unhulled sesame seeds*
1 *cup sunflower seeds*
½ *cup shredded coconut*
½ *cup dates or other fruit*

Naturally Great Teas

That Can Make You Feel Good

All over the world people bend with genial anticipation over steaming cups of tea. Teas are mood lifters, health givers, stimulants, soothers and healers. Fortunes are told from tea leaves and weighty agreements sealed with a sip of a fragrant brew.

Tea tasting is a science and, in many cultures, the person knowledgeable about teas is held in high esteem. But it's not only the Chinese or Indian teas most familiar to us that are accepted as everyday beverages. Countless types of herb teas, ranging from aromatic to sweet to tart, are equally popular in many families. In European and South American countries the menus of restaurants, coffeehouses or *Konditoreien* carry at least two or three herb teas in addition to coffee, so-called black tea and hot chocolate. Among the most popular ones are peppermint, chamomile and mate.

Persons dropping in at a friend's house are often given a choice of teas. Will it be fresh peppermint, lemon verbena or bergamot picked fresh from the herb garden near the kitchen door? Or perhaps a tea made from dried herbs, fruits, flowers or from such seeds as anise, rosehips, flax and fennel is more appealing?

Aren't the rest of us missing something? Let's get better acquainted with the uses of herb teas. They are fragrant and tasty. They don't contain caffeine. And what's more, they help in combating indigestion, colds and other ailments.

Peppermint tea and papaya tea are known to soothe upset stomachs and ease menstrual cramps. Chamomile is an honored sleep inducer, and it's not addictive.

301

Some people have success in treating a cold that has settled in their bladder with an hourly schedule of drinking herb teas. Goldenseal, chaparral, lemongrass, Spanish eucalyptus, and bearberry leaf teas are said to be good for that purpose. To induce the sweat that helps drive out a cold, try tea made from dried linden blossoms.

Trees often provide the basic ingredient for a tea, sometimes the bark, often the leaves, in some cases the root.

A Tasty Time-Honored Spring Tonic

Sassafras tea is a good example. That time-honored spring tonic comes from the root of the sassafras tree. Users say it helps to cleanse the body of winter sluggishness. A common theory is that it thins the blood and thereby improves circulation. Whatever it does, it tastes good.

You don't need much sassafras root to make a good tea. Just put a few chips of it into a pint of water, cover, bring to a boil and let simmer for about five minutes. (The tea should be bright orange and fragrant.) Strain and drink, with a spot of honey if you like. Don't discard the bark; it can be used for about six brewings, getting better each time.

What about Ginseng?

Another tea root, ginseng, the ancient Oriental helper for all ailments, is making a comeback. The alleged power of ginseng to improve sexual performance and endurance—so far unproven—is the key to its current popularity.

The juices of onion and garlic have highly antiseptic properties. A syrup made of cooked, strained onions, sweetened with honey, is a most effective cough medicine. Garlic soup also helps combat colds.

Nasturtium is not only a very pretty flower and an insect repellent, it also tastes good in salad and the tea made from it has remedial properties for such ailments as sore throats and skin problems caused by poor metabolism. But heat diminishes the flower's healthful properties. So make a cold nasturtium tea. Just crush leaves, stems, flowers and seeds and soak them in water overnight. Then strain, and your drink is ready.

The variations in taste that teas provide present intriguing possibilities for any food lover to explore. Their health-giving attributes make teas even more desirable. Why limit yourself to the familiar? Be as creative in your beverage choices as you are in choosing foods. They are natural joys of living.

Appendix

Main

Meal Menus with a Purpose

When a family sits down to dinner, it's a sure bet that few of the diners are aware of the planning and effort involved in getting the food to the table. But the cook knows only too well. For many cooks, menu planning is the most important and time-consuming part of the job.

If there are a few heavyweights in the family, weight-control dishes are likely to be featured. If money is tight, menus must be planned with the budget in mind. When the cook works outside the home, quick-to-cook meals can be a lifesaver after a hard day. Many, if not most, of us cook the way we do for definite reasons. The tough part is coming up with different and interesting meals that will accomplish our purposes.

In the following section we offer a variety of main meal menus that will help with that chore. More than that, there is no need to consult a variety of cookbooks to get the meal together. Recipes for all of the dishes in each meal are right here in *The Natural Foods Epicure*. Whether you need to plan a no-meat meal or want ideas for elegant entertaining, whether you're a top-of-the-stove cook, or want an all-in-the-oven menu, you'll find it here plus much, much more. All natural, all delicious.

Menus for All-in-the-Oven Meals

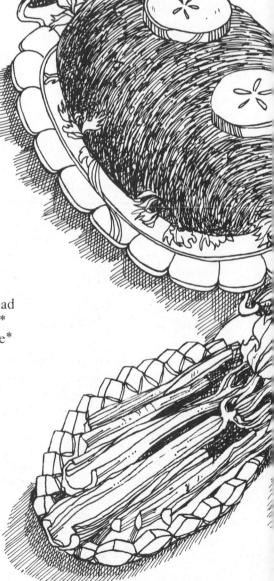

Applesauce Meat Loaf*
Baked Potato
Fitness House Spread*
Carrot and Celery Sticks
Bulgur Raisin Custard*

Lamb Cassoulet*
Tossed Green Salad
Tomato Dressing*
Apfelkuchen Souffle*

Orange Marinated Pork Roast*
Baked Pumpkin Ring*
Tossed Green Salad
Savory Yogurt Salad Dressing*
Fruit Cup
Wheat Sprout Candy*

Carrot Peanut Loaf*
Baked Onions and Bulgur with Raisins*
Tomato and Lettuce Salad
Sunflower Mayonnaise
Winter Pear Crunch*

Green and Red Pepper Casserole*
Wheat Soybean Casserole (omit cheese)*
Romaine and Spinach Salad
Lemon Dressing*
Cherry Ice Cream*

Kugelis (Lithuanian potato pudding)*
Oven-Baked Sausage*
Carrot and Cabbage Slaw
Baked Apples

Beef Stew with Plums*
Baked Parsnips and Carrots*
Watercress, Romaine and Endive Salad
Basic Oil and Vinegar Dressing*
Indian Pudding*

Menus for Calorie Counters

Fish Kebabs*
Parsley Potatoes
Korean Spinach Salad*
Blueberry Yogurt*

Baked Chicken, Quince and Butternut Squash*
Cauliflower Vinaigrette*
Apricot Soup*

Zucchini Frittata*
Green Bean-Sunflower Seed Salad*
Applesauce (unsweetened)*

Curried Apple and Veal on Whole Grain Toast*
Kohlrabi Slaw*
Half Grapefruit

Carrot Soy Loaf*
Broccoli Mustard Relish*
Blackberry Soup*

Alfalfa Sprout Gazpacho*
Stir-Fried Turnips with Beef*
Brown Rice
Watermelon

Buckwheat-Stuffed Cabbage Rolls*
Tomato Sauce*
Steamed Zucchini
Carrot Yogurt Sorbet*

Menus Featuring High-Fiber Foods

Cashew Carrot Soup*
Cottage Cheese Buckwheat Squares*
Fried Okra*
Brown Rice
Grapes

Rye and Lentil Pilaf*
Braised Celery Hearts*
Radish, Carrot and Apricot Relish*
Pineapple Pudding*

Okra Soup*
Soybean-Cabbage Casserole*
Celery, Green Bean and Tomato Toss*
Carob Bran Cake*

Bran Vegetable Meat Loaf*
Basic Gravy*
"Bubble and Squeak" (English cabbage
    and potato hash)*
Steamed Carrots
Strawberry Salad*

Buckwheat Cholent*
Glazed Turnips*
Celery and Zucchini Sticks
Apricot Prune Apple Tart*

Buckwheat Groat Patties*
Tomato Sauce*
Zucchini in Yogurt Sauce*
Sauerkraut Onion Rolls*
Cherry Custard Cake*

Caribbean Banana Soup*
Blackberry and Cantaloupe Salad
    with Cottage Cheese*
Buckwheat Kasha Bread*
Fitness House Spread*
Carob Nut Brownies*

Low-Budget Menus

Oatmeal Soup*
Spinach Cheese Blintzes*
Marinated Green Bean, Celery
    and Radish Salad*
Lemon Orange Gelatin*

Parsley Pesto*
Steamed Carrots
Iceberg and Escarole Salad
Soy Salad Dressing*
Raw Apple and Black Walnut Cream*

Peanut Butter Soup*
Millet Lentil Loaf*
Stir-Fried Cabbage*
Crepes Suzette*

Mushroomburgers*
Scottish Scones or Bannocks*
Stir-Fried Bean Sprouts*
Apple Pie with Whole Wheat and Rice Pastry*

Madras Chicken Curry*
Brown Rice
Okra Curry*
Sliced Oranges and Bananas

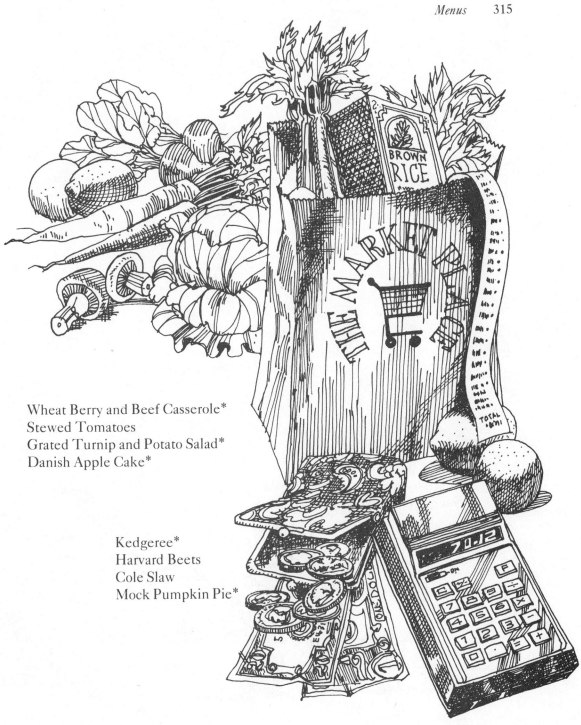

Wheat Berry and Beef Casserole*
Stewed Tomatoes
Grated Turnip and Potato Salad*
Danish Apple Cake*

Kedgeree*
Harvard Beets
Cole Slaw
Mock Pumpkin Pie*

No-Meat Menus

Kale and Kidney Bean Bake*
Green Salad with Radishes and Raw Cauliflower
Beet Dressing*
Coconut Yogurt Cheese Pie*

Sunflower Carrot Patties*
Tomato Sauce*
Steamed Broccoli
Whole Wheat Macaroni Salad with Cheese Dressing*
Coconut-topped Orange Slices

Tomato Quiche*
Bulgur and Lentil Pilaf*
Spinach and Raw Mushroom Salad*
Sunflower Seed Cookies*

Cold Beet and Cucumber Soup*
Black Bean and Rice Bake*
Wheat Germ Muffins*
Orange Flowers (whole orange cut into
      wedges but left intact at the bottom)

Kidney Bean Curry*
Curried Cabbage*
Brown Rice
Zucchini, Pepper and Tomato Relish*
Strawberry Cheesecake Pie*

Sweet Potato Soup*
Mexican Garbanzo Beans*
Cauliflower Salad*
Cranberry Galette*

Swiss Chard Soup*
Dried Lima Bean Casserole*
Carrot and Cucumber Sticks
Cold Berry Souffle*

Special Dinner Party Menus

Garden Soup*
Pork Prune Roll-Ups*
Himmel und Erde (mashed potatoes with apples)*
Steamed Green Beans
Cucumber Vinaigrette*
Jelly Roll*

Peanut and Cabbage Curry*
Curried Potatoes with Yogurt*
Brown Rice
Apple and Apricot Chutney*
Key Lime Pie*

Russian Barley Soup*
Baked Stuffed Whole Fish*
Zucchini, Corn and Tomato Saute*
Green and White Salad (greens and shredded
        cabbage, cauliflower and green onions)
Basic Oil and Vinegar Dressing*
Strawberry Custard Pie*

Orange Borscht*
Bulgur *Couscous*
Sliced Tomatoes and Cucumbers in Yogurt
Seedless Grapes
Carrot Confection*

Chanfaina of Liver*
Corn Souffle*
Brussels Sprouts in Mushroom Sauce*
Sliced Tomatoes on Watercress
Lemon Dressing*
Spiced Plums in Wine*

Winter Squash Soup*
Chicken Breasts in Sour Cream Aspic*
Avocado, Orange and Onion Salad with Molasses Dressing*
Baked Banana Pancake*

Grapes Turkey Mornay*
Boston Lettuce
Watercress Dressing*
Lemon Sherbet (milkless)*

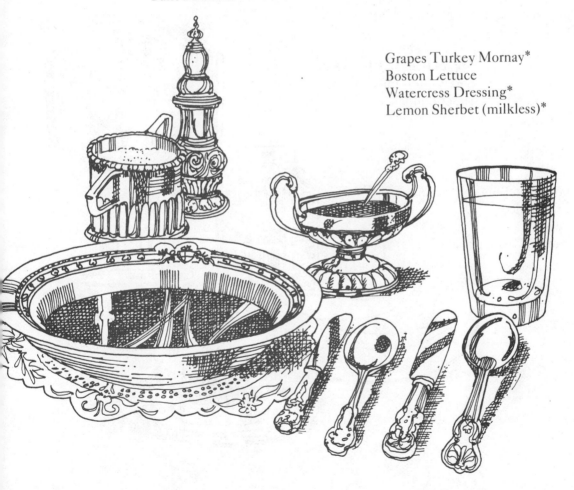

Time-Saving Menus

Egg Foo Yung*
Brown Rice
Braised Swiss Chard*
Papaya Shrub*

Soy Cheeseburgers*
Spinach and Cabbage Salad
Basic Oil and Vinegar Dressing*
Buckwheat Groats
Fresh Berries with Yogurt

Apple, Beet and Tuna Salad*
Barley-Buttermilk Biscuits*
Super Fudge*

Stir-Fried Beef and Watercress*
Brown Rice
Peas
Banana Cashew Shake*

Fish Filets Sauteed in Egg*
Bulgur
Sliced Tomatoes and Cucumbers
Sunflower Oil Dressing*
Seedless Grapes in Yogurt

Beef and Sprout Patties*
Parslied New Potatoes (in their skins)
Carrot Sticks, Radishes, Cauliflowerets
Avocado Grapefruit Soup*

Fresh Herb Omelet*
Canned Beet and Green Onion Salad
Cottage Cheese Dressing*
100% Whole Wheat Bread*
Pineapple-Carrot Shrub*

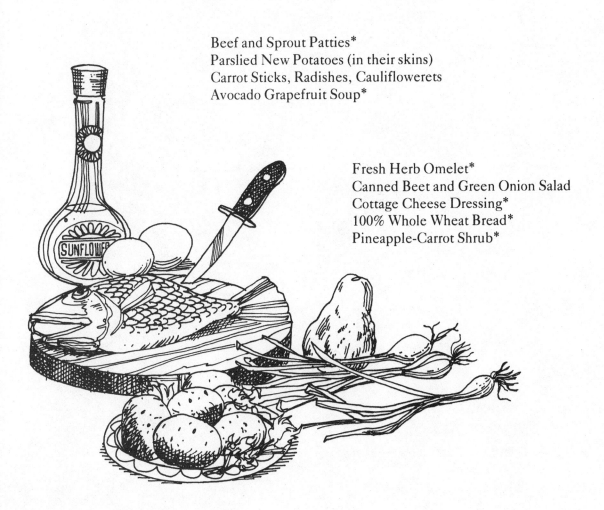

Make-Ahead Dishes

When time is a major factor in meal preparation, some cooks depend on dishes that can be made ahead of time. These need only be quickly heated or merely whisked out of the refrigerator, ready to serve. Listed below are a number of *The Natural Foods Epicure* recipes that lend themselves particularly well to the make-ahead idea. You will find that for these dishes, the time lapse tends to enhance the flavor.

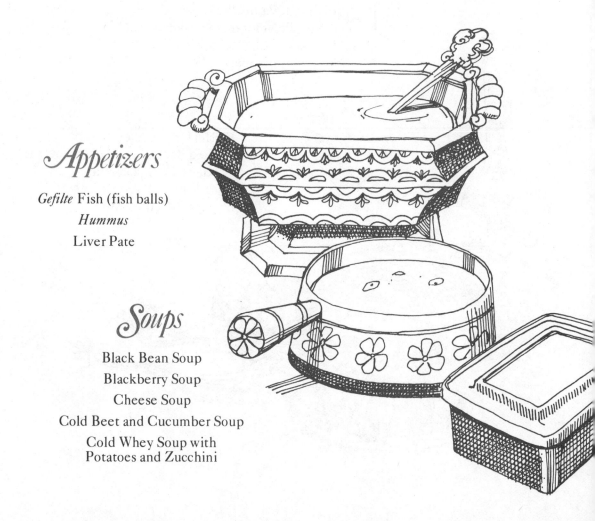

Appetizers

Gefilte Fish (fish balls)

Hummus

Liver Pate

Soups

Black Bean Soup

Blackberry Soup

Cheese Soup

Cold Beet and Cucumber Soup

Cold Whey Soup with
Potatoes and Zucchini

Salads

Broccoli Mustard Relish
Cauliflower Vinaigrette
Cucumber Vinaigrette
Eggplant Salad
Green Bean-Sunflower Seed Salad
Herbed Soybean Salad
Jellied Avocado and Cheese Ring
Navy Bean Salad

Main Dishes

Boiled Fresh Tongue
Buckwheat-Stuffed Cabbage Rolls
Chicken Breasts in Sour Cream Aspic
Jellied Avocado Tuna Loaf
Kidney Bean Curry
Lamb Korma
Mexican Garbanzo Beans
Rolled Eggplant Italian
Spinach Lasagna
Steak Tartare
Turkey Bulgur Casserole

Desserts

Carob Cottage Cheese Pie
Danish Apple Cake
Key Lime Pie
Noodle Kugel
Rhubarb Fool
Spiced Plums in Wine
Strawberry Soft Yogurt Ice Cream
Thick Custard
Walnut Torte

Menus for Top-of-the-Stove Meals

Lamb Korma*
Brown Rice
Curried Broccoli and Carrots*
Watermelon and Onion Salad*
Oat Candy*

Boiled Fresh Tongue*
Potatoes, Carrots and Cabbage Wedges
        simmered in Tongue Broth
Tossed Green Salad
Emerald Dressing*
Peach Fritters*

Chinese Chicken Livers*
Brown Rice
Avocado Watercress Salad with Tamari Dressing*
Plum, Peach and Nectarine Compote*

Dutch Kale with Potatoes and Sausage*
Pickled Beets
Wheat Berry *Muesli*

Hopping John (black-eyed peas, rice and pig's feet)*
Steamed Collard Greens
Skillet Cornbread*
Cranberry-Applesauce*

Chick-Pea and Cabbage Soup*
Sprouted Wheat Tabouli*
Strawberry Soup*

Lentil, Rice and Prune Pilaf*
Steamed Carrots
Cucumber and Walnut Salad*
Peach and Cantaloupe Soup*

Bountiful, Beautiful

Add to the list of joyous American traditions the Sunday brunch. The concept is unique to this country, and it is hard to define. The dictionary suggests that brunch is one late morning meal eaten in place of two. But that is like describing the British afternoon tea as "a cup of flavored hot water, light amber to deep brown, served with sugar and lemon or milk." The social occasion and the accompanying food are much more important than the beverage. In the same way a brunch really means much more than merely two meals in one.

When people are invited to a brunch or give a brunch or go to a restaurant that serves a brunch, they have a definite idea of what it should be. It won't be just juice, eggs and coffee. Those items might be served in deference to the breakfast overtones, but they'll come with plenty of other food that will push them into the background. And that food will be interesting and special—perhaps crepes folded over creamed chicken or a fruit mixture, omelets filled with surprising additions, sausages, light meats, eggs Benedict, grilled organ meats, cheese or liqueur souffles, exotic juices, punches, teas and coffee mixtures. A brunch is an event!

We have devised a group of brunch menus that make the most of naturally great foods and provide some ideas you can use for the Sundays to come. They will certainly help build your reputation as a person who knows that the meaning of "brunch" has blossomed and grown into a lot more than it was when Webster first set out to define it.

Brunches

Mushroom Crepes*
Eggs on Curried Rice*
Kidneys en Brochette*
Sunflower Seed Muffins*
Jellied Avocado and Cheese Ring*

Eggs Moppioli*
Zucchini Dollar Cakes*
Sliced Tomatoes
Gefilte Fish (fish balls)*
Rice Flour Muffins*
Oat Crepes* filled with strawberries, topped with yogurt

Baked Tomatoes and Eggs*
Sprouts and Avocado Crepes*
Herbed Triticale Casserole Bread*
Eggplant Salad*
Fruit Compote

Broccoli Cheese Pie*
Sweetbread Mushroom Curry*
Buckwheat-Groat Souffle*
Banana Cornbread*
Green salad with orange segments in it
Spicy Yogurt Dressing for Fruit Salad*

Naturally Great

Dippers

Bran Sesame Crackers
Cheddar Chips
Chive Wafers
Garbanzo (Chick-Pea) Sprout
    Snack
Oatmeal Crackers
Old Country Soft Pretzel Sticks
    (rye)
Peanut Cornmeal Snaps
Soul Food Crackers
Sprouted Wheat Sticks
Whole Millet Crackers

Dippers and Dips*

Dips

Avocado Banana Dressing
Avocado Spread
Brazil Nut Sauce
Cottage Cheese, Date and Nut
    Filling
Curried Avocado Filling
Eggplant Dip or Dressing
Hummus
Kidney Bean Dip
Lima Bean and Sesame Dip
Sunflower Seed Spread or Dip
Walnut Cheese Spread
Walnut-Onion Dip or Spread
Wheat Germ Spread

(See Index for Recipes)

Handy Kitchen

Equipment for Cooking Natural Foods

Apple Corer and Slicer

This is a German-made gadget which cuts apple-pie-making time in half.

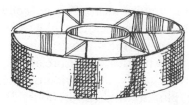 

Chinese Wok

The traditional *wok*, made of cast iron, can only be used successfully on a gas range, not an electric one. However, the Oriental technique of stir-frying can be done quite well, using a large stainless steel or cast-iron skillet over any type of heat.

Crockery Pot

One of the most convenient, energy-saving cooking utensils is the slow cooker. Some natural foods require long, slow cooking, especially grains, legumes and the tougher, cheaper cuts of meat. This piece of equipment has a definite place in your kitchen, especially if you are working outside the home. (For complete information, see "Cooking with a Crockery Pot.")

Electric Blender

A blender will grind nuts, make bread crumbs, sunflower seed meal, oat flour from rolled oats and it will even make mayonnaise. It is the fastest way to puree any food and does the best job of liquefying food. The number of buttons is not important; they only affect the speed of the blade, and two speeds, fast and slow, will do what's needed. But the quality of the motor is very important, because a blender gets a lot of use in the natural foods kitchen. The most useful type of blender comes apart at the base, allowing for ease in emptying and in washing the blade. Also, a pint-size canning jar with regulation size mouth will fit onto this type of blender base, making the job of grinding small seeds, herbs and spices, simpler.

Electric Mixer

A simple hand model electric mixer speeds up certain short-term processes, like whipping cream, beating egg whites or whipping mashed potatoes. Some wheatless yeast breads require 5 to 10 minutes beating in an electric mixer to develop the gluten in the rye flour. In such cases, a stationary model with a bowl, a flat beater or even a dough hook attachment is the best tool to use.

Food Mill

This is a hand-operated tool for pureeing apples, tomatoes or any cooked vegetable or fruit. In some ways it has been superseded by the electric blender or by the tool known as the Victorio Strainer or the Squeezo Juicer, a well-made, hand-operated appliance which extracts juice or puree and discards the unusable part of the food, all very neatly in one operation.

Grain Mill   There are basically three types—large electrical units, small hand units and units that attach to appliances such as mixers. Check your appliance to see if there is a grain mill attachment available for it. Whole grain flours are widely available for purchase in natural food stores and co-ops. Often these outlets are equipped with grain mills for processing the grain you buy. If you want to buy grain in quantity, I think it is a worthwhile investment to buy your own mill to make flour. Freshly milled flour tastes better and it is the most nutritious.

Ice Cream Freezer   The only way to know for sure what is in your ice cream is to make your own. Manufacturers are not required to list all ingredients or additives. Inexpensive ice cream freezers, both hand operated and electric, are available. These require ice and salt, which could be considered a disadvantage. I know of only one electric ice cream freezer (Salton) now on the market which fits into a refrigerator-freezer, making ice cream in an hour if you like the soft variety. The texture is very good, and the machine is not expensive. There is one drawback—only one quart can be made at a time. However, with a 20-minute wait, the freezer can be reused to make another quart.

Juicer

This is important for those who drink a lot of vegetable and fruit juices and want to avoid any additives which may be in those sold commercially. Also those who have an abundance of fruits or vegetables available find them useful.

Mention should also be made of the steam juicer. This three-section appliance is placed directly over the surface unit of your range. The fruit is placed in the top perforated section which is the steamer. Water is placed in the bottom section and heated. As the fruit steams, the juice drips through to the middle section, the juice kettle, and is forced through a hose into the sterilized bottle. No further preserving is necessary.

Knives

The paring knife, the chef knife (sometimes called French knife with triangular blade, comes in different lengths, handy for chopping, slicing), the bread knife with saw teeth, the carving knife (slicer), and perhaps a boner, if you plan to bone meat, are the basic knives you will need.

Meat Grinder

If you want to buy fresh meat by the cut and then grind your own hamburger, this piece of equipment is a necessity. It allows you to control the leanness of your meat and you are assured of its freshness. A meat grinder is also useful for grinding leftover cooked roasts or poultry for hash, croquettes or spaghetti sauce. You can choose from hand-operated and electric meat grinders, those which clamp onto counters or are held by suction, those made of metal and plastic, and some grinders attach to appliances.

*Nut or Coffee
Grinder*

This is handy for grinding small seeds, herbs and spices.

Shredder

Most of the good machines which are made specifically to shred and cut vegetables into cubes, strips and slices come only in institutional sizes. However, some home appliances have convenient shredder attachments. Many people prefer the old-fashioned hand shredder. Whatever your preference, some kind of shredder is necessary if you want to make cole slaw, grate vegetables for salad, shred cheese or make potato pancakes.

Sprouter

There are many types of sprouters on the market. For the average-size family, simple quart jars are adequate and can be covered with nylon mesh or cheesecloth, held on by a rubber band. Wire mesh lids which fit these jars are also available. They range from fine to coarse, according to the type of seed being sprouted.

Vegetable Steamers

There are bamboo and ceramic vegetable steamers available. I find the most practical (and least expensive) one to be a collapsible metal type that fits several sizes of pans.

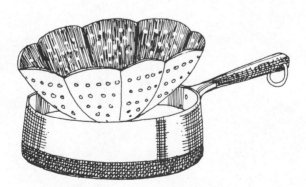

Wire Whisk

Use this to avoid lumps when combining liquid and dry ingredients.

Wooden Spoons

Long and short handled spoons are necessary for stirring in metal pans, to avoid scratching them.

Yogurt Maker

Commercially made yogurt is expensive, sometimes has a strong, often sour, flavor or may contain sugar and artificial flavors and coloring. Making your own yogurt is the only sensible way for true yogurt lovers. Some are very resourceful at yogurt making, successfully using oven pilot lights, radiators or even the top of the TV as a heat source. However, for well under $20 you can be assured of foolproof yogurt making by purchasing one of the many good yogurt makers which are available.

Pots and

A heavy skillet comes in handy for browning meats, cooking hash to the crusty stage, for pancakes and omelets. Cast iron is the best material for this kind of utensil because it maintains and holds an even heat.

A double boiler is an important item for keeping food at a warm, not hot, temperature, particularly for creamed foods which are apt to stick and burn and for those which have egg in the sauce, to prevent overcooking.

Waterless cookware, if you can afford it, is the best cookware. Very little water is required for cooking vegetables when it is used. Purees like fruit butters, for example, can be cooked slowly for a long period without the danger of being scorched.

This cookware is very heavy because the sides as well as the bottom are constructed of an

Pressure

The pressure cooker has a definite place in the natural foods kitchen. It is the most efficient method of cooking beans because it does not require that beans be soaked before being cooked and it cuts down the cooking time to about one-quarter of that needed to tenderize the beans by the conventional method of boiling them on top of the stove. For example, chick-peas and soy-

Pans

inner and outer layer of stainless steel with a core of carbon steel or aluminum, sandwiched between, which allows for even heat penetration. Some waterless cookware has an aluminum base which absorbs heat quickly and distributes it evenly. This base has stainless steel bonded to it for added strength and to make cleaning easier.

The cookware covers have a rolled or beaded edge which fits a rim on the pans. During the cooking process, a partial vacuum is created which seals cover to pan, allowing for very little escape of moisture.

Whatever brand you choose, the heavier the pots, the better the quality and the higher the price. But they will last a lifetime. So far as I know, all brands are sold through a representative of the company, not in a store.

Cooker

beans, which require 3 to 4 hours of stove-top cooking, will be tender, not just crunchy, in 45 minutes (chick-peas) and 25 minutes (soybeans), when cooked in a pressure cooker.

True, you must remain in ear-shot of the cooker while using it, so as to detect any change in the steady rocking of the pressure regulator. And to conserve your fuel, it is important to determine what is the most efficient way to use the pressure cooker on your range. The manufacturer's booklet isn't necessarily your best guide on this matter. On my electric range, I find the best method is to put my 6-quart cooker on the largest surface unit, turning the temperature to high. The regulator soon starts to rock and there is quite a loud hissing noise. I quickly lower the temperature to medium-high and after another few minutes, I lower the temperature still more, until I get it as low as possible, still maintaining that steady rocking of the regulator. After the first few times you use the pressure cooker on your stove, you'll know how to adjust the temperature. Of course you must set the timer from the moment the pressure regulator begins to rock.

When the time is up, remove the cooker from the heat and run cold water over the side of the lid not letting any water get into the vent. When the hissing sound has stopped and the lid is cool to the touch, lift off the pressure regulator and open the lid. Some recipes direct that the food be left in the cooker on the turned off burner and be allowed to cool down of its own accord.

If during the cooking process the pressure regulator stops rocking, it is either because the heat has been turned too low or because the vent pipe has become clogged. If the latter is the case, simply remove the cooker, cool it under water as

described above, remove the lid and wash it. Then resume cooking.

Adding one tablespoon of vinegar to the pot when cooking foods which tend to froth, such as soybeans, split peas, brown rice or applesauce, will in most cases prevent this from happening.

Wheat berries, whole rye and triticale also cook much faster by pressure. Some prefer cooking meats and vegetables by this method. In my experience, it is difficult to avoid overcooking vegetables when they are done in this way. Pressure cooked meats do not retain the same texture or flavor as roasted meat, and in most cases, I prefer to roast meats in the oven or to cook them in the crockery pot.

One other important function of the pressure cooker deserves mention: processing canned vegetables and fruits. The pressure canner saves valuable time and fuel. Traditionally, it has been used only to process low-acid vegetables which require a higher temperature than that of boiling water to kill harmful microorganisms. But increasingly, the pressure canner is being used to process high-acid foods such as peaches and tomatoes as well as low-acid foods, because of saving time and fuel. Of course, for this, a large pressure cooker is necessary and these can be quite expensive. Whether or not this is a necessary tool for you depends on how much canning you do.

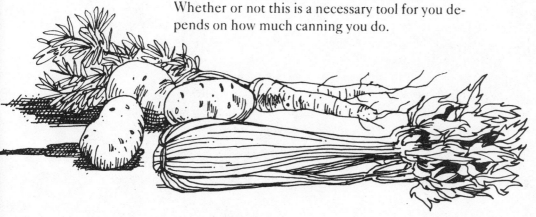

Cooking with a Crockery Pot

Surely the most popular recent development in cooking aids is the crockery pot, or slow-pot cooker. It is, in fact, a variation on the traditional hospitality pot which held an honored place in early America's country kitchens. It simmered along on low heat all day on the back of the wood-burning stove, always ready with a meal for unexpected guests. It also provided many a family meal.

In today's style of living the idea of having a potful of appetizing food, ready and waiting when the working husband and wife arrive home in the evening, is undeniably appealing. Some Americans willingly "set up" the crockery pot before leaving the house in the morning, or sometimes even the night before, knowing that once it's done, final preparations for dinner will be minimal: put a salad together, butter the rolls and you're ready to eat.

If you are planning to do some crockery cooking, here are some important points to bear in mind:

• Place vegetables in the pot first, with meats on top, since vegetables cook slower than meats in these utensils.

• Browning meats is seldom necessary except to remove excess fat. Fats will not bake off in a crockery pot as they would in an oven.

• All moisture is retained in the crockery pot during the cooking process, so the amount of liquid required in recipes for other types of cooking can be cut by as much as half. This means it is important to leave the pot covered. Wait until the suggested cooking time is up before testing. Heat inside builds slowly, and everytime the unit is uncovered enough heat escapes to slow the cooking process even more.

(continued on page 344)

Naturally Great Recipes that Can Be Adapted to the Crockery Pot

BEEF
Applesauce Meat Loaf
Beef Stew with Plums
Buckwheat Cholent
Stuffed Beef Heart

CHICKEN
Chicken Paprika
Coq au Vin (Chicken in Wine)

LAMB
Braised Lamb Shanks
Lamb Cassoulet
Lamb Korma
Ragout of Lamb

PORK
Hopping John (black-eyed peas, rice and pig's feet)
Pennsylvania Dutch Pig's Stomach

MEATLESS
Rye and Lentil Pilaf
Split Peas with Barley

• Don't worry about the foods that might be done before the predicted time. Since no moisture escapes, and since cooking is so slow and gentle, foods are not likely to be spoiled by some overcooking.

• Cooks new to the crockery pot may find that because of the moisture retained in the pot the residual juices are too thin to use as gravy or in making a sauce. The solution is to take off the cover and remove the solid contents, turn the setting to high and let the remaining juices evaporate and thicken. Or, if you want to use the full amount of liquid, make a *roux* (equal parts of flour and melted butter), add it to the juices and let it simmer.

• Most cooks have to get the "feel" of a new stove before they can produce their best dishes. The same is true of the crockery pot. The most important, and only mysterious element, is timing. So if you are new to this appliance, expect that foods will get done a little earlier or a little later than predicted, until you learn how *your own* crockery pot behaves.

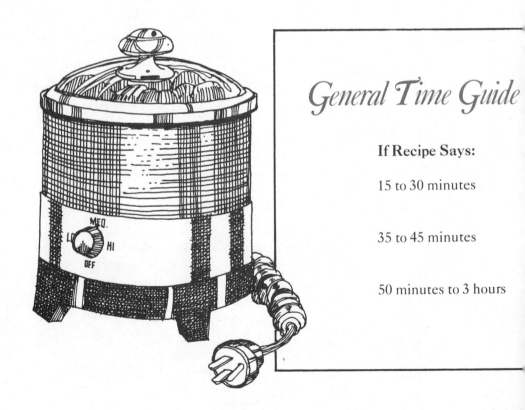

General Time Guide

If Recipe Says:

15 to 30 minutes

35 to 45 minutes

50 minutes to 3 hours

Even the same model pots, made by the same manufacturer, cook at slightly different speeds. Line surges and other peculiarities of electrical current are blamed for the variations in cooking times, which can be as much as two hours.

The cooking times given in recipes or manufacturers' manuals are only suggested times. When directions say, "Turn to low and cook 6 to 8 hours," translate that to mean that 6 hours is the soonest the food could be done; 8 hours the latest. For a crockery pot to cook foods in close-to-estimated times, ideally it should be half-full.

• Low temperature in a crockery pot is figured to be 190° to 240°F.; high temperature, 300° to 340°F. Cooking time can be cut in half by turning from low to high.

• Crockery pots are good for cooking meats, stews and casseroles of all kinds and rice or bean dishes that ordinarily take a long time to make. They are not suitable for cooking fish, best cooked briefly.

for Converting Recipes

Cook in Crockery Pot:

1½ to 2½ hours on high or
4 to 8 hours on low

3 to 4 hours on high or
6 to 10 hours on low

4 to 6 hours on high or
8 to 18 hours on low

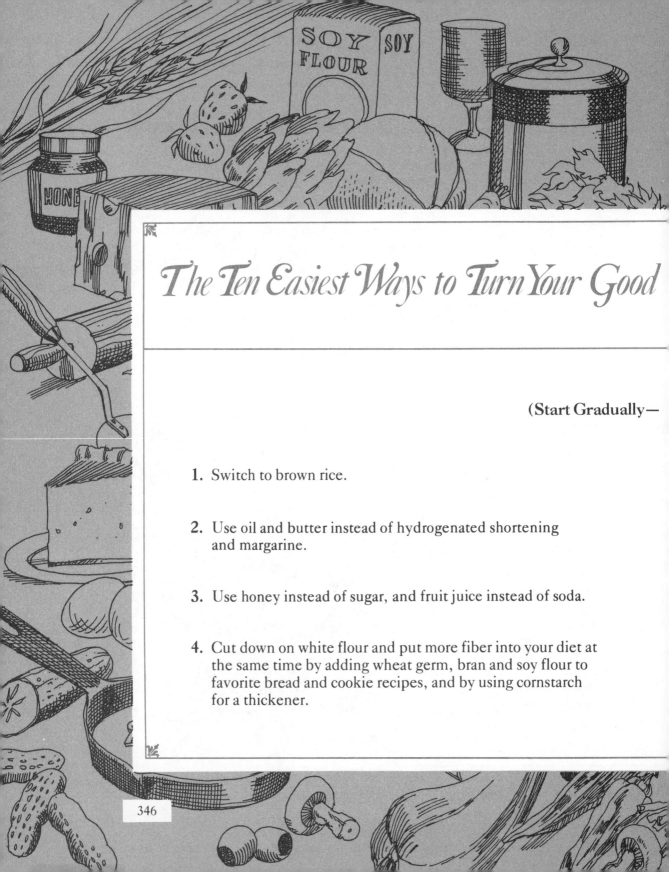

The Ten Easiest Ways to Turn Your Good

(Start Gradually—

1. Switch to brown rice.

2. Use oil and butter instead of hydrogenated shortening and margarine.

3. Use honey instead of sugar, and fruit juice instead of soda.

4. Cut down on white flour and put more fiber into your diet at the same time by adding wheat germ, bran and soy flour to favorite bread and cookie recipes, and by using cornstarch for a thickener.

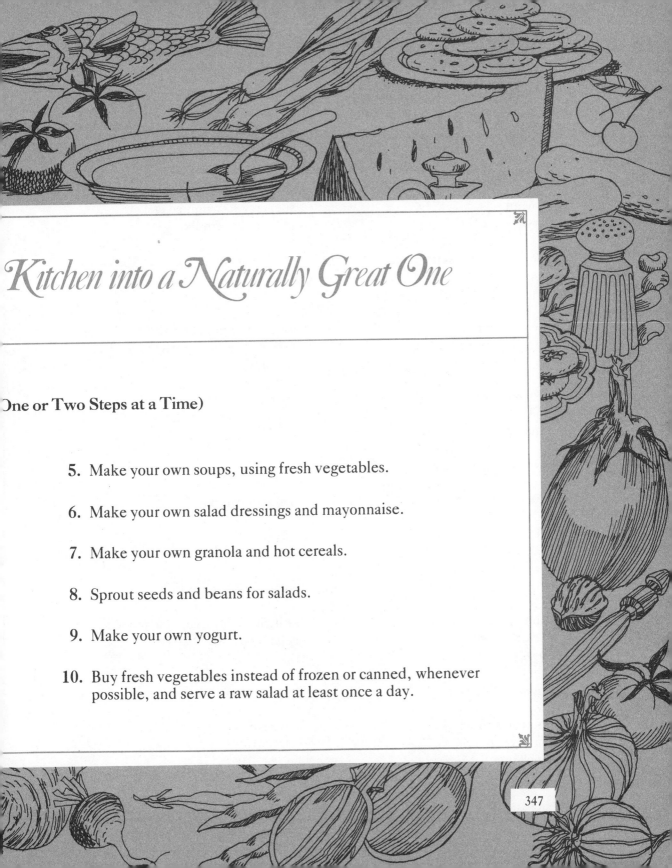

Kitchen into a Naturally Great One

(One or Two Steps at a Time)

5. Make your own soups, using fresh vegetables.

6. Make your own salad dressings and mayonnaise.

7. Make your own granola and hot cereals.

8. Sprout seeds and beans for salads.

9. Make your own yogurt.

10. Buy fresh vegetables instead of frozen or canned, whenever possible, and serve a raw salad at least once a day.

yogurt	for	sour cream, whipped cream, milk or buttermilk
fresh or frozen vegetables	for	canned vegetables
yogurt cheese	for	cream cheese
wheat germ whole grain bread crumbs	for	crushed cornflakes, crushed graham crackers or white bread crumbs
chicken fat oil butter	for	shortening, lard or margarine
whole wheat pasta	for	white pasta
Fitness House Spread	for	margarine or butter
herbs kelp	for	salt
herb teas	for	coffee or black tea
unflavored, unsweetened gelatin powder agar	for	artificially flavored, sweetened gelatin powder
tamari soy sauce	for	Worcestershire sauce
pure maple syrup honey molasses	for	pancake syrup

for Ordinary Ingredients

cornstarch whole wheat flour rye flour oat flour brown rice flour barley flour	for	white flour when used as a thickener
fruit butters	for	jelly or jam
carob	for	chocolate
bulgur brown rice buckwheat groats	for	white rice or instant rice
honey molasses diastatic malt (in bread)	for	white or brown sugar
whole wheat flour rye flour oat flour barley flour brown rice flour buckwheat flour soy flour (in combination with another whole grain flour) millet flour cornmeal (finely ground) ground nuts	for	white flour when used for baking bread, cookies and cakes

When the Spice Is Right,

Flavoring foods with herbs and spices, one of the most delightful and creative aspects of the culinary art, began as a dire necessity. In the days when canning as a means of preservation had yet to be discovered, and modern methods of refrigeration had not even been dreamed of, spices and herbs came to the rescue by retarding spoilage and masking off-tastes of foods that were not as fresh as they should have been.

When travel horizons began to widen, those returning home longed to bring back samples of the exotic fare they had tasted—cheeses from Switzerland, fruits from Spain and grains from Egypt. Flavorings used in various parts of the world—the sweet and the tart, the hot and the mild, the pungent and the

the Taste Is Brighter

subtle—were introduced with these imports. Eventually their original purpose to preserve and disguise was forgotten. The attractive tastes these herbs and spices imparted to homegrown foods as well as the imports solidified their position as basic ingredients of fine cuisine.

Over the centuries refinement and experience have taught us how to use herbs and spices to turn an ordinary dish into a culinary masterpiece. We all know it can be done. Most cooks have had the experience of inquiring about the special quality of an admirable concoction, only to learn that its success is due to a pinch of clove, a hint of garlic or a dash of curry.

Cooks at every level of expertise find working with both the familiar and exotic herbs and spices an imaginative challenge. New cooks are delighted to discover the special value a clove of garlic rubbed on the side of the bowl can add to a salad, and chefs of long experience can still be exhilarated by what a pinch of cinnamon can do for a tomato sauce and how a few strands of saffron can raise a soup to new heights.

If you are a salt-and-pepper cook don't deny yourself the pleasures of creative seasoning any longer. Start now by adding elegance to one of the dishes you plan to cook today. You'll see that buttered carrots profit mightily by mixing in some freshly chopped mint leaves just before serving; chicken sauteed with sprigs of rosemary becomes a memorable dish; a bit of clove cooked with red beets demonstrates a perfect marriage of flavors.

If you are using fresh rather than dried varieties of herbs, use about three or four times the amount recommended in the recipe, since the dried ones are much more concentrated in flavor. Both herbs and spices should be kept in tightly closed containers as the air robs flavor. When aroma or color fade, replace them, for spices that have aged too much simply won't give the expected flavor when added to a recipe.

Don't be afraid to experiment, but remember this basic rule: less is better. It's easy to overseason foods. Bear in mind that if you are eating lamb with a mint sauce, you want to taste the lamb as well as the sauce. It's much easier to add more flavoring than to remove what is already there when it's too strong.

In the following pages we describe some of the common favorite herbs and spices along with some special and unusual ones, just to give you an idea of the range of flavorings available.

Allspice

This is not a combination of spices, but a simple berry usually dried and sold in powder form. Allspice has a sharp flavor that suggests a combination of cinnamon and cloves. It is primarily used in baked dessert dishes such as pies and cakes and occasionally appears in meat recipes.

Anise

The taste of the aniseed is sweet and spicy. It is classed as one of the four great hot seeds. The pleasant licoricelike flavor and aroma of anise make it especially welcome in cakes, soups and drinks.

Many Westerners are surprised to see anise appear so frequently in Chinese cuisine, but it has been used in the Far East for centuries and is actually much more common in everyday Oriental dishes than in our own.

Use anise to perk up the taste of soup by adding a few seeds as it cooks. Those who ordinarily add cinnamon or nutmeg to applesauce will find aniseed a delightful change. A simple innovation in salad dressing calls for stirring a teaspoon of aniseed into a cup of yogurt and pouring it over fruit or greens. Or add some seeds to softened cream cheese to use as a cracker spread or on any sweet bread.

Basil

Basil imparts a delicious clovelike flavor to bland vegetables and soups, salad dressings and egg dishes.

But use it carefully if it is new to you, because basil is powerful. It is one of the few herbs that increases in flavor when it is cooked. At the same time fresh basil may be chopped coarsely and added liberally to raw tomatoes that are to be served as a salad or in sandwiches, and it makes a terrific spread when chopped and added to fresh butter.

Versatility is one of the shining values of basil, for it can make an impact on so many dishes and marries so well with any number of fresh foods. Try basil on any of the summer vegetables or use it in your favorite sauces and stews as the French do.

Bay Leaf

This is a classic flavoring that appears in certain traditional recipes literally by definition. For example, a true court bouillon, the stock in which fish is poached, requires a bay leaf. The leaf is an important part of the *bouquet garni* used in stuffings and in roasting fowls. Many marinades for poultry and game, especially venison, call for bay leaves. A single bay leaf added to an old-fashioned vegetable soup or stew can turn it into a gourmet meal. Bay leaf is welcome with vegetables such as artichoke, eggplant, and even steamed or boiled potatoes.

The *bouquet garni* which is used for so many dishes ordinarily contains two sprigs of parsley, two of chervil, one of marjoram, one of thyme and one-half bay leaf. It may seem that the bay leaf proportion is small in relation to the other items, but the flavor of this strong herb deepens as it cooks, particularly when it is shredded. Most fresh leaves soften as they cook, but the bay does not, so be sure to remove the leaves before serving.

Caraway

Here is one of those so-called utility herbs. This pleasant flavoring is among the best known and most frequently used in virtually every part of the modern world. It has an enjoyable and distinctive flavorsome tang that makes a tasty addition to rye bread and cheeses and it even serves as the base for a German liqueur called *Kummel*.

Caraway seeds can be added to cakes, puddings and cookies, but the seeds are especially compatible with apple dishes of almost every kind and are staples in rye and black breads. A favorite middle-European dish consists of boiled cabbage to which bacon drippings and caraway seeds have been added. Try caraway in the vinegar you use for pickling beets.

Chervil

People call it "the gourmet parsley," since it has a more delicate flavor than parsley. It is well known to food experts as a good basis for any herbal salad. The French make chervil soup and many of that country's famous sauces are based on this herb. Because its scent is similar to the fragrance of myrrh, one of the offerings of the Magi at the birth of Christ, chervil is also known as *Myrrhis*. Chervil often turns up in recipes for sorrel or spinach soup and it adds special flavor to fish, eggs, meats or vegetables.

Since chervil is a mild-flavored herb, it is used in the same quantity as you would use a vegetable in soup, for instance, so you need plenty of it. Dried chervil should be stored away from light, since the herb will turn yellow or grayish in a short time if exposed to light. Also it must be kept in a tightly closed container because it will pick up the slightest moisture above normal humidity and become stale. You can use chervil in any dish where parsley might be used. *Bearnaise* sauce requires chervil and it should also be put in any of the vinaigrette and wine sauces. Chervil is especially good in salads where its flavor is most noticeable because it is raw.

Chili Peppers

Some people use them only as spices or for pickles, stews and the like. But not all chili peppers are so hot that you can't breathe after you swallow a bite. There are different kinds and some of them are extremely sweet and meaty. Hot ones, when used in small amounts, add a welcome fiery excitement to goulash. You can also buy chili peppers in dried and ground form.

Chives

Some cooks really believe that chives are one of the most indispensable herbs for daily use. They offer a great improvement to salads, raw vegetables, cheeses and omelets. Added to sour cream, chives are familiar to Americans as part of a topping for baked potatoes, and many soups and sauces would be missing a vital ingredient without chives. Try chive butter—chopped chives mixed with butter—as an excellent addition to grilled meat or fish. Chopped chives make an excellent garnish for cream soups and chowders and they lend a lovely color to hollandaise sauce.

Cinnamon

You might be surprised the first time you encounter the flavor of cinnamon in tomato sauce, but to the people of Greece and Armenia, it is an essential ingredient. Used sparingly, it adds an exotic and interesting touch to familiar pasta dishes. In the Middle East, cinnamon is regularly used in meat dishes, particularly lamb. In this country we are more likely to find cinnamon in sweet potato dishes and with winter squash. Of course the flavor zips up any home-canned fruit or fresh fruit mixture. And fresh pineapple with a bit of cinnamon added is irresistible.

Depending on how it is to be used, cinnamon can be purchased in stick form or as a powder. In either form, the sweet-pungent aromatic quality is the same and its presence in any dish will not go unnoticed.

Cloves

The most readily identifiable of the spices, cloves appear in an endless variety of sweets, and they add a welcome flavor to meats, vegetable dishes and fruits as well. The deep, spicy flavor of cloves originates in a dried bud that is available whole or as a powder. They are a classic addition to baked ham, fine cooked with beets, peaches and apples. Ciders, mulled wines and teas are all enhanced by cloves.

Curry

The confusion about curry has persisted for the longest time. Is there or is there not a curry plant? Most knowledgeable people agree that there isn't and that all curries are actually spice mixtures.

Noble medieval diners "peppered up" their gamey meats with the newly discovered spices from the Orient. Especially popular was a mixture of coriander seeds, turmeric, cardamom, cinnamon, pepper and caraway seeds, all ground and mixed. That was their curry. In India, virtually every village and individual family, has its own special mixture, depending on which spices are grown in the area. *Garam Masala* (see Index) is a good example of this.

But most curries have a basic similarity in taste, and it seems that a single ingredient delivers that taste. Some people say it is turmeric, some think it is an herb, similar to rosemary, others claim that it comes from a relative of the citrus tree, and some talk about a curry leaf tree. Whatever it is, most people have a definite initial response to this saucy flavoring: love or hate. If you are one of the latter, give curry a second chance. Be aware that to be an authentic curry, it does not have to be hot. The success of a curry lies in the combining of spices with vegetables or meat to create the most delicious dish. As a beginner, add a pinch of curry to any cream soup, to potato salad or to scrambled eggs.

Dill

In Scandinavia, dill is as popular as parsley, but the middle-European countries also find it almost indispensable in their cuisine, particularly for pickling cucumbers and for brightening the flavor of bland vegetables. Both the herb and the seed are used, depending on the cook's desire for a more or less sharp flavor.

The most frequent use for the dill herb is with fish, salads and certain vegetables. If the fresh leaves are finely chopped and mixed with cream cheese they make an unusual spread. One of the main reasons for dill's popularity is that it improves rather than dominates the flavor of the foods on which it is used. It is one of those herbs that can be used generously without ruining the dish. Add it to cottage cheese for a tangy snap. To make dill vinegar, simply soak a few dill leaves in vinegar for a few days.

Fennel

Quite a few plants do double duty as a vegetable and a flavoring herb. Fennel, also known by its Italian name *finochio*, is one of these. From head to root, this is a delightful addition to nearly every kind of cooking. Its stalk bulges to a bulbous form right above the ground, then fans out into several smaller stalks ending in tips of light, feathery leaves similar to dill. The stalks, both thin and thick parts, can be served raw as a snack or appetizer, in a salad, or lightly steamed as a delicious hot vegetable with a unique taste. The leaves, chopped, can be used to flavor salads, dressings and soups; and, finally, the seeds, resembling anise in looks and taste, can be used in making a soothing tea.

Garlic

This pungent favorite has been in the kitchens of the world for so long that it appears in a Chinese book dating back to 1,000 B.C. and is known to have been used by the Babylonians around 3,000 B.C. It is even part of the ancient Hebrew Talmudic law which stipulates that it be used in certain dishes and on certain occasions. There is certainly a reason why it has persisted for so long. No chef would dream of starting a salad without first cutting a clove and rubbing it around the inside of the salad bowl. But a finely chopped clove of garlic will spark a soup, and a joint of lamb, mutton or pork is vastly improved in tenderness and flavor by adding garlic. (Simply skin a few cloves and insert them in incisions made in the fatty exterior of the meat before roasting.) Garlic butter (made by blending together a quarter pound of butter and four macerated garlic cloves of average size) makes a heavenly sauce for chicken and certain kinds of seafood, and is a wonderful coating for croutons.

The smell of garlic on the breath does present a problem for some people. If you like garlic, cultivate a taste for parsley, which is said to sweeten the breath. Simply chew a sprig or two at the end of a garlic-rich meal.

Ginger

The sweet hot zing of gingerroot fits into a variety of dishes that range from appetizers through main courses to desserts. It is most familiarly used to flavor cooked fruits, pastry, sauces and some Far Eastern meat dishes. It is an indispensable ingredient in some stir-fry dishes. Ginger works well with carrots, onions, peas, apples and peaches.

You can buy whole gingerroot fresh or dried or in powdered form. Fresh gingerroot should be kept in the freezer as it is highly perishable. When you want to use frozen or dried gingerroot, just break off a piece, peel, then grate or chop. If you're using powdered ginger, remember to keep it tightly covered as ginger is especially susceptible to flavor loss when exposed to the air. Remember, too, that it is a strong flavor and it takes a bit of experience to find just the proper amount to use.

Lemon Balm

Its crushed foliage smells like lemons and that's how it got its name. In the summer a few leaves added to fresh fruit juices, particularly orange juice and iced teas, provide a cool and fragrant flavor. Lemon balm can be freshly chopped or whole-dried and its leaves may be used in salads, egg dishes, and chicken and fish dishes where the delicate lemon taste adds a distinctive flavor. Try rubbing leg of lamb with lemon balm leaves just before roasting. Its flavor is mild so lemon balm can be used lavishly.

Marjoram

Traditionally, sweet marjoram has been a symbol of youth and beauty and happiness. It has a strong, sweet, yet spicy flavor and is essentially a meat herb. Strong meats like venison are also improved by being rubbed with marjoram before roasting. Its characteristic flavor comes out best when used in stuffings for fowl or any kind of ground meat. Made-up meats, such as meat loaf and sausage, particularly benefit from the special flavor of marjoram. Marjoram can easily overpower other flavors so it should be used discreetly. For a satisfying snack, sprinkle a few cut-up leaves of fresh marjoram on lightly buttered whole wheat bread and broil it lightly to make a flavorful herb toast.

Mint

If you think of hard candy wafers or chocolates when you think of mint, remember that green mint plants were used in the kitchen long before candy was even invented. There are many members of the true mint family, but the best known are spearmint and peppermint. In India the plant is particularly cherished for its pleasant, fresh fragrance. A room can be scented simply by hanging a bunch of mint in the doorway and this is a common practice in India and other hot countries, for the aroma creates the impression of coolness.

It is impossible to pinpoint the single most common use of mint. There's mint tea, mint jelly, or mint sauce, mint mixed into a salad and dressed with oil and vinegar; mint combines well with peas and beans, new potatoes, beets and spinach; and it is a vital ingredient in Kentucky's famous mint julep. It also adds marvelous flavor to roast meats, particularly lamb and chicken.

Mustard

The tiny mustard seed provides a disproportionate amount of spicy flavor and a fresh dimension to cooked dishes, salads, sauces and sandwiches. No self-respecting French restaurant would serve a salad whose dressing did not contain a dash of dry mustard. And who can deny the contribution good mustard makes to a ham sandwich or a hot dog? The hot, sharp flavor works well with celery, potato salad, cucumber pickles and in cheese dishes.

Nasturtium

Here is a food that has never realized its potential in the United States. The entire plant has a spicy, yet delicately pungent flavor. Both the flowers and young leaves are fine for salads and sandwiches, used in the same manner as lettuce. The seeds also make an excellent snack and the Chinese have relished pickled nasturtium seeds for centuries. To make them, simply gather seed clusters when about half grown, leaving some of the stems still attached, clean the seed clusters and put them in a jar, covering them with freshly boiled cider vinegar. Seal the jar tightly and store in a cool place.

The custom of eating nasturtium petals and using them for tea and in salads also comes from the Orient. The flowers do not dry well however and they should be used while they are still fresh. On the other hand, the leaves may be dried and used all year round as garnishes for food and chopped up for mixing in spreads.

When you use nasturtium leaves, be aware of their strong peppery flavor. If you use chopped leaves in cream cheese (two teaspoons to a quarter pound of cheese is about right) do not allow the mixture to stand for a long time since the nasturtium will turn the cheese bitter. For an unusual salad, combine beets, apples, sorrel and nasturtium leaves and pickled nasturtium seed pods.

Nutmeg

The sweet, slightly sharp, spicy and pervasive flavor of nutmeg is hard to mistake. Traditional pumpkin pie almost demands this ingredient. The seed can be bought whole or ground into a powder. Carrots, beets and applesauce benefit from a dash of nutmeg. Use it sparingly and canvas the family for a consensus on nutmeg. It is one of those love-it or hate-it flavorings.

Oregano

The pungent flavor of this herb is particularly identified with the cooking of southern Italy. Many Americans first came into contact with oregano as an ingredient in the sauce for pizza pie and spaghetti dishes. Sparingly added, the leaves of fresh or dried oregano impart a zesty smell and musty-sharp flavor to sauces and salads. It is a flavorful garnish for beef and lamb stews and gravies and particularly good with tomato juice.

Pepper

According to an old saying, a little pepper can't do any harm. It is so good in so many dishes.

Pepper berries are the fruit of a tropical vining shrub growing mostly in India, Malaya and the East Indies. The berries, which are ripe when they turn red, are picked and dried just before ripening for so-called "black pepper." If you buy these berries ("whole peppercorns"), they will last almost forever. But once they are ground, they quickly lose much of their pleasant bite. That's why a peppermill is so nice to have; you grind only as much pepper as you want to use each time, leaving the full-flavored, unused peppercorns intact.

The "white pepper," somewhat milder than the black, is made from the ripened berry that has had the outer covering removed. It is used for aesthetic reasons in dishes such as white sauces, where the little black sprinkles would be unattractive.

For an unusual dessert, try "peppering" a fresh fruit salad as they do in India.

Rosemary

Rosemary is one of the most fragrant of herbs with a flavor that is both sweet and savory. It is equally at home in jams and jellies and meat dishes and fish. One of its most famous uses is with chicken sauteed in olive oil. Rosemary wine can be made according to an ancient recipe by soaking a handful of six-inch tips in half-a-gallon of white wine for a few days. If you try that, keep the wine in the refrigerator, since it spoils quickly.

Rosemary can be purchased in the form of dried and chopped leaves. However, if it is available fresh, the cuttings from a new growth can be laid directly on lamb or pork roasts and poultry to add flavor.

Rosemary has been described as "a cross between sage and lavender with a touch of ginger and camphor." Because of its sometimes overpowering flavor, rosemary should be used sparingly, especially if dried. For a unique taste experience, add chopped fresh rosemary to fresh fruit salad.

Sage

Experienced chefs talk about "toning down" sage with parsley. Like rosemary, sage, either dried or fresh, must be used with caution. Its strong aromatic smell and somewhat bitter astringent taste can dominate foods in which the herb is used. For a special omelet combine chives and chopped bacon with sage, mix with the eggs and when the omelet is finished garnish with a tiny sage sprig. Like bay leaf, sage is good with stuffings for wild or domestic fowl and works well as a flavoring for sausage.

If you are an adventurous cook, whole leaves, fresh or whole-dried, can be wrapped around lamb and veal for an unusual dish. Sage also has a reputation for adding a delicious flavor to summer fruit drinks and to fresh fruit salads.

Sorrel

Sometimes called sour grass, sorrel is a favorite of the Europeans as a lemony addition to soups, sauces, salads and vegetable dishes. A special sauce can be made by chopping fresh sorrel, soaking it in vinegar for a few hours, then draining and adding melted butter to serve with fish, scrambled eggs or hot potato salad. Add whole sorrel leaves to spinach or to turnip greens while they're cooking.

Summer Savory

Anyone on a salt-free diet would welcome savory as a marvelous substitute flavoring. It can almost be used as a spice since it has a pleasant, strong and slightly peppery taste. Europeans are especially fond of summer savory in all green bean dishes. For some reason it has a special faculty for enhancing the flavor of that vegetable. Summer savory also adds a special kick to cabbage and brussels sprouts. Savory developed a reputation back in the sixteenth century as a help to indigestion, and this property is still noticeable when savory is added to dishes which are usually difficult to digest, such as cucumber salad, pork and sausage. Be careful with the quantity of savory. Start with a little and increase amounts to suit your own taste.

Tarragon

They call tarragon the lord of all culinary herbs. The French consider it of supreme importance and it forms the basis of such famous sauces as *bearnaise*, hollandaise and *mousseline*. It is identified with sophisticated cooking. Use chopped tarragon leaves to enhance a French dressing or sprinkle the chopped leaves on green salads. To bring out the flavor of a fine steak or grilled fish add tarragon leaves while cooking.

Experienced cooks warn that the delicate fragrance of tarragon gives way to a strong tang which only comes out if too much tarragon is used. Be careful to stick with judicious amounts until you gauge the effect of this herb on the food you add it to.

Make your own tarragon vinegar for salads and other culinary needs. Simply fill a wide-mouthed bottle with fresh sprigs of tarragon then soak them in fine-quality vinegar or white wine. Remember to use a light-flavored vinegar so as not to stifle tarragon's relative mildness.

While tarragon is good with a lot of foods, cauliflower, for some reason, benefits especially from a sprinkle of tarragon. Also, those who make their own tartar sauce will find that this herb is indispensable.

Thyme

The flavor of this herb is characterized as "outspoken" and it can easily overpower more delicate herbs as well as foods it is combined with. In one of those strange happenings that often relate to foods, thyme was once considered an emblem of courage and soup made from thyme and beer was given as a cure for shyness.

Because thyme helps with the digestion of foods, it is the herb to use with fatty meats such as lamb or pork. It is an essential part of the *bouquet garni*. A little goes a long way so it should be used with great care. Try thyme in thick soups such as bean, minestrone, lentil or split pea. Think of it as you would think of oregano and marjoram. Experts suggest adding thyme to bread and biscuit doughs, or flavoring homemade croutons with the minced leaves.

Honey, a Pleasure

The very idea of honey is inviting. It is synonymous with soothing, smooth, softness and a sweetness that has the essence of fields and gardens built right in. It has the same kind of appeal and mystique that wine has. Connoisseurs can identify the honey source by the type of bloom and where it grew, just as knowledgeable wine lovers can pinpoint the grape and the vineyard that produced a vintage wine.

So honey is much more than a mere sweetener. It is a table pleasure to be savored, an experience. Don't settle for the first jar of honey you happen to pick up at the supermarket. Some of these contain corn syrup. Shop around, test a variety of flavors and look for economical purchases. Often the best quality of honey in the largest size for the least price is available at natural food stores. Try honey with morning toast, on fruit, in tea, as a sugar substitute in baked goods, particularly homemade breads. Stop at roadside stands that offer raw honey for sale. Keep tasting for those delightfully surprising differences in flavor and texture.

You don't have to go to a far country to find the finest honey. Grapefruit honey from Texas is one of the smoothest and most delicate of all honeys. Tupelo, from our own magnificent trees of that name in the South, is known to be a connoisseur's choice. We have an impressive range of other honeys—from the strongly flavored and distinctive sage, buckwheat and wildflower varieties to the milder honeys, clover and alfalfa, to name just a few.

In ancient times, all honey was wild honey and it was usually eaten with the comb, though some people punctured the comb and let the liquid drip into containers leaving the comb behind. Today centrifugal force is used to extract the liquid honey from the comb, then it is

to Be Savored

strained to remove all solid sediment, and pasteurized (which is un-necessary since honey keeps for years without pasteurization).

Honey is a natural sugar (combined levulose and dextrose, both quickly absorbed by the bloodstream). It is used as a food and flavoring, a food preservative, a mild laxative and sedative, an antiseptic and a quick source of energy. It contains some vitamins and minerals and has 1,600 calories to the pound—second only to dates among natural foods. Honey is one of the very few unrefined sweeteners available com-mercially and can be substituted for white sugar in any recipe by using it in about half the quantity of sugar called for. In the recipes in this book, honey is the sweetener most often used.

Vegetable Oils

Most cooks have had some experience in cooking with vegetable oils. In general they find the oils easier to work with and generally more versatile than lard or butter or other solid fats. But there's more to be gained by using vegetable oils than mere convenience. For one thing they offer a wide variety of flavors that can add to the appeal of a dish; for another, they are demonstrably better for your health.

The term "fats" usually refers to both solid and liquid fats, while "oils" simply indicates a fat in a liquid state at room temperature.

Unsaturated fats are liquid fats. Among them are peanut, safflower, soybean, cottonseed, corn and olive oils. (Cottonseed oil is not recommended due to cotton being the crop most heavily sprayed with pesticide in the United States.) The important point to remember is that liquid fats usually have a high content of unsaturates (desirable) and a low content of saturates (less desirable).

for Easy Cooking

Saturated fats, in general, are solid fats. This group includes fats from all meats, butter and lard, as well as hydrogenated cooking fats. It is generally recognized that when solid fats are not balanced by enough polyunsaturates they can contribute to the development of cardiac problems. What is recommended is not the elimination of solids fats—but an increase in the *ratio* of unsaturated liquid fat to saturated solid fats. In addition, health experts say that the *total* fat consumption should be reduced.

Although most consumers have come to prefer refined oils because they are tasteless, odorless and light colored, crude oils are gaining popularity because consumers who try them find them excellent for salads, for flavoring and for cooking at low heat. They contain the natural taste and odor of the seeds, nuts or beans from which they're derived.

Substituting liquid vegetable oils for shortening in baking requires very little change in cooking methods. Either crude or refined oils can be used at low temperatures. At moderate and high temperatures, or when a tasteless, colorless oil is preferred, a refined oil can be used, but it's important to note the difference in the various refined oils that are available.

Some of the best-known brands of commercial vegetable oils are partially hydrogenated, as indicated by the words, "specially processed," on the label. Other oils are available which contain no hydrogenated fats whatsoever. These nonhydrogenated oils are also preferred because they do not contain the preservatives and additives (e.g., propyl gallate, methyl silicone, citric acid, etc.) used by most commercial oil makers to prevent rancidity and lessen spattering and foaming.

For general cooking use, some nutritionists recommend alternating the use of several different vegetable oils to provide a variety of the essential fatty acids. The consumer can mix his own or use the blend of oils offered by some firms. A wide variety of oils is available in addition to those already mentioned, including rice bran, sesame, sunflower, almond and apricot oils.

How to Convert

Preheat oven to 350°F.

Cream shortening and sugars together. Beat in eggs and vanilla. Combine flour, salt and soda, mixing well, and add along with oats and nuts to wet mixture.

Drop by teaspoon onto lightly oiled cookie sheet, leaving approximately 2 inches between cookies. Flatten with a wet fork and top with a piece of nut if desired. Bake in preheated oven for 10 minutes. Cool on rack.

Yield: 4 dozen cookies

Basic Oatmeal

Original Recipe

1 *cup shortening* . . . .

1 *cup brown sugar* . . . .
1 *cup white sugar* . . . .
2 *eggs, beaten* . . . .
1 *teaspoon vanilla* . . . .
1½ *cups all-purpose flour* . . . .

1 *teaspoon salt* . . . .
1 *teaspoon baking soda* . . . .
3 *cups rolled oats* . . . .

½ *cup chopped nuts* . . . .
nut pieces for top of cookies (optional) . . . . .

Notes on

1. To approximate the consistency of the shortening, I use butter (also for its flavor), to which I add oil, in order to lessen the amount of saturated fat. For 1 cup of shortening you cannot just substitute ½ cup of butter and ½ cup of oil because oil absorbs more flour than butter does. So I use ⅓ cup of oil and ½ cup of butter.

2. Molasses and honey have twice the sweetening power of sugar so when they are used instead of sugar in a recipe, use half as much as the amount of sugar called for. Molasses is a good substitute for brown sugar as they have a similar flavor.

a Recipe

Cookies

Converted Recipe

. . . . . ½ *cup butter*
⅓ *cup oil*
. . . . . ½ *cup molasses*
. . . . . ½ *cup honey*
. . . . . 2 *eggs, beaten*
. . . . . 1 *teaspoon vanilla*
. . . . . 2 *cups whole wheat flour*
*(rye flour may be
substituted)*
. . . . . 1 *teaspoon salt*
. . . . . *(omit)*
. . . . . 3 *cups rolled oats*
*(ground briefly in
electric blender if not
commercially processed)*
. . . . . ½ *cup chopped nuts*
. . . . . *nut pieces for
top of cookies (optional)*

Preheat oven to 350°F.

Grate butter into flour. Add oil, mixing it in lightly with a fork. Add oats and salt, working the mixture lightly with your fingers as you would pastry. In a small bowl, combine eggs, molasses, honey and vanilla. Stir this wet mixture into the dry ingredients and add the nuts, mixing well.

Drop by teaspoon onto lightly oiled cookie sheet, leaving approximately 2 inches between cookies. Flatten with a wet fork and top with a piece of nut if desired. Bake in preheated oven for 10 minutes. Cool on rack.

Yield: 4 dozen cookies

Converting Recipes

3. Whole wheat flour (or rye flour) does not absorb as much liquid as white flour. For this reason and also to compensate for the fact that I use liquid sweeteners (honey or molasses) instead of dry (sugar), the amount of flour has been increased.

4. I omit the baking soda in most cookie recipes as a leavener is not needed.

5. Rolled oats which are sold by natural foods distributors are sometimes too coarse to be used for oatmeal cookies, unless they are first processed briefly in an electric blender.

Your Recipe Now Serves

2	4	6	8		Key for New Measurement
1	2	3	4		½
1½	3	4½	6		¾
3	6	9	12		1½
4	8	12	16		2
5	10	15	20		2½
6	12	18	24		3

Desired Number of Servings

Pints

Key Number

Original Measurement	½	¾	1½	2	2½	3
⅓						1
½	¼		¾	1	1¼	1½
1	½	¾	1½	2	2½	3
1½			2¼	3		4½
2	1	1½	3	4	5	6
3	1½		4½	6	7½	9

Teaspoons

Key Number

	¹/₂	³/₄	1¹/₂	2	2¹/₂	3
¹/₈	¹/₁₆	³/₃₂	³/₁₆	¹/₄	⁵/₁₆	³/₈
¹/₄	¹/₈	³/₁₆	³/₈	¹/₂	⁵/₈	³/₄
¹/₂	¹/₄	³/₈	³/₄	1	1¹/₄	1¹/₂
³/₄	³/₈	¹/₂	1¹/₈	1¹/₂	1⁷/₈	2¹/₄
1	¹/₂	³/₄	1¹/₂	2	2¹/₂	3
1¹/₄	⁵/₈	¹⁵/₁₆	1⁷/₈	2¹/₂	3¹/₈	3³/₄
1¹/₂	³/₄	1¹/₈	2¹/₄	3	3³/₄	4¹/₂
2	1	1¹/₂	3	4	5	6
2¹/₂	1¹/₄	1⁷/₈	3³/₄	5	6¹/₄	7¹/₂
3	1¹/₂	2¹/₄	4¹/₂	6	7¹/₂	9
4	2	3	6	8	10	12

Original Measurement (left vertical axis label)

Tablespoons

Key Number

	½	¾	1½	2	2½	3
1	½	¾	1½	2	2½	3
1½	¾	1⅛	2¼	3	3¾	4½
2	1	1½	3	4	5	6
3	1½	2¼	4½	6	7½	9
4	2	3	6	8	10	12
5	2½	3¾	7½	10	12½	15
6	3	4½	9	12	15	18
7	3½	5¼	10½	14	17½	21

Original Measurement

Cups

Original Measurement

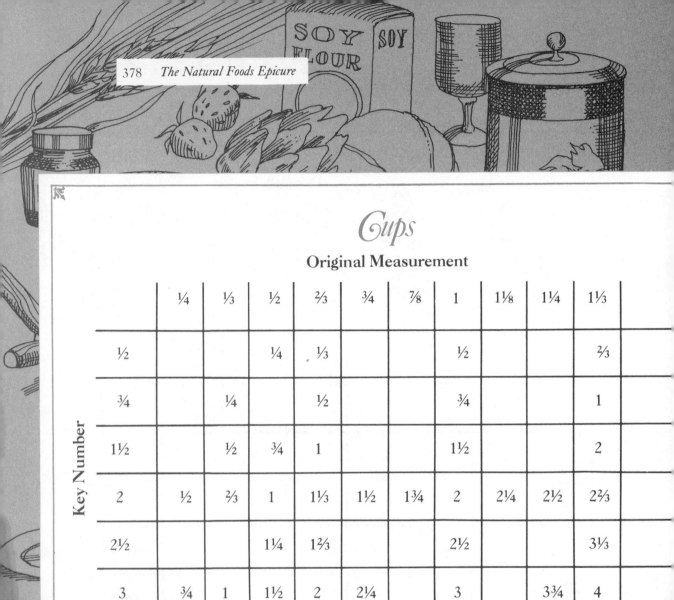

Key Number	¼	⅓	½	⅔	¾	⅞	1	1⅛	1¼	1⅓
½			¼	⅓			½			⅔
¾		¼		½			¾			1
1½		½	¾	1			1½			2
2	½	⅔	1	1⅓	1½	1¾	2	2¼	2½	2⅔
2½			1¼	1⅔			2½			3⅓
3	¾	1	1½	2	2¼		3		3¾	4

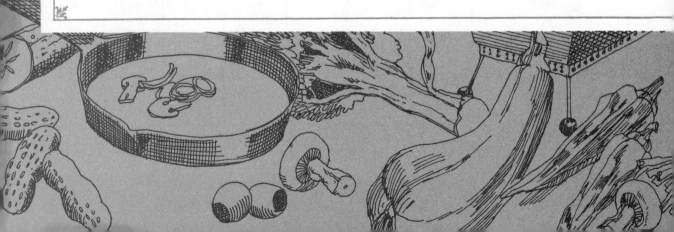

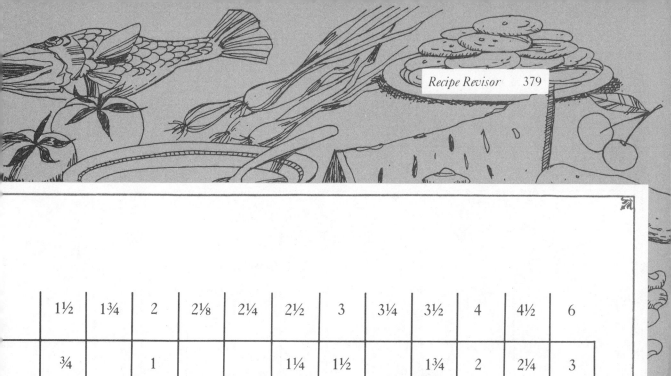

1½	1¾	2	2⅛	2¼	2½	3	3¼	3½	4	4½	6
¾		1			1¼	1½		1¾	2	2¼	3
		1½				2¼			3		4½
2¼		3			3¾	4½		5¼	6	6¾	9
3	3½	4	4¼	4½	5	6	6½	7	8	9	12
3¾		5			6¼	7½		8¾	10	11¼	15
4½	5¼	6		6¾	7½	9	9¾	10½	12	13½	18

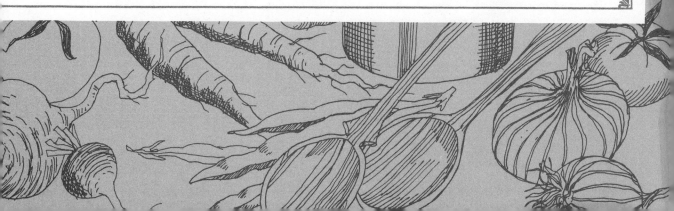

Ounces

Original Measurement

	1	2	2¼	2½	3	3½	4	4½	5	6	7
½	½	1	1⅛	1¼	1½	1¾	2	2¼	2½	3	3½
¾	¾	1½			2¼		3	3⅜	3¾	4½	5¼
1½	1½	3	3⅜	3¾	4½	5¼	6	6¾	7½	9	10½
2	2	4	4½	5	6	7	8	9	10	12	14
2½	2½	5	5⅝	6¼	7½	8¾	10	11¼	12½	15	17½
3	3	6	6¾	7½	9	10½	12	13½	15	18	21

(Key Number — row labels in left column)

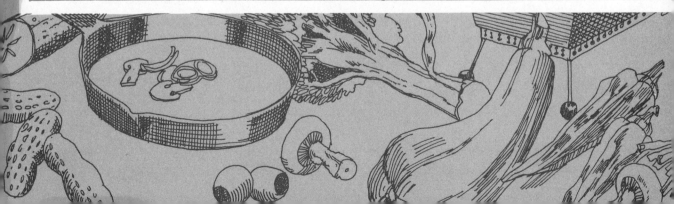

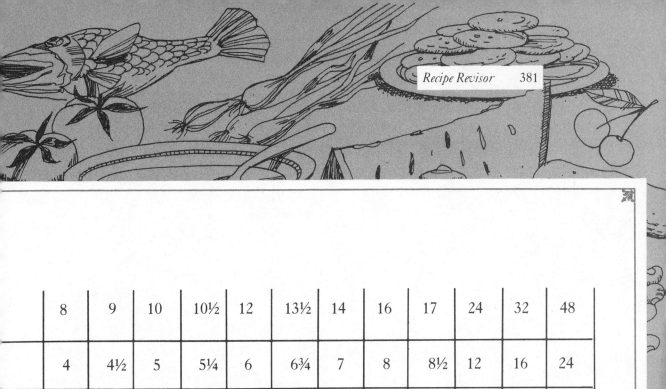

8	9	10	10½	12	13½	14	16	17	24	32	48
4	4½	5	5¼	6	6¾	7	8	8½	12	16	24
6	6¾	7½	7⅞	9	10⅛	10½	12	12¾	18	24	36
12	13½	15	15¾	18	20¼	21	24	25½	36	48	72
16	18	20	21	24	27	28	32	34	48	64	
20	22½	25	26¼	30	33¾	35	40	42½	60		
24	27	30	31½	36	40½	42	48	51	72		

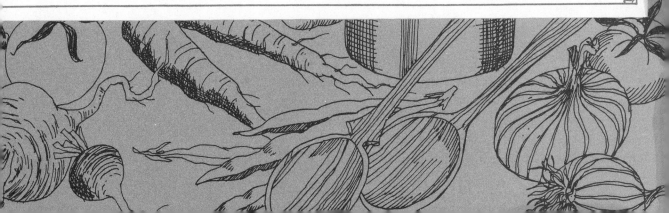

American Standard to U.S. Metric Mass (Weight)

	Milligrams	Grams	Kilograms	Ounces	Pounds
1 ounce =	2835	28.35	.028	—	—
1 pound =	"Lots"	454	.454	—	—
1 milligram =	1	.001	.000001	—	—
1 gram =	1,000	1	.001	.032	.002
1 kilogram =	1,000,000	1,000	1	.000032	2.2

Conversion Charts

Metric Conversions for Length

¼ inch   =   .63 centimeter

½ inch   = 1.25 centimeters

1 inch   = 2.5 centimeters

2 inches = 5.0 centimeters

3 inches = 7.5 centimeters

4 inches = 10.0 centimeters

6 inches = 15.0 centimeters

12 inches = 30.0 centimeters

American Standard to
U.S. Metric Fluid Volume

	Milliliters	Liters
1 teaspoon =	5	.005
1 tablespoon =	15	.015
1 fluid ounce =	29.56	.030
¼ cup =	59.125	.059
½ cup =	118.25	.118
1 cup =	236	.236
1 fluid pint =	473	.473
1 fluid quart =	946	.946
1 gallon =	3,785.4	3.785
1 milliliter =	1	.001
1 liter =	1,000	1

U.S. Metric Fluid Volume
to American Standard

1 milliliter =	.068	tablespoon
1 milliliter =	.034	fluid ounce
1 milliliter =	.004	cup
1 milliliter =	.002	fluid pint
1 milliliter =	.001	fluid quart
1 milliliter =	.0003	gallon
1 liter =	67.68	tablespoons
1 liter =	33.8184	fluid ounces
1 liter =	4.227	cups
1 liter =	2.113	fluid pints
1 liter =	1.057	fluid quarts
1 liter =	.264	gallon

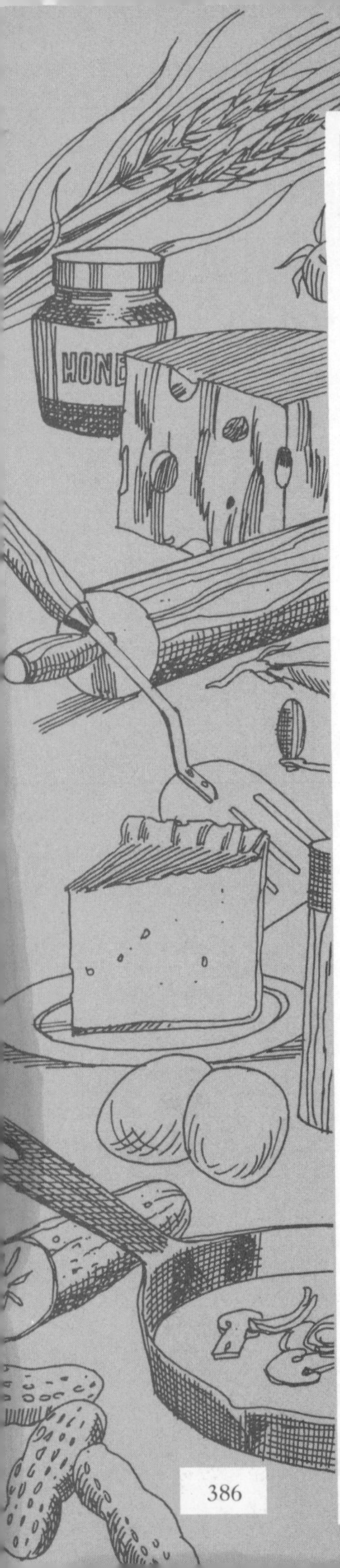

Liquid Measure
Volume Equivalents

60 drops	= 1	teaspoon
1 teaspoon	= ⅓	tablespoon
1 tablespoon	= 3	teaspoons
2 tablespoons	= 1	fluid ounce
4 tablespoons	= ¼	cup or 2 ounces
5⅓ tablespoons	= ⅓	cup or 2⅔ ounces
8 tablespoons	= ½	cup or 4 ounces
16 tablespoons	= 1	cup or 8 ounces
¼ cup	= 4	tablespoons
⅜ cup	= ¼	cup plus 2 tablespoons
⅝ cup	= ½	cup plus 2 tablespoons
⅞ cup	= ¾	cup plus 2 tablespoons
1 cup	= ½	pint or 8 fluid ounces
2 cups	= 1	pint or 16 fluid ounces
1 pint, liquid	= 16	fluid ounces
1 quart, liquid	= 2	pints or 4 cups
1 gallon, liquid	= 4	quarts

Approximate Temperature Conversions

Fahrenheit	Centigrade (Celsius)
−10°	−23°
0°	−17°
32°	0°
115°	46°
130°	54°
212°	100°
234°	112°
244°	117°
250°	121°
250°-275°	121°-133°
300°-325°	149°-163°
350°-375°	177°-190°
400°-425°	204°-218°
450°-475°	232°-246°
500°-525°	260°-274°

To convert Fahrenheit into Centigrade, subtract 32, multiply by 5, divide by 9. To convert Centigrade into Fahrenheit, reverse the formula: Multiply by 9, divide by 5, add 32.

Index

N